STEP
UP

STEP UP

CONFIDENCE, SUCCESS AND
YOUR STELLAR CAREER IN
10 MINUTES A DAY

PHANELLA MAYALL FINE
and ALICE OLINS

Vermilion
LONDON

1 3 5 7 9 10 8 6 4 2

Vermilion, an imprint of Ebury Publishing,
20 Vauxhall Bridge Road,
London SW1V 2SA

Vermilion is part of the Penguin Random House group of companies
whose addresses can be found at global.penguinrandomhouse.com

Copyright © Phanella Mayall Fine and Alice Olins, 2016

Phanella Mayall Fine and Alice Olins have asserted their right to be identified as the
authors of this Work in accordance with the Copyright, Designs and Patents Act 1988

This edition first published in the United Kingdom by Vermilion in 2016

www.penguin.co.uk

A CIP catalogue record for this book is available from the British Library

ISBN 9781785040528

Printed and bound in Great Britain by Clays Ltd, St Ives PLC

Penguin Random House is committed to a sustainable future for our business,
our readers and our planet. This book is made from Forest Stewardship
Council® certified paper.

Contents

To

Lulu, Pearl, Tallulah – our daughters.
May your unicorns always be within reach.

Noah, Otto, Bear, Richard and Toby – our little and big men.
Success isn't measured in pounds and pence.
Be free. Be you.

Step Up Career To-Do List

1. Read this book (figures . . .).
2. Be committed to completing workouts: one a day = new skill in a week. DO IT.
3. Be open to self-reflection, personal ambition and feeling EMPOWERED.
4. Celebrate uniqueness as a woman.
5. Embrace notion of change. Because change makes you fly.
6. Accept that it's OK not to know the logistics of how newly energised career will pan out, i.e. don't get bogged down in details (N.B. advice in book will get you there).
7. SHARE THIS BOOK WITH MEN IN LIFE.
8. Swot Step Up's values.
   a. If all of us push our careers forward, we'll reap the rewards and allow our daughters to proceed in calmer work waters.
   b. Gender equality does not mean gender sameness.
   c. Dig your own definition of success.
9. Diarise girls' night on Saturday (AKA enjoy time away from work).
10. Note to self: stop comparing self to best friend. Or sister. Or woman at work who seems to Have It All. She doesn't.

Now let's get started . . .

CHAPTER 1

The Truth About Women (and Men)

There are a lot of depressing statistics out there about how men dominate the workplace. Did you know that there are more FTSE 100 CEOs called John than there are FTSE 100 CEOs who are women?

Welcome to our book. We are delighted that you're here. Even though we opened with that appalling John statistic (no offence, Johns), this isn't a book about beating men to the top. Or even getting to the top, if that isn't your bag. It's the perspective of two young women just like you, who want to celebrate our womanhood and have rocking careers. We are here to:

|1| Lend a hand in defining your own breed of success (we don't all want to be CEOs).
|2| Give you the skills and know-how to elegantly glide northwards.
|3| Explain how to tread your own path as a woman – we're a minority in the workplace, that's leverage in our minds.
|4| Beef your confidence.
|5| Beef your earnings.
|6| And make you happier too.

Indeed, the act of writing this book has neatly encompassed all the themes within. For us to have been able to fill all these pages, we've had to strip back and start at the beginning again. There was a working partnership to build and nurture; a bucketload of confidence to fill; we needed to learn to effectively (and modestly) take advice from others; then there was all the planning involved in getting 90,000 words on paper, and that's before we even got to a shared ability to self-promote, network and digitally switch off. And don't even get us started on Instagram…

You see, from where you're standing, with this book in your hands, it probably looks as though we're two established authors who proceeded to publication without a notable obstacle ahead. The truth is, we've endured just as many ups and downs as you. We all struggle in our careers, just as we all also have the capacity to shine. To be able to get to somewhere great at work, somewhere fulfilling and enjoyable, takes grit, pain and plenty of resolve. We wouldn't wish our painful first weekend of writing on anyone. But we've been there now, we've done it, we moved on and here is our book for you. We see it as a travel guide to a better and more gratifying career, by two holiday reps who are on your side and doing it too.

You see, this book doesn't just divulge the secrets of female career success; it also acts as a practical guide. Whether you're a doctor, gymnast, banker or tech prodigy, as long as you're a woman, to some degree or another you'll be susceptible to the same forces, checks and choices as all other working women out there. We see this as a good thing. Yes, we'd like to move to a place where gender doesn't define our chances of success. But gender keeps things interesting – and that's why we're advocates of women. Nobody wants a working world filled with identikit drones. Plus, empirically speaking, diversity also equals prosperity. So, for many many different reasons, women should feel freer at work.

THE IDEA

So why this book, and why now? Well, let's start at the beginning. Phanella's day job involves coaching and training hundreds of women in large companies to get ahead at work. About a year ago, she received an email from a woman in Colombia. This woman had just watched one of her online female leadership training presentations and felt compelled to get in touch. 'I have been profoundly affected by what you had to say,' she wrote in an email. 'Where can I find out more?'

Alice's day job is an altogether different kettle of fish; she is a journalist with tenures at some of Britain's most esteemed newspapers and style publications. We have been friends since our early twenties (just when our respective careers were starting to form) and before Phanella received that seminal email, we'd already spent many hours (and digested many bottles of wine in the process) talking about women and work. With the email from Colombia as the spur, we tried to find some relevant literature; rather predictably there was nothing quite right – nothing youthful, academically sound, stylish and enjoyable enough. Nothing that combined hours of real-life experience, current research and stories of success or paid respect to the constraints of time that we live our modern lives by. So, we decided to write that book ourselves. Yes, it was an extreme answer to a simple request, but what convinced us to do it ourselves was simple: timing.

THE MESSAGE

Women's careers aren't just in the ether, they're on the front pages of newspapers, inside glossy magazines, on the radio, across the internet and they're being discussed on a daily basis in governments all around the world. It's amazing that there's so much buzz around women and careers; people are really talking about women's rights at work, and attitudes are changing. Things are getting really exciting for women at work – and that's why we wrote this book.

Sure, if you look at gender-split job statistics, the situation is pretty much as depressing as it's ever been. But – BIG BUT – the John stat doesn't account for what's swirling around the media, and is inside the meeting rooms and minds of career folk (women and men) across the globe. Women have been legally entitled to the same respect, pay and job titles as our male friends and peers for many years and slowly but surely the reality is catching up with the legal framework.

We want equality, but we want something more than that too: we want to stay uniquely and wonderfully female. The same pay, yes, opportunities, of course, but we don't want to have to abandon our femininity at the office revolving door. For us, gender parity does not imply gender uniformity. As two passionate and impassioned women, we embrace our distinctive peculiarities and you should too.

The *Step Up* message is based on the idea that while everyone deserves to be received and treated equally at work, women must do it their own way, because being a woman is part of what makes you, you.

Gender is an emotive and complex subject and, as such, here's a little disclaimer: there will be times in the book where it might feel as though we're using a large gender generalisation brush. We apologise in advance. We are acutely aware that the very act of gender generalisation is part of the reason that there are now barriers that need dodging in the pursuit of straightforward female career success. It's tricky: science, research and received wisdom all tell us that men and women are different beasts and yet the very admittance of this fact fuels the fire of discrimination.

So we'll keep things simple: this book is the realisation of two women's shared vision for female career empowerment. Our sphere of interest is careers, but many of the skills and subjects that we discuss transcend all areas of life. We don't want you to abandon your wonderful, crazy female traits, we want you to harness them so that you can crack open your own style of success and proceed to a happier and more fulfilled work you.

As we've listed above, we will educate you on the skewed internal dynamics of the working world (this might be painful), and then explain the skills you need for lasting career success. Once you know them, we'll give you space and workouts in which to practise these new work progression talents, and while you're at it, we'll keep things colourful by way of our Women at the Top anecdotes. There's no subject that the Hemsley sisters, Kirsty Young, Bobbi Brown *et al.* can't make transfixing and inspirational.

But first of all, that little question of difference.

THE DIFFERENCES
We'll start with science because no one can argue with that. The side-by-side vision of a naked female and a naked male validates the simple fact of life: we are different versions of the same species. There's the obvious stuff and then there are the mysterious workings inside our heads.

Our brain is arguably the most important thing about us. It makes us human and is the instigator of everything that we think and do. It's our life control centre, and science tells us that for men and women there are brain wiring variations. In the past, we've been wedded to the notion that men have better connectivity within each hemisphere, whilst women have better connectivity between the hemispheres. In an everyday sense, this explained why men excelled at spatial awareness and women at social cognition and multitasking.

Neuroscience is notoriously complex but the latest large-scale research shows that gender brain differences may not be as clear-cut as we were led to believe. While some recent studies suggest no significant difference in crucial parts of the brain at all, the most recent research leads to the centre of the brain – the hippocampus, the part associated with emotion and memory. This is usually larger in men than women, but, without wanting to get too technical, some women have a larger, more male-style hippocampus and some men have one that is smaller and more female in style.

This suggests the idea of a continuum of femaleness to maleness for the entire brain. This is relevant to the book, because it delivers the concept of range: scientists found that the majority of the brains studied were a mosaic of male and female structures, meaning there is no one type of male or female brain. We like this because it validates our own stance of overlap. The most successful person in the workplace, research says, is the woman who retains her female brain but who isn't afraid to borrow some stereotypically male traits when the opportunity requires it.

Success isn't about pitting yourself against a man, it's about learning to be your best – it's about finding your place on the continuum and making it rock. Interestingly, brains aren't fixed organs, they are constantly evolving and changing as we age, depending on how we use them.

Neuroplasticity, as it is called, in part explains why little girls end up studying languages and the arts and little boys get filtered into STEM (Science, technology, engineering and mathematics) subjects that frequently lead to more lucrative careers. Repetition reinforces the networks within our brains: baby girls and baby boys might start off with exactly the same brain software, but over time, as we unwittingly encourage boys towards Lego and trucks and girls into social situations that require capable communication skills, the map of association in our childhood brains is sculpted so that the function of the hardware is constantly altered by experience. We lead our girls to dolls and our boys to the top of trees, and then we wonder why society ends up treating women and men differently.

Hormones also play a part in this lifelong divide, as does parental nurture. More interestingly, though, this has a much more subtle impact – it defines what we believe about ourselves. We self-stereotype against ourselves as women, and then we live up to these restrictions. There is a recent study using Asian-American women that perfectly illustrates the point. The group was divided and set a maths test. Just before the test commenced, half of the group were reminded that they were Asian, invoking the stereotype of Asians having a high maths ability. This half did better in the test.

However, when they were reminded of being female (which invokes the stereotype of poor maths performance), they scored lower on the test than the control group.

The point is that while men do tend to outperform women in assessments of mathematic ability, for example using the test results of American SATs exams, in reality women aren't actually worse at maths (see p. 7), we're just stereotyped into thinking that way. In the workplace, this presents (in the main) as women not reaching for leadership positions, or being too conservative in their entrepreneurial expectations for the simple reason that we (wrongly) believe that we don't belong at the top.

Of course, what Step Up is all about is finding your own definition of 'top'. We aren't all professors in waiting, but we should all be able to imagine ourselves where we really want to be at work. Not where society or our stereotyped brains expect us to land. That's the reason why we just got all scientific on you, because today, you are the product of many forces.

Your career brain, the one you rely on to muster confidence, the one that assists you in awkward networking situations, pay negotiations and everything else in between, may not currently be on your side and that's in part due to stereotyping and nurture. When you know the reasoning behind where your brain is at, it allows you to make positive changes (keep reading this book) to redirect those channels – to change the hardware, so that your brain (your unconscious thinking) is aligned to your reach-for-the-stars career dreams.

THE CULTURE

So that's what's going on in your head, but what about external influences? The gender pay gap, the glaring disparity between the number of women at entry-level jobs versus the number higher up the tree, these markers aren't just the result of our curiously wired brains.

How about where we live? To explain this one, we again need to defer to maths testing. One huge recent study of student assessments, which reviewed the results from a quarter of a million fifteen-year-old students across forty countries, categorically proved a link between female maths ability and prevailing gender equality. In countries with the highest levels of gender equality (as measured by a political-empowerment index and an index of women in the labour market), the gap in maths performance, which usually favours the boys, completely disappeared. In fact, in Iceland, which has one of the highest levels of gender equality, the girls actually outperformed their male peers. What this tells us is that something as basic as your home country will shape the path along which you tread at work.

Unconscious bias is another biggie in the external players. In fact, it's a fundamental influence on the female career, and because of this, we've given it lots more space in Chapter 9. Still, it's important that we mention it here. There's nothing wrong with carrying some biases around, it's just that the ones against female career performance keep us down. Before 1970, women made up less than 10 per cent of musicians in most top symphony orchestras. Then, blind auditions were introduced; when the judges weren't able to see the gender of the musicians playing before them, something remarkable happened: women suddenly accounted for 40 per cent of the orchestras. The only explanation is unconscious bias.

We are all at fault. We hold unconscious biases against ourselves and against other women too. Even ardent feminists aren't immune; the power of this unwitting thought process surpasses all reason and belief. Although we can't alter it completely, when we know it is there, unconscious bias becomes a lesser beast.

THE BIG (LITTLE) ONE

Now, to the biggest of the big: BABIES. Yes, full disclosure here, we both have them, there are five little Step Uppers between us. These children are wonderful, they're magical beings that have interrupted, shaped and inspired our career journeys to date. During the process of writing this book, people who know us (even some of our dearest friends) assumed that as two mothers writing a book on careers, it automatically meant this would be a tome on (and only for) working mothers. Perish the thought. Not that we don't love being working mothers, we do, we just don't have that much to say on the subject. Our children don't define us, they enhance us.

We will let you draw your own conclusions on whether this misplaced assumption was unconscious bias or stereotyping. Whichever way you look at things, nothing defines gender like reproduction. Women are the only ones who can carry, deliver and breastfeed a family's offspring, and so women are really the only ones who bear the brunt of Offspring Career Modification. Sometimes, children can be an absolute bonus. The incredible **Kirsty Young**, who currently presents *Desert Island Discs* and has worked for nearly all of the UK's media channels, thinks that since having children she has become more focused, strategic and successful.

'I had been a workaholic, but then I had children and I realised that if I'm going to leave this tiny person in the care of someone else, I'd better be doing something that I really love and am good at. Strangely, having children has made me a lot more focused and ruthless in the choices I make in my career.'

For all the ups and downs, children put women in a new camp: CAMP MUM. We are the ones who take time off to actually have the baby, and once they are here, we are more likely to want to work flexibly so that we can spend more time with them too. In fact before the baby is even born, it's women who have to announce the pregnancy and carry the bump around the office for nine long months. All of these components conspire to make others (and ourselves for that matter) treat us differently. Although many countries have made strides in how parents share the leave away from work, there is still overwhelming inequality at home.

Women continue to do a disproportionate share of childcare and home-centric chores and we are more likely to be affected by the challenges of juggling home and work responsibilities. Editor of *Red* magazine **Sarah Bailey** says this on the matter. 'Unless we empower men and dads, and inspire and encourage them to take on 50 per cent of the domestic load, women in partnerships with kids can't be true powerhouses.' The point is that making 'sharenting', as many now call it, the norm rather than negotiable is a vital step on the road to gender equality.

If you want the domestic stats, here they are:

> At entry-level jobs, women are nine times more likely than men to say that they do more childcare.
> These women are also four times more likely to say they do more chores.
> In households where both partners work full-time, studies show 41 per cent of women do more childcare (as opposed to sharing the load – for comparison, just 3 per cent of men report doing more than their share) and 30 per cent report doing more chores.
> In younger generations, although household chores are split more evenly, women under thirty still do a majority of childcare with 45 per cent of women taking on the lion's share of childcare vs. just 5 per cent of men (the rest have been listening and see it as equally shared).
> Working women are 60 per cent more likely than working men to have a partner who works full-time, with this disparity increasing to 85 per cent at the executive level.
> In our *Step Up* study (more of which later) the vast majority of women who had made it to very senior levels in the very high-demand legal world had husbands who didn't work or worked part-time flexibly from home.

In short, this data tells us that whatever their position, women have more to do at home than men, and we're less likely to have someone else at home supporting us while we captain the ship unless we're already at the very top level. Babies, children and family structure all impact on how we work, and the ways in which we do or don't succeed.

In France, the culture is very different and women aren't subjected to as much Camp Mum discrimination. There, women typically return to work very quickly; this is the norm, because childcare is state supported, work hours are capped and employees enjoy plenty of holiday allowance. As a result, France has one of the best maternal work rates in the world: in 2012, it was 75 per cent. Because it is accepted that French women will go back, they aren't marginalised so acutely for having children. In Japan though, where working hours are arduously long and sexual discrimination isn't as quiet as it should be (i.e. silent), the same percentage of women leave the workforce for over ten years after having their first child.

THE ZEITGEIST

Part of this global variation is due to culture, and part is the result of government initiatives and the attitudes that boil away within influential companies. Like we said at the very start, timing is key. And hallelujah, now is a good time to be a woman at work. It isn't perfect but things are certainly changing. Just last year in the UK, the government-backed Davies Review – having already helped eliminate all-male boards in the FTSE 100 – stipulated that a third of all board seats at Britain's top 350 companies should be held by women by 2020.

And in California, the 2015 Equal Pay Act means that women now have the right to equal pay for substantially the same work as a man and can also ask for disclosure of what men are being paid in similar roles. This should please Oscar-winning actress **Jennifer Lawrence**, as the problems of gender inequality don't just affect the ordinary.

Last October, in a heated essay she wrote for her friend Lena Dunham's Lenny Letter newsletter (Dunham also pops up later in the book), Lawrence took a brutal stance on pay inequality in Hollywood. In her response to the Sony hack, which revealed that she had earned considerably less than her male co-stars in *American Hustle* despite her major role in the film, she said:

'When the Sony hack happened and I found out how much less I was being paid than the lucky people with dicks, I didn't get mad at Sony, I got mad at myself. I failed as a negotiator because I gave up early. I didn't want to keep fighting over millions of dollars that, frankly, due to two franchises, I don't need.

'But if I'm honest with myself, I would be lying if I didn't say there was an element of wanting to be liked that influenced my decision to close the deal without a real fight. I didn't want to seem "difficult" or "spoiled." ... 'I'm over trying to find the "adorable" way to state my opinion and still be likeable! Fuck that. I don't think I've ever worked for a man in charge who spent time contemplating what angle he should use to have his voice heard. It's just heard.'

For the record, *Forbes* ranked Lawrence as the highest-paid female actor of 2015. Since the Sony leak, she made headlines again for negotiating a higher salary than Chris Pratt, her co-star in *Passengers*. While Pratt earned $12 million for the film, Lawrence netted $20 million upfront. Jennifer Lawrence, you are our hero.

What she says, and what she implies, is what this book aims to counter: that because many women struggle with confidence and because things aren't intrinsically fair, many women aren't treated equally in the workplace.

Yes, there are plenty of differences between men and women, some innate and some imposed. But this isn't a book about the sexes; this is a book about women for women. Yes, society favours male progression, but don't let that hold you back. Remember, success is so much sweeter when you've had to be steely — when you aren't the Prodigal Son.

What we want with this book is to empower you to be a go-getter in the skewed world we call work. Because when we learn to be successful along our own unique paths, we'll be collectively more powerful and we will positively impact society.

THE PRACTICALITIES

Right, the preaching is over. For all the big talk, at its heart, this book is about making small career changes. Networking, negotiating, dressing the part, building your personal brand and getting the most out of social media are just some of what's waiting for you in the chapters ahead. We promise to give you the lowdown on why these are all relevant and potent tenets of career success and then provide you with the tools to make these part of your brilliant everyday.

And better still, *Step Up* career enhancement is as quick as it is effective. We are acutely aware that time is something many of us struggle to find, which is why this book had to work in small, bite-size slices. Ten-minute slices, to be precise.

The ten-minute-a-day *Step Up* regime is based on the empirical fact that our greatest successes in life are generated during our shortest portions of time. At the gym, we call this High Intensity Training. And as two HIIT fanatics, we've channelled those same principles of short, intense drills in our book.

We know that you are as time poor as you are ambitious. You already have a job to maintain, a busy social life, possibly children in tow; then there's the body to hone, the newspaper to read … Time is precious. That's why the *Step Up* daily workouts require just ten minutes of your time, because finding career success needn't take all day.

In the workplace, success and effort are inversely proportional. For years, economists have debated the exact ratio of effort to output: some say 80/20, others 99/1: We Say Ten Minutes a Day.

It's hard to believe, but research shows that positive career behaviours (we have hundreds waiting henceforward …) are far more significant than hard graft alone. And from our own experience helping thousands of ambitious women, we know that when you commit to *Step Up*'s five allotted ten-minute workout slots, by the end of a given week, you will already feel more assertive exercising your new skill. Whether it's networking or learning how to use the influence of others, our philosophy is Read, Rehearse and then Realise. It applies to all of our themes within the book and as such, each chapter has five separate *Step Up* Workouts to shortcut you towards new solid and relevant career progression tools.

TIME TO STEP UP

Sitting at the core of this book is our belief that each of us should work towards our own breed of success. How do you succeed as a woman today, and how do you succeed as you? We aren't scared to talk about our gender, to be defined by it even. As we've already said, our gender makes us interesting – we're a minority in the workplace and that gets us noticed. So don't hand back the mantle and try to work like a man. Instead, encourage the men you know and work with to also get involved in the debate; educate them to champion the cause, and get them fully involved at home. Whichever way you look at it, things aren't equal and refusing to talk about being a woman does a disservice to women. It impedes those below us looking for role models, and it quietens the equality debate. Being a woman is your trump card, and we're going to show you how to play the game.

CHAPTER 2

Defining Success

THE BACKGROUND Success Is a Unicorn

S uccess, like so many of life's big concepts, is a wily beast. It's a mythical creature that lives inside our conscience – a vision and a state of mind. Sometimes, when the going is good, success treats us well; it buoys up our confidence and puts butterflies in our tummies. When the shit hits the fan, though, success can be cruel and cunning. It sits impassively on our desks, stirs our insecurities and makes us feel blue.

Success is a unicorn: difficult to see, sometimes fleeting, exhilarating … most of all hard to capture. That is one of its problems. Success is the cornerstone of our careers – and for that matter, our lives – but most of us haven't figured out our own take on the matter.

This chapter will help unravel what success actually means (and looks like) to you. And once you know that, you will be ready to employ the tools in the rest of the book to make that unicorn yours.

The fact that we are women complicates the subject of success. Because even today, when our sisters have achieved inconceivable brilliance, society still has a pitifully straitjacketed and * clears throat * male-biased interpretation of success.

According to the *Oxford English Dictionary* (i.e. God), success in the workplace is: '*The prosperous achievement of something attempted; the attainment of an object according to one's desire: now often with particular reference to the attainment of wealth or position.*'

You see, what the OED did there? With '*the attainment of an object according to one's desire*' it made us think that success today is a personal endeavour, and then wallop, it slapped us with a big, old-fashioned limitation: 'now often with particular reference to the attainment of wealth or position'.

While becoming Top Dog and earning enough to sustain a lifestyle peppered with five-star holidays and four-ply cashmere can be markers of modern-day female success, many women aspire to success's subtler sides: balance, authenticity, satisfaction and timing are just as valid as big bucks and killer job titles. Success is a multifaceted unicorn and yet from the outside looking in, success remains a predictable (male) workhorse.

This book is based on the principle that your success is unique to you. It doesn't matter what your age is, where you work or whether you've just thrown in the corporate towel and are about to launch a goji berry-themed food blog from your garden shed; the same rules for discovering – and re-evaluating – your individual variety of success still apply.

In this chapter we will give you a set of tools that should help you define your success – visualise that unicorn. What does she actually look like and how does she fly? Because when you know where you are heading (or riding) then you will be better placed to meaningfully digest the rest of the book, not to mention achieve everything you want out of work, and life. This is the start of something new – and thrilling.

WHAT Understanding Our Differences

There is no point comparing eggs with bacon: as we've already pointed out, women and men are built differently. The wonder of delivering new life into this world is a female-only pastime, whilst men have the upper hand when it comes to peeing on the go. Eggs and bacon work brilliantly on the same plate, but eggs and bacon need to be prepared using different cooking instructions. In short, it's OK for your definition of success to have a female tinge.

UPBRINGING

We all learnt lessons as children, young adults and even as the people we were yesterday, that continue to shape the way we think, our sensitivity levels, our resilience, our kindness, the intensity of our don't-give-a-damn swagger and, crucially, the vision of how we want our lives to turn out: our success.

'I think about confidence a lot,' says **Sharmadean Reid MBE**, founder of cult nail mecca WAH London, who has been named as one of the fifteen people who will define the arts in Britain by *Vogue* magazine. She is just thirty-one years old, and has become a business guide and mentor to many aspiring, female-run start-ups. 'I've met so many people in business and something that is so unfathomable to me is the way they um and ah about an idea; I just get on and do it. I often wonder why I am that way – and I've come to the conclusion that it's because my family have always been supportive of me.'

Sharmadean is different to many of the women she mentors, many of whom don't, for example, aspire to live life in the public eye. The point is, when we are able to accept these differences, we take our first step towards achieving a new type of career liberation and freedom. Whether it's between the female sisterhood, or across the gender divide, difference is a bonus, not a hindrance. Who wants to work in an office of automata? And here at the start, when we are grappling with our own definitions of success, especially in light of what society expects from us (to tread the well-beaten male path), it is worth acknowledging the sex divide.

Men have been more dominant in terms of meaningful, high-achieving careers for many more decades than women, and the legacy of this imbalance still exists today. Physically, men are the stronger sex, so back when supermarkets didn't deliver, they left the cave and killed the cow to be able to provide for their families. Women, on the other hand, stayed sheltered and nursed the babies.

Neanderthals, for the record, became extinct around 40,000 years ago. Yet the balance hasn't exactly found its equilibrium. We might have got the vote and won the freedom to choose whichever career we please, but we still work within a framework set out by men. Linear career trajectories, bullish definitions of success and rigid, pyramid-style hierarchy structures all suit the type of adult who was born with a need to beat his chest and climb the highest tree. This can be a problem for many women, especially ones who struggle with confidence and assertiveness. Thankfully, things are changing; barriers are starting to crumble and the landscapes against which many of us work are becoming more fluid and opportunistic.

But still, to be able to possess an honest and attainable vision of success, we need to be able to embrace the brilliance of what being a woman really means. Once we've done that, we can craft our unique career vision within its wonderfully female and multidimensional parameters.

So, lesson number one, don't compare yourself to the men in your life. And perhaps more importantly: don't pit yourself against your female peers either. Because when it comes to defining and then capturing our own breed of success, comparisons are nothing short of poison. Women's emotional complexities make us brilliant, but also confuse the issue. Take it from us; if you are trying to suppress your own definition of success whilst at the same time attempting to conform to the different types of successes expressed by friends and colleagues, not to mention your place of work and society, then you are going to feel so confused and pressurised to act in a certain way that it would be impressive if you were even able to just log on in the morning.

What you need is a nice shiny clean slate, because following other people's dreams will leave you eternally unfulfilled, not to mention completely detached from your magical success unicorn.

TIMING

Another marked difference between men and women is how our careers pan out over time. The female career trajectory, when you look at it in terms of timing, is a complicated graph: an image of the Alps mountain range makes a neat analogy. The many summits and troughs, as well as all the time gaps in between, tell the stories of how our work and personal lives interact. As an aside, when men plot their career/time graphs, the results are usually a lot more, ahem, straight and phallic.

Time is a crucial variable when we define our success, because for many of us, children and family will at some point impact on our climb. For many working women Everest is a long slog. At the start though, men and women tend to enter the workplace on a pretty even footing. We've all just graduated or got past the first hurdles of our careers, and we're all knuckling down in the day and partying too hard at night. Even though life at the lower end of the career ladder can be frustrating, there are advantages to all being on the same page.

And because women are having children later, this has meant an extension of this phase by a few years. Today, the typical woman gives birth to her first child at thirty years old, compared to twenty-six years old forty years ago in both the UK and Australia (twenty-six now and twenty-one then in the US). Usually, we then push out a selection of offspring and temporarily become overwhelmingly obsessed with love and poo.

For many women, in terms of work, a child represents a big fat trough. We are not anti-children: children are the highest peaks in our Books of Life, but work and life don't always sit neatly on the same page. And once a woman has a child, there is often something other than work lurking at the back of her mind. And while we're talking family pressures, the care of ageing parents can become another complication to speedy and lofty female career aspirations (love you Mum and Dad).

The balance does shift later on in life, because for us women the summit calls again when we're in our forties and fifties, and we forge ahead in our careers. This is just around the time that men realise there's more to life than work, and they ease off their ascent to smell the flowers.

For many working women our lives dictate our career climb – not the other way around. And while we do eventually reach our personal peak, we have often done so in a way that has responded to the patterns of our personal lives.

Men, on the other hand, are usually driven by Summit Fever from the off: singularly focused on their career achievements, they have hiked northwards through each layer of the corporate pyramid in their quest for career fulfilment. Male successes are usually measured by making money and bagging promotions and that makes things difficult for the rest of us.

Current research has revealed a shift though, as men who make up Gen Y and to some extent Gen X, begin to take their cues from our zigzagged career graphs. These men, the ones at parent/baby coffee mornings who have taken advantage of their entitlement to split paternity leave (whey hey, six months away from the grind!) or work a four-day week to embrace their passion for vintage trains, now have career trajectories with a few more lumps and bumps.

Men might be broadening their horizons, but most organisations – both public and private – still operate on the traditionally sequential, Summit Fever career model. The best thing to do when we find ourselves caught in these rigid, male-biased offices and careers is to reinforce and hold tight the subtler facets of our personal success.

Have a read of these three parameters of career success that the Kaleidoscope model (more on that just a bit further on) suggests are relevant to consider at all stages of our careers. Perhaps they are useful questions to ask yourself now?

CHALLENGE: What is your need for challenge, career advancement and self worth?
BALANCE: What are your and your families' requirements when it comes to balance, relationships and caregiving?
AUTHENTICITY: What about me?! How can I be authentic, true to myself and make genuine decisions, at work and at home, that fit seamlessly into my life and definition of success?

THE ACADEMICS EXPLAIN

The most accepted – and we believe, relevant – model of women's careers is the Kaleidoscope career model. The Kaleidoscope career is one created on our own terms; it is defined not by a corporation but by our personal values and our overall life choices. It says, and

TRADITIONALLY FEMALE VS TRADITIONALLY MALE/CORPORATE

	EARLY PHASE	MIDDLE PHASE	THIRD PHASE
Traditionally female	**Challenge** Balance Authenticity	**Balance** Challenge Authenticity	**Authenticity** Challenge Balance
Traditionally male/ corporate	**Challenge**	**Authenticity**	**Balance**

Based on work by Mainiero and Sullivan 2006

we tend to agree, that like a kaleidoscope, our careers are dynamic and constantly in motion; as our personal lives change we should be perfectly able to alter our careers accordingly.

What the research around this model tells us is that men traditionally work through their lives in a parallel manner (they thrive on the undeviating mountain climb) while women have tended to juggle everything at the same time.

In the Kaleidoscope's eyes, followers of the traditionally male path successfully compartmentalise their lives: which means that during the week they are able to solely focus on their careers and on Saturdays and Sundays they then focus on family. Interestingly, this research also says that while they are expert time dividers, many aspire to have a more blended, female-style approach to life.

You don't need us to tell you that women, in contrast, are often Queens of Kingdom Multitask. We are able to, and often feel emotionally obligated and energised, by juggling all elements of our lives all at the same time.

The most recent large-scale studies put into words what we've just covered – and what's probably swirling around your head. That women overwhelmingly tend to have complex career trajectories and much more nuanced definitions of success. And as such, we place more value than men do on individual achievement, pursuing a passion, receiving respect and making a difference and less on titles and training. Fewer women list wealth as an aspect of personal or professional success, although (clearly) it is still important to us.

The most common factor of success for both men and women is a desire to enjoy rewarding relationships. However, where the simple fact of having a family indicates success to men, women want to feel they have a *good family life*. Women are also more likely to talk about the importance of friends and community. For the majority of us, balancing a career and family is a major concern and it's one that complicates our notion of success.

Award-winning baking teacher and founder of Pretty Witty Cakes, **Suzi Witt**, has thousands of students based in nearly fifty countries around the world. A former City lawyer, having children completely changed her path. 'It was a no brainer,' she says. 'If I opted to go back to being employed I felt that I would never have the life I wanted. This was because becoming a parent had fundamentally changed me and what I wanted out of life.'

It is important to understand not just how our careers are shaped but also what boxes they might be forced to squeeze into. Research tells us that despite the kaleidoscopic nature of our lives, for women to reach senior management positions we still need to operate within a traditional, typically male career framework. To reach senior levels in corporate careers – a traditional definition of success, even if it is one we personally might eschew – studies show that women need to display high-career centrality, work continuously without career breaks (straight up Everest) and either accommodate their family responsibilities to fit around their work lives or remain childless in order to succeed.

Women who have reached this kind of role have typically been driven and worked continuously and full-time – anyone? No prizes for predicting the academics' conclusion that the perpetuation of this stereotype is hugely detrimental to women trying to meaningfully engage in their dual roles of career and family responsibilities.

As an aside, this may not be the case for you. Its presence in the top tiers of corporate careers, however, will in some way affect us all. Even in very creative industries, if you want to reach the top, at some point there's an expectation that you need to put in long hours of face time and that isn't always conducive to living our multifaceted, Kaleidoscopic lives.

This conflict is the crux of what makes defining our own success so problematic. Yes, we have more complex lives and careers and our unicorns are infinitely more colourful. What this all means in an everyday sense though is that women are subject to more stresses on our focus, jobs, values and relationships than men.

In addition, reaching traditionally successful roles often requires us to suppress that richness. This is not to say that we can't reach those lofty heights. Even those of us with the most vivid kaleidoscopes, those who want to meaningfully engage with our families, can do it. It is you this book is designed to help. But it is also here to help those for whom this isn't success. Those of us for whom passion, balance and authenticity dictate a different path. We may be baking different-shaped cakes, but we all need the same ingredients. When we understand where we are coming from – how our careers are shaped, what we are working with and against – defining that path becomes clearer and, suddenly, we are ready to achieve.

TO SUM UP

Men and women, women and women, you and your best friend, we are all different beings with different pet unicorns. Being different is good; it's what makes us stand out and shine. Don't ever be afraid to hold up your own breed of success.

And don't feel that being a woman is somehow a duff hand either. Yes, things might be less straightforward, but our world of possibility is sparklier too. While society continues to encourage men into traditional roles, we are more liberated. Count the number of male fashion bloggers or stay-at-home dads. Summit Fever can be a straitjacket and it's one we rarely wear.

Despite her choice to aim straight for the top, **Caroline Kuhnert**, Head of Ultra High Net Worth Emerging Markets Clients at global powerhouse UBS, acknowledges this freedom. Responsible for UBS's business with the super-rich in the Near and Middle East, Africa, Central Europe, Eastern Europe and Latin America (plentiful, as you can imagine), Caroline plays big. But it could have been different.

'Women have broader interests. When things get tough in the markets, you remember that you like to paint, are charitable or would like to have children. Women also have choices. Many men don't have, or don't feel they have, the same choices. They just have to get on with it,' she says. 'If you want to get ahead at work, accept that there may be tough times ahead and grit your teeth. Or take another path and be happy with it. But above all, don't be a victim. We need to make our choice and follow it through.'

Let this book be your call to arms. Your moment to avoid victimhood and make a deliberate choice, whatever that choice might be. You really can change where you are heading and the way that you are heading there, as long as you stay in touch with your notion of success every moment of your career. Alternatively, if you know where you are heading let this chapter cement that vision before you use the rest of this book to make it happen.

WORKOUT Your Success

This one needs a couple of friends. Grab a drink each and imagine you are about to make a presentation to a group of seventeen-year-old girls, perhaps your former selves, on the definition of success.

Now spend ten minutes discussing in your group what you believe that definition should be.

What you'll find: you won't agree. Even though you may not have fully articulated or even thought about it yet, you and your best friend will have different initial reactions to defining your visions of success.

Rejoice in your difference but understand the importance of defining your own vision rather than somebody else's.

HOW TO Find your Breed of Success

YOUR SUCCESS METRICS

Okey dokey, so hopefully by now you have started picking out unicorn names and have some kind of workable notion of what success is in your eyes.

In order to define something though, we need to be able to measure its outline: what metrics are you going to use? **Arianna Huffington**, co-founder of the *Huffington Post*, has three: money, power and the third – well-being (which encompasses wisdom, wonder and giving). Is she right? 'The current definition of success – in which we drive ourselves into the ground, if not the grave, and in which working to the point of exhaustion and burnout is considered a badge of honour – was created by men. It's a model of success that's not working for women, and it's not working for men either.'

But of course there could be many more. What about personal challenge, expertise, honesty or even resilience – the ability to fail and then get up, dust yourself down and start all over again? It all depends on your personal core values.

Part of knowing where you are heading – the definition of your success – is being able to vocalise these metrics to others. And you can't know those until you're aware of your core values. These are likely to stay fairly constant, although they can evolve over time. For example, as we age, we may focus more on altruism and balance and place less value on money and power. If something starts to feel out of balance or not quite right in your career, the first step is to return to your values and check they are still aligned with your success plan.

VALUES – Your Life Hashtags

Ah, values. Yes, here is one of those words you expect to find in a conventional career self-help book. We apologise in advance for the clichéd diction, so instead, let's call them your ultimate life hashtags.

Draw to mind the nicest current photograph you own of yourself, the one where your skin looks all dewy and that wrinkle between your eyes has been obscured by a helpful lock of hair. Now, mentally post that photograph on your favourite social media channel: if this photograph was the only way of telling the world the story of who you are, which hashtags would you choose?

#Kind
#Driven
#Family gal
#Independent
#Diligent
#Hungry for money
#Sociable
#Queen Bee

If you're not a social media type, then think of your values as the oars of a boat you're rowing towards success. These oars keep you afloat and also ensure that you are heading in the right direction. Rowing boats that glide on still, cool waters are a thing of beauty. Underneath though, the oars are pounding the wake; the oars – your values – work in unison, to underpin your career boat race.

Values, in non-boating terms, are the moral indicators that we believe are important in the way that we live and work. It's values that determine our priorities; and, deep down, they are the measures we use to tell ourselves whether our lives are turning out the way we wanted them to. Helpfully, research tells us that if we align our work values with our personal ones, we are much more likely to feel fulfilled. So that's only one set of hashtags, or oars, to concentrate on then.

Like many of the concepts in this book, values are often unconscious and are not something we always articulate or realise that we even hold. This is what makes them tricky. We all spend so much time living and working on autopilot that our values get lost in the mix of washing our hair and clearing the inbox.

It would be impossible, not to mention exhausting, to accurately think through every command that shoots from the grey matter into our arms, legs and thoughts. Thus, we spend a hefty proportion of our time going through the motions and processing things in a mildly oblivious manner. When it comes to our careers, however, this is dangerous. Especially, when things aren't working out the way we (unconsciously) planned them to. It is at times like these, times like now, when you might want to hit the reset key on your career #values.

So how do we know if we're working within our core values? Well, happiness and fulfilment are good indicators, but these are nebulous and hard to measure. If, for example, you are achieving external measures of success – money, power, an office with a riverside view – but still don't *feel* successful, then it is likely that you are not being true to your personal values of morality and charity. Likewise, if your family is everything, but you are racking up over sixty hours a week with your feet under the desk, then you don't need to be a psychiatrist to work out that you're going to feeling dissatisfied, no matter what the rewards.

Or, do you thrive on the company of others, but are currently working alone? When we row our boats using oars that don't fit we end up feeling down, unmotivated and possibly even resentful of our careers. Not just that, we also allow ourselves to venture down a path that will never lead to success.

VALUES – HOW?
A good way to unearth these mysterious life hashtags is to consider your past. When were the times at work (or in your personal life) that you felt happiest, proudest and most satisfied? And when were the times that you achieved great things but your heart felt flat? If you invest in some self-reflection (mirror optional), your seminal list of values should start to unfold. When you realise that authenticity and expertise are up there near the top, write them down. Start a list of hashtags – spend time thinking back across your experiences to date, and they will lead you to a new understanding about how and why things matter.

Once your values list starts emerging, try this workout to help fill in the gaps.

WORKOUT   What Do you Value?

Find two coloured pens and a piece of paper.

(2 minutes) Draw a graph with time along the bottom and fulfilment or happiness along the side. Use the first colour to draw a line reflecting your work fulfilment over time. Reflect high points like getting a job you really wanted, and low points, like not quite making it through those tough exams.

(2 minutes) Now take the other colour. With this one, plot your life. Highs and lows as before. Now sit back and reflect. Where are the peaks, what about the troughs? What do they have in common? Where do they coincide? Start to understand what matters to you. In other words, your values.

(6 minutes) Each of these meeting points should highlight a few of your values. Try to identify ten values, ten reasons why work (or life) really felt great. If you have more, think about whether they are really separate. For example if you have compassion, generosity and altruism, you could conflate them to say that concern for others is important to you. Once you have your list, try to put them in order. If it's tricky go through each one, compare and move it up or down depending on how it fares against the one above. Where you struggle to decide, compare them in real-life scenarios. For example, with adventure vs. intellectual challenge: would you rather take up an overseas project similar to one you have done before or take one that's trickier but closer to home?

WORK TYPE

At this point, it is worth taking a moment to think about everything that we have already covered: success and society, climbing trees as little girls, timing, kaleidoscopes and now values. Be prepared, there is more to come. Success – and its meaning to you today – is an intricate subject. Don't rush this chapter. To be able to clearly and effectively unlock your personal success story takes time. It certainly requires more than a quick muse over a lukewarm canteen cappuccino.

When we are able to clearly formulate and express our core values, we become empowered, which is one of the aims of our book. But values won't finish the success puzzle; next we need to tackle our work type. Yes, we know, we know; we've just spent several pages banging on about the importance of being an individual in this whole achieving-your-success Nirvana, and now we're trying to impose some kind of general classification system? It sounds bonkers, we know, but bear with us.

We *are* individuals, but most of us work with other individuals and, at some point, we need to consider ourselves within this context. When we know our work type (perhaps you're a Climber, or someone who aspires to be an Expert), it adds a new dimension to our success game – we have more purpose.

There's no point trying to become the next board member if your personality suits the solitary role of an award-winning scientist. Identifying our work type also helps to normalise our quest: to understand and accept that we are not the only ones who don't aspire to be the boss helps us to make peace with our success definition, particularly when comparison rears its ugly head.

To give these personality types a bit more, er, personality, we've assigned to each a well-known female success story. While we certainly don't want you to compare yourself to JK Rowling, or any of the others, giving each a face should bring them to life. When you read through, make sure you do so with yourself (not your flatmate or mother) in mind.

KARREN BRADY – The Climber

We've all seen *The Apprentice*. Karren Brady, like many climbers, is interested in the big job title, a degree of status that could induce cold sweats among non-climbers and a pay packet that allows for regular and bountiful expeditions to Harvey Nichols. Brady-ites are highly competitive and want to combine material success with enjoyment at work. Having said that, some women in this category are more focused on beating the competition and goal busting than pure work status.
GENDER SPLIT – MEN DOMINATE

MARIE CURIE – The Expert
Women like Curie are primarily interested in becoming experts in
their field (scientist Curie was the first woman to receive a Nobel
Prize for her pioneering research into radioactivity). Curie groupies
crave recognition for their achievements and aspire towards technical
expertise over status or pay.
GENDER SPLIT – WOMEN DOMINATE

MARGARET THATCHER – The Influencer
We aren't making any kind of political statement here; whatever
her shortcomings the Iron Lady perfectly encompasses the role
of Influencer. Driven by the degree of organisational influence
that they can achieve, Maggie-ites want to leave their mark on
an industry – their legacy and impact gets them out of bed in
the morning.
GENDER SPLIT – EQUAL MIX

JK ROWLING – The Self-Improver
Today, Rowling might be a literary superstar, not to mention the UK's
best-selling living author, but when she started she was predominantly
motivated and inspired by realising her potential. JK-ers are primarily
interested in personal challenge and self-development; they also crave an
ability to balance their work with their personal lives.
GENDER SPLIT – WOMEN DOMINATE

These women are an impressive bunch; not only do they neatly
illustrate these four key work character types, they are also a fantastic
reminder of how women can and do achieve many different kinds of
success across many different spheres.

What's likely is that you've probably found elements of yourself
(figuratively, if not literally) in several of the categories. Don't worry;
you are not a lost soul with little hope of finding lasting career
success. You are normal. Even our category namesakes each possess
elements of one another in terms of their career personalities. It is
normal, nay good, to have a nuanced picture of yourself and your
work style. The reason these categories are useful is to give our

successes parameters. Once we know that we're, say, part Influencer and part Climber, it should relieve the pressure to be an Expert and Self-Improver too.

PAINTING YOUR VISION

Now comes the really exciting stuff. Once we are clear on our personal values and where they stand on the work personality categorisation chart, we can think big. Because who doesn't love a bit of blue-sky thinking? The daily grind can stifle even the most resolute free spirits: the same commute, the same desk, the same egg mayo sandwich for lunch every day … it's not exactly rousing stuff. To get ahead, though, we need to be able to shelve the minutiae of work life and look to the future in all its Technicolor glory. No one succeeded in life by just focusing on the here and now.

Please enter … your Career Vision Painting, or CVP as we like to call it. The academics, just so you know, call this a Career Vision Statement, but we're taking a more creative, visual approach.

A CVP is a personal work manifesto, realised as a beautiful oil painting. To be able to build that image, we need to picture ourselves in our ultimate job. At this point, we don't need to focus on how we'll get there (that'll stunt the imagination, plus we'll address that later in the book), instead just paint a vision in your head of you doing the job that you aspire to.

Chances are you've never done this before. That's the funny thing about careers; we spend our childhoods imagining what we'll be when we grow up, then we grow up, take the first good job going our way, and pretty much just wing it from there. That is why exercises like this virtual painting session are crucial, and enjoyable too. Let your mind and brushes go in whichever direction they choose; don't quieten any voices – just go wild!

You'll soon find that your imagination has formed a vision that is really very happy indeed; if you think freely enough, and still within the context of your career, you should be able to actually see yourself in a place where you'd be truly content to end up work-wise.

Now here's the cringey bit: find a willing volunteer (partner and/or best friend fulfil this role perfectly) and articulate this vision to them. You might feel stupid, but saying it out loud – describing the painting – will clarify what you're thinking, and make it seem more possible. Plus, this exercise gives you something tangible to work towards.

Because once that picture is painted, you can start to imagine how the painted – successful – you will act and feel. If you really want to be the boss, don't just visualise yourself in the boardroom, delve deeper:

'When I am the boss,' you could tell yourself, 'I will feel strong and powerful, but I will also retain empathy for and interest in my younger employees.'

'When I am boss [see, this is fun], my day will start early, I will work alone at home, have a quick stop at the gym, and then it'll be straight to the office for a summit meeting with my amazing team.'

'When I am boss, I will wear Miu Miu prom dresses in the summer and something dark and elegant from Dior when it's cold…'

If you're struggling, try looking to your role models to help piece together your image (turn to Chapter 5 for more on how to identify these). Make-up guru **Bobbi Brown** certainly looked close to home when she was seeking her inspiration. 'I've always dreamed big and been determined to reach my goals – whatever they might be. I learnt a lot from my grandfather, Papa Sam. He moved here from Russia when he was a boy and he worked his way up selling newspapers and ladies' handbags, and eventually he became "Cadillac Sam", one of the biggest car dealers in Chicago.'

Like Bobbi, what you're aiming for is an inspirational image of success rather than a restrictive list of self-imposed expectations to weigh you down. And don't be limited by your current role either. If you are a nurse but your core values of autonomy and entrepreneurship (Karren Brady + JK Rowling) mean you have a strong drive to launch your own business, then this is a valid Career Vision Painting. Go with what feels right and true to you and you'll be more likely to achieve it – don't worry, we'll work out how to get you there later on in the book.

Without a CVP, we reside in a passive place that is not conducive to happiness or fulfilment. By just buying this book you have proved to yourself that there is more out there; so put the gear stick into first, and right now, drive yourself out of inertia and into a sunny and proactive frame of mind.

Here is a neat workout to help give your imaginative play a bit of structure.

WORKOUT CVP

Now get creative.

(1 minute) Reread your core values and remind yourself of your work type.

Remember this is a long-term vision not a short-term thing – don't be limited by your present, we are imagining a best future. Remember also that things will ebb and flow in your career – but where do you want to end up?

Now write.

(3 minutes on each question)

1. If absolutely no obstacles stood in the way of your achieving it, what would you most like to attain in your career?
2. Who are the people you most admire? What is it about them or their careers that attract you to them? Is there something about what they have or do that you want for your career vision?
3. Imagine yourself in the future at a point in which you have achieved great career success. What is it that you have accomplished? What does your life look like?

Just to reiterate, without a clear Vision Painting (or Statement), your career will end up feeling like one of those very long, very delayed commutes home. A map is a good way of bridging the space between the here and now and that beautiful image in your mind's eye.

If you have ever been stuck between stations on the London Underground, then you'll know the panic and disorientation that can manifest itself when you are paused inside a dark tunnel and you have no idea how you'll be able to get off. Perhaps you have that same panicky feeling now when you think about your job and where it is going?

When you are young, it's kind of fun to not have any type of direction. Back then, it felt OK to ride around on Planet Job frivolously hopping on and off your tube train ... It is important that we all have times in our career (usually they are early on) when we experiment with different jobs and in different fields. But this career recklessness isn't sustainable if you want to achieve fulfilment and success. What you need is a map to work out how you're going to reach your unicorn.

Gemma Bellman, Managing Director (at just thirty) of our favourite beauty and wellness site Get the Gloss and creator of her own successful app, BeautySpotter, didn't get where she was by staring out the window and counting sheep. No, she had a clear vision from the off.

'In every one of my decisions there's been an element of planning, but of course always mixed in with a large dose of chance. The journey is different for each of us and largely depends on whether we want to follow a more traditional career path or go down the entrepreneurial route. I've always been drawn to both, so I try to be very structured about the way I approach an entrepreneurial project. I started off somewhere that was highly structured, at Goldman Sachs, where I knew I would get a great grounding, good skill set and start building my network early on. I was then pulled, by the heartstrings I suppose, to a more creative role at L'Oreal, where I learnt important lessons in business and retail, and I then combined this range of experience to launch get-the-look app, BeautySpotter. All of this forms part of a broader drive toward certain goals but is always shaped by the opportunities and challenges presented at the time. When an exciting opportunity came up – as it did for me as MD at Get the Gloss – I couldn't wait to get started. So I guess I've learnt that even when something hasn't been written in your detailed plan from the start, if it works with where you want to get to, go for it!'

Of course, there will inevitably be delays and detours in everyone's journeys, and probably, as there has been for Gemma, there will be some moments of unexpected opportunity too; but when we at least know the final stop, then we have somewhere concrete to aim towards. As we've said, later on in the book we'll help you plan your route – now though, hold that Career Vision tightly, because when the end point is in sight, we are much more likely to arrive in one piece.

Oh, and don't start chipping away at the painting when we're not looking. We know what you did there, you started thinking big, and then you doubted yourself; everything looked a bit too scary and impossible to achieve. The point of a CVP is to unhinge ourselves from succumbing to internal limiting beliefs. We all have these pesky and intrusive thoughts that manifest themselves in our subconscious; what we need to do is learn to quieten the voices. Try putting them somewhere very dark and very far away (inside that Underground tunnel?) and keep them totally separate from your work happy place.

Negative thoughts sabotage career success. Everyone fears ridicule; we're all guilty of some prohibitively short-term thinking; ditto, following someone else's dream, suffering the pressure of tradition-bound choices and being too narrow in our focus. It's how we manage these fears that is key to achieving success.

If you are still struggling to envisage your ultimate job, then try this workout.

WORKOUT Visioning the Past

Sometimes it is most helpful to look to the future, but hindsight is also a beautiful thing.

Imagine you are sitting at the head of the table at your eightieth birthday. You're looking back fondly at a life you have lived fully and well.

Now think about what is creating that warm, satisfied glow you feel. Ask yourself where you went, what you did, where you lived, who was in your

WORKOUT **Visioning the Past** continued

life, what you did for others and what your life felt like. What's important: is it wealth or family, autonomy or recognition, balance or altruism? What is it that would make you feel – particularly in a work sense – that it has been a life well lived?

Grab a piece of paper and pen, set a time for ten minutes and silence your internal editor (we know her well). Now write. When the timer dings, consider what you've revealed about your vision.

How will you create the life you can be happy with fifty years from now?

SHORT-TERM PLANNING – The Big Five

Defining your own success is a multifaceted notion that as we've already shown draws as much on academic research as it does on the way we are raised, our character traits, and our ability to project ourselves into the future. These are all vital parts of the puzzle, but what about the individual pieces?

We say, start with the edges first. Setting short-term career goals allows us to turn that Career Vision into something attainable – something that we can logically get our heads around. Rome was not created in a day, despite the expectations of Constantine the Great (male, sadly). Likewise, successful careers need time and structure.

Stepping stones are a much-trodden (sorry) but useful analogy for getting from here to your unicorn. Very few people achieve their ultimate career goal in one fell swoop. Usually, we take a series of smaller leaps that in some capacity or other feed into the final piece in the puzzle.

It is fair to say (and good to know) that sometimes these leaps don't feel like progression. If the final goal is overseeing the foreign department at work, then you're going to need to take that job in Kazakhstan for a year, even if it's not a promotion you wanted. It's just as important to gather vital skills as it is to glide northwards up the job tree, so instead of being impatient, think strategically.

When we break down our Career Vision Painting into digestible three-year plans it makes success more attainable – and probably more enjoyable too (after all, no one likes stumbling around in the dark). Three years is a helpful amount of time, as it can cope with both realistic achievements and a good dose of aspirational goals too. We suggest thinking about where you want to be in three years, and then work backwards across the stepping stones, to where you are today. If you need to, look over your values and your vision, and remember to incorporate both, in some capacity or another, into each step.

If you are doing all of this in your head while flicking through the book, then stop. Research tells us that those who actually write their strategy or goals down score more winners than those who don't. If you need to, go out and buy yourself a nice new notebook, something that you can keep in your top drawer and enjoy adding to it over time.

Here are some tips on how to make a first-rate three-year plan. Think of this as your very own personal business plan. Include the elements below and make it detailed enough to follow but flexible enough that chance can still work its magic.

> BE SPECIFIC: is it clear what your stepping stones actually are?
> BE MEASURABLE: how will you know when you've leaped to the next stone?
> BE AWARE: might your stone-stepping impact on others – your partner, for example?
> BE REALISTIC: are your stones too slippery? Can this route actually be achieved?
> BE TIMELY: when are you going to make the final, three-year leap?

AFTERTHOUGHTS
The Here and Now
As we've now explained, when it comes to planning for success, each one of us requires an elegant blend of aspirational vision and realistic frameworks. By now, your success bag should be overflowing: oars, hashtags, unicorns, a self-portrait, the Underground map, each one of these is a valid component of your Super Success Story.

Think big, yes. But, of course, work hard too. The late, multi-award-winning architect **Zaha Hadid**, who spoke to us before her unexpected and tragic demise, emphasised the importance of industry. 'Architecture is a very tough profession,' she told us. 'Every architect you talk to has it very, very difficult. Now I've achieved the success, but it's always been a very long struggle. In the early years we worked all night to establish ourselves. It requires constant focus and commitment.'

When we combine our vision with hard work and the plethora of skills awaiting you in the rest of this book, we're sure you'll be riding that unicorn before you can say glossy white mane.

For those whose current position is at complete odds with their ultimate self-portrait, then try creating a temporary success appendix. We must always keep an eye on the organisation in which we are currently working, because no matter what our ultimate definitions of success actually are, when we aren't working towards success in our current employer's eyes, we start treading on thin career ice.

Got a touch of the Rowling about your vision, but stuck in a Thatcherite place of work? Then make sure you use your time today to build the skills that will help you realise your end dream of opening a restaurant or writing a bestseller, whilst making sure you understand how your line manager defines success. It can be a balancing act, but it's worth the struggle if you are contemplating a complete departure from the here and now.

If success in your organisation today is a predictable – and frustrating – blend of the male and the linear, where steady progression through the ranks is the order of the day and that's not you, then focus on the elements of the company, and your job, that resonate most strongly. Otherwise, you risk others seeing you as someone who lacks commitment and motivation, despite the fact that you're completely dedicated to your role, if not the ancillary politicking it entails. Careers are as much about managing people and situations as they are about being the best.

Timing (Part Deux)

If you've ever owned a pet, then you'll know the work involved. Your success unicorn is no different: it will not feed itself, nor will it polish that graceful, twisted horn. What we're saying is that your success story needs regular tending. To be able to sit back in old age and feel content that your career turned out the way you had hoped it would (the dream scenario), you are going to need to keep that unicorn in tiptop condition. Not every day, or even every week, but at regular intervals throughout the year remember to think objectively about your job, your overarching career, and what you consider success to be at that moment in time. It will change, you see, and that's OK as long as you keep on top of things.

We think it's wise to set aside some time each year – New Year, your birthday (or is that too depressing already?), September – to revisit this chapter and your definition of success. Adjustments to oars and hashtags (think of these as Operating System Updates) will help keep you on the correct route. It might be worth rereading this chapter right now in fact, because what's clear to us is that finding our versions of success is not exactly clear at all. Having said that, when it's in your grasp, be firm in the way that you attack that end goal.

This is the beginning of your new work story: if you build strong foundations now, the rest will feel decidedly breezier.

WORKOUT Evaluate Your Success

Just as regular reviews are essential in the workplace, personally checking you're on track is crucial too. To this end, now we're going to complete a personal review.

(10 minutes) Schedule a ten-minute meeting with yourself. For this, you're going to be your own boss.

Set out the goals you're going to track.

Now evaluate how you are doing with reaching your goals. Specific things to evaluate might include how close you are to defining your

WORKOUT Evaluate Your Success continued

vision or, if that vision is defined, how you're moving towards it. What have you changed? What are you working on? What has worked and what hasn't? And finally, set small goals to work towards for the next meeting and beyond.

Now schedule this meeting to occur in one month, and to recur every month after that. Make the meeting with yourself non-negotiable. Self-evaluation is a powerful motivator and reinforcer of change.

THE TIPS

Devoured the chapter, mastered the workouts, now it's time to spend ten minutes a day implementing our tips into your daily work routine:

|1| Be a fearless female

Remind yourself to embrace what makes you female – the pros and the cons career-wise. Then make peace with it. More likely than not you will have a more nuanced definition of success than your male friends, more of an eye on your kids than your partner. Embrace it. Your femininity is brilliant. It affords you choice, emotional depth and better wardrobe choices in equal measure. If you start to doubt it, remind yourself. Every morning look in the mirror and affirm the brilliance of you and the success you are striving for. Whatever the words you choose, positive affirmation is proven to improve wellbeing and drive away and reduce stress.

|2| Hone your vision

A vision is crucial. If yours still isn't clear despite these workouts, look externally. Reread your favourite novels, evaluating what makes your favourite characters so dear to you. What about the well-known women you admire? What about them makes you tick? Crystallise these insights and use them to edit your vision statement until it sets your ambition on fire.

|3| Stay flexible

But, as we've said, the vision might change. Watch for it. Keep a copy pinned to your wall or readily to hand in your Evernote app. If you sense that you and your vision are out of whack, don't be afraid to work at a redefinition. You know the bumps in the road we've talked about, they can upset that vision too. When necessary, revisit the workouts and amend the vision to suit today's you.

|4| Look around you

Don't lose sight of your environment. Your own definition of success is crucial. But that of your workplace or industry is crucial too. Have an eye on both not only to appreciate where you stand in the mix, but also what you might need to do to get heard.

|5| Silence your critic

The biggest enemy of defining success is your inner critic. Whether she manifests as the devil on your shoulder or the voice of 'compare and despair', lock her out of this conversation. This is just step one on your path to greatness. If she starts to get mouthy, silence her with the fact that we're about to put the tools to get there in your hands.

CHAPTER 3

Internal Influences

THE BACKGROUND

T his chapter will help you to identify your internal strengths and your internal shortcomings so that you can accept who you are, realise where you need to make changes and harness what you already have in bucketloads. You are a brilliant work in progress; now it is time to get inside your head – inside Planet You – to take that brilliance and raise it ten-fold.

Whether you are a policewoman, a partner at an international law firm, a primary school teacher or a ballerina, if you want to fly your success unicorn anytime soon, you need to cultivate a proven set of personality traits, behaviours and capabilities that flourishing career women tend to possess.

Darcey Bussell and Helena Morrissey don't just share a neat brown bob and a penchant for pearls. They are also both in ownership of a similar set of characteristics that influence how they work; we don't have to know them to be crystal clear that they both have drive, determination, impressive stress tolerance levels and a host of other important character traits. What we're saying is that to be able to do great things at work – to attain that Career Vision – you need these too.

Every successful person in the workplace needs to manage the same basic demands. Not, at this point, the demands of time and balance (jump to Chapter 10 for more on balance); no, these pressures are the ones that swirl around our brains – that impact on how we feel at work.

We aren't robots, just as we aren't perfect specimens either. All of us have insecurities and flaws and to realise our career dreams, we need to line up certain books in our personality libraries so that we have the words and knowledge to cope at work. What goes on inside our heads is an ultimate game changer. Happily none of us are born mistresses of successful thinking; much of it is learnt. And now we're going to teach you too.

Darcey and Helena will both have been – and still are – subjected to a similar array of demands when they go to work in the morning. These are the same stresses, by the way, that you face too. For ease, we have divided the character traits, ways of thinking and states of mind needed to face these demands into two neat teams: strategy and emotions. Together they cover the complete spectrum of Internal Influences that dictate how well you do at work.

Your mind is the most powerful organ in your body; this chapter will get it onside and working harder so that you're able to fly that unicorn into the blue.

Strategy: how you think about work
> **You plan your career:** You know success requires forethought.
> **You are ambitious:** You know foresight and confidence go hand in hand with planning to conquer challenges and achieve future goals.
> **You enjoy your job:** You choose the right career, find your flow and make the most of what you've got.

Emotions: how you cope at work
> **You are conscientious:** You are hard working, careful, painstaking, meticulous and scrupulous – working by your inner sense of what is right.
> **You are resilient:** You reside happily in high-stress environments.
> **You have ego strength:** You believe in yourself no matter the obstacles.
> **You are assertive:** You are straightforward in your communication style.
> **You have empathy:** You understand and relate to the feelings of others.
> **You have energy:** You bring vitality and enthusiasm to your work.

As a postscript, ego strength and assertiveness are both elements of confidence. Confidence is so crucial (some believe it is the most important trait). and can be such a common problem area for women. that we've given confidence its own chapter – coming up next.

These lists look daunting in print so don't go putting big fat crosses where they're not required. Remember, all of this is a process. So take a moment to reread these traits and really think about where your strengths and weaknesses lie, because these two lists form the basis of everything we're about to discuss.

In short, if you want to get ahead you need to have a smooth blend of confidence, resilience and energy – as well as be intuitively self-aware (much more of which later).

Men, by the way, have an almost identical set of traits for success. Energy, empathy, focus and the ability to tolerate stress all feature heavily for them too. What's interesting though is that the only non-direct comparison in studies of successful working people across the sexes is confidence. In the main, men just don't suffer our female-style confidence crisis. The confidence gap is something that women must manage and it's a key theme in this book. When we can have full trust in our thoughts and ourselves, as well as truly believe in our own powers, then we'll achieve our success and consequently help bridge the gender divide.

We are going to start with an exploration of the emotions list, because for many, this is where most Internal Influence glitches lie.

EMOTIONS
Conscientiousness
Happily, what we lack in confidence, women make up for in conscientiousness. You only need to look at Jane Austen for the evidence.

One of the most widely read writers in English literature, Austen, despite her biting irony and brilliant exploration of women, received little personal fame from her work. But, she remained doggedly determined – she was conscientious. And her conscientiousness has left the rest of us an unmatched legacy of literature.

Being conscientious (this trait includes timeliness, diligence and self-control) is one of the most important personality factors when referring to success, because conscientious people are better at setting goals, are more organised and happier to follow the rules of the game.

As an aside, Austen wasn't exactly lacking in the areas of ego strength, assertiveness (a female writer, fancy that!), empathy, energy (she wrote and published *Sense and Sensibility*, *Pride and Prejudice*, *Mansfield Park* and *Emma* in just four short years) and confidence either. She lived at a time when women weren't encouraged to work, let alone succeed. So we can only believe that it was her strong will and passion (her Internal Influences) that kept her going.

Stress Tolerance
Women are expert stress heads. And this complicates things immensely. We are literally the bright light towards which stress moths hover. And stress can be a big stress when it comes to work.

But stress can also be a driver for brilliance when you know how to harness its fiery, panicky power. Redirect stress and it will, surprising as it sounds, become your ally – your career cheerleader even. But until you can sing and dance with stress, it can feel like one of work's biggest enemies.

Women and men experience different types of stressors in the workplace. For example, women tend to get all hot under the collar when it comes to work relationships. We're guilty of misinterpreting what the boss has just said, or taking to heart a flippant comment made by one of our favourite colleagues. We access our emotions more easily, and at work, this can become an obstacle to getting ahead. Men, as a comparison, get stressed about money and mistakes, which by the way are just as restricting as relationships, they just present differently.

If your team got a grilling from the boss, the fallout would be different between the sexes. The men would most likely take it on the chin and then carry on unfazed. The women – you know what we're going to say here – would spend the rest of the day in varying states of panic, palpitations and fear. We find relationships at work stressful: fact.

The grilling didn't bother the men, not because they don't care about their colleagues, or the boss's opinion for that matter, but because their stresses lie in different spheres. As we've said, what they worry about are the financials and work mistakes, which is hardly surprising, because whether or not they actually bring home the majority of the bacon (all hail the female breadwinner), men are still programmed to think of their role as being The Provider.

For women, by contrast, emotions are stress number one. Then there's the fact that women's lives are just more stressful. We've got more going on in them, because we tend to dive into the intricacies of work and life to a greater degree than men. We expand the roles of friend, carer (women tend to do more caretaking at work as well as at home), manager, confidante, mother, wife and mentor so that each is as fulfilling as the next. This is admirable and stressful in equal measure: when stresses bubble beneath our everyday workload, it makes us anxious and uncreative. Put bluntly, stress stops us from fulfilling our potential.

The good news is that once we have stress in our hands and we know why it's there, we can harness its energy to greater ends. Try and think of yourself as a furnace; we know it's not the most glamorous analogy, but the idea is that your furnace stress heat could be driving new challenges, networking or promotions.

Having a higher stress tolerance – or learning to increase your stress tolerance – is an advantage, especially when you can redirect the heat. Those who cope better with this daily burden of stress achieve more and do better at work; they're also happier and less likely to quit. We say, learn to process stress positively.

Once you reframe your stress, manage it more effectively and dump the rest in some sort of tension recycling system (one day we'll be able to sell this excess energy back to the National Grid), then your journey through work and life will be immeasurably improved.

Energy
The upshot of being – let's face it – busier than men, is that we're frequently tired. Exhausted even. But success isn't sleepy. Women

who do well are disproportionately energetic in comparison to their lethargic peers. And again, it's not innate. Sucesssful women's adrenal glands don't secrete caffeine; they weren't born with more bounce. Energy is something that can – and should – be cultivated.

Melissa and Jasmine Hemsley, bloggers, authors, TV chefs and global health gurus, demonstrate that energy every day. Fuelled by their healthy relationship with food and exercise, they frequently find themselves working seven-day weeks. The way Jasmine refuels her waning reserves is to acknowledge it.

'It has been a total pleasure to work on this business, which is our passion – and the last few years have been plenty of hard work – more graft than glam! It has been all-consuming, exciting and gone far beyond the small seed idea of having a family-run wellness company with food at its heart. The passion gives you energy but you have to check in with yourself constantly as you can easily work 24/7 as new and exciting opportunities and ideas pop up. Sometimes you just have to block out a day in the diary: no appointments whatsoever. It has to be like that, because otherwise you will totally burn out. So if I am tired, I say I am tired. If I feel exhausted, I give in to it, go home and go to bed at nine o'clock – and you feel brand new the next day. When you're exhausted it can be easy to get swept up into "but that could lead to that" or "I don't want to upset them." Ultimately you run the risk of spreading yourself too thin and not sticking to your career plan.

'Sleep and proper down time is the big thing that always get compromised in a busy career. We work with so many people who think they can't go to bed early because they might miss out on something, or it's boring, or nobody else does it so why on earth should they need more sleep. I have to remind myself constantly that if I want to get somewhere faster I have to sleep more!'

Jasmine doesn't think that going to bed early is boring, and we don't either. Energy has bounds and while Jasmine might be able to take on more than the average woman, she gives herself time off, and you should too.

Empathy

The last of our essential emotions, empathy is something most of us have in spades. Crying at the news? Tick. Feeling our best friend's break-up as viscerally as if it were our own? We've all been there. This is good news. Most of our inbuilt empathy cylinders fire on full throttle all the time. Successful women embrace their compassionate natures – and it pays dividends. Success isn't about being like a man, it's about harnessing the things that make us women and working with them in the best way we can. Empathy is our friend because she helps us understand and respect our peers and ourselves.

STRATEGY

Enjoyment

Anita Roddick, one the UK's most visionary and pioneering female entrepreneurs before her death in 2007, put it like this: 'To be successful you have to believe in it with such a passion that it becomes a reality.' Positive psychology tells us that happiness leads to success. And not just at work either; when we are happy, our health, wellness, family life, energy and spirit all thrive. We cannot expect to be at our best and kick those balls into touch if we drag ourselves into work every morning.

Ask yourself this: do you think about your job and smile? Go on, do it. Sit there for a moment and run through a typical day in your work life: how's that facial expression? If there's a wash of contentment across your face, then you're well placed. A happy working woman will progress further, because she enjoys what she does. If your forehead is in deep frown mode, then you need to consider what it is about your career that's inducing this grimace. When our hearts aren't in our work, the outcome is grim.

To explain more deeply the importance of career happiness, Step Up has carried out a body of research in the field of law. Law is an uncompromising and challenging industry, which is why we chose it for this study. We concluded that if very senior female lawyers, despite their punishing schedules, were still happy, then they were on to something magical.

What was clear from the lawyers that we talked to, of whom all continue to battle the aforementioned stressors as well as the added pressures of this intense sphere of work, was that they *loved* their jobs. Moreover, the interviewees themselves identified that the pleasure they derived from their work was the exception not the rule.

Lawyer **Tamara Box** is Global Chair of the largest team at international firm Reed Smith. Alongside her many industry awards, she is also a founding member of the 30% Club, which successfully campaigns for female representation on FTSE boards. Alongside her phenomenal energy and empathy, she also loves her job. 'Enjoying my work has had a huge bearing on what I've achieved. When you feel that your work is fun, you will be much more successful at what you are doing,' she says. 'I won't tell you there aren't a few days where I don't think, "I could do without this day." But by and large, I love what I do. I love having the opportunity to meet incredible people, to go to amazing places, to be a part of challenging transactions, to see other people achieve success, to get to be part of a transformation. To me that is exciting. So for me every single day is a lot of fun. I'd like to think that if it ever stops being fun, I would find something else to do.'

MP and previous Education Secretary and Minister for Women and Equalities, **Nicky Morgan**, agrees that drive and passion have been crucial to her success in equal measure: 'I joined the Conservative Party myself at just sixteen,' she explains, 'and I've always know that politics was something I was deeply interested in. I had a fantastic career in law and loved working in an environment that was intellectually very demanding. But eventually I realised that the call of politics wasn't going to go away and that's when I made the decision to stand as an MP – and once I had done that, I didn't give up until I was there on the green benches.'

We wholeheartedly agree with Nicky and Tamara: when we are passionate about what we do, the rest – our unicorns – will follow.

Planning
Passion and planning don't seem like obvious bedfellows. But passion plays out in plans of action and unless we know where we are heading, that passion will eventually pass.

A skill for planning is not just obvious, it's easy too, and if your planning head and your ambition head can get talking, then you'll have the Holy Grail of success: work focus.

As we have already mentioned, when we have a vision of success and set out broadly how we are going to achieve it, then that success is more likely to grow wings. If, on the other hand, we aimlessly head forward, we're in danger of missing the right turn to the top.

'Whatever the mind of (wo)man can conceive and believe, it can achieve,' said American personal success author Napoleon Hill. No one plans in concrete, so don't worry if things change and evolve. Take Hill's sentiment loosely, but take it seriously, because problems arise when we don't have a plan at all.

Of course, there's an argument to say that the most successful people have careers that are joyfully unplanned. These extraordinary stories usually involve a lot of luck – and no one can plan for that. Likewise, there's a danger in over-planning, which we'll come to later. For most women, though, planning doesn't come naturally. So clean your success binoculars and take ten minutes to look into the future and think about where you want to be heading. And don't just do it now because we're telling you to, make planning and foresight a regular exercise, because it's a key ingredient in playing out those career dreams.

Ambition

Very successful women (that's you, Thatcher, Brady, Rowling and Marie Curie) tend not to feel fear – they are ambitious without restriction and this drives them forward.

Sheryl Sandberg in her book, *Lean In*, talks through the importance of ambition in the success formula. What Sandberg says is that ambition is a difficult word for many women because while success and likeability are positively correlated for men, strong-minded ambition makes women the bêtes noires. As a man gets more successful and powerful, he becomes the Dude. As a woman gets more successful and powerful, she becomes the Devil. Sheryl calls this the Ambition Gap. This is true in some instances, but we think the success and likeability story is more complex than that.

Women, we say, are ambitious for what they want, but what they want is often impacted on by how they are treated by others. This means that women will follow their own paths to success (and those paths may not always be traditional), but their paths to success are often stunted. Basically, we redefine our success to make it more attainable and less scary. Think about that ambition you held as a newbie at work, or what you imagined you'd do at work when you were a child. We bet that those dreams – those ambitions – were bigger than the ones you have today.

Ambition is a tricky concept for women because it doesn't fall within the modesty norms that we've been taught to live by. Even today when we are filling our daughters with drive and smash-through-the-brick-wall power, our biases mean girls remain praised by society for being more passive. And this leads to unconscious submission at work. Plus, once we throw a lack of confidence into the mix, and any other of the Internal Influences that we're talking through here, it's no wonder we struggle to imagine ourselves achieving our goals, or even having the same goals as our male peers. What we're saying is that you need to strip back that tightly bound corset of humility and reach for the stars.

So that's the Internal Influences background covered. What we hope you're now clear on is how vital it is to get things straight inside your head, because what you *feel* impacts on how you work – and how others perceive you too. What you're aiming for at this point is an uncluttered foundation onto which you can build your career empire. But you can't get constructing until you've dug out some self-awareness.

AIMS Self-Awareness and Being True to Number One

Many successful women were not born with bravado or even ego strength. But they are all self-aware – they all truly know themselves (and how they fare in the emotion and strategy chart) and they work according to their own set of truths. No one has every career-busting character trait naturally within themselves: but if you know that what you lack in energy, you make up for in assertiveness, then that's a solid start.

For many career scientists, knowing where your strengths lie is all just theory until you've cracked self-awareness. This is why many consider it to be the most important quality for career success: we can't make changes and improvements to ourselves until we can meaningfully understand our personal strengths and weaknesses.

Do you think tightrope walker Philippe Petit, him of the daring (and illegal) high-wire traverse between New York's Twin Towers in 1974, entered into this world possessing poise, fearlessness, balls (in a non-physiological sense, of course), a head for heights and elegance? He did not. He might have had a natural aptitude for balance, but to be able to walk unaided on a piece of dental floss at 1350 feet above the ground, Philippe needed to be acutely self-aware. By knowing every fibre and feeling within himself, he could then intermingle the traits that came naturally with the ones that he needed to learn.

'As a creative person I have things I go back to again and again I have obsessions,' says accomplished architect **Deborah Saunt**, whose latest project is leading a team of landscape designers, traffic engineers and lighting specialists in the 'West End Project' to transform the Tottenham Court Road area, a major urban design proposal for Camden Council.

'I know what things preoccupy me and these things invite me to look back at my work so that I can understand what I've been doing and why. My background, the environment in which I was raised, both my time as a child in Africa and Australia, as well as the political influences of my grandfather, have made me who I am today.'

When she is discovering a new site for one of her buildings, Saunt walks around with her camera at hip level – eye height for a child – so that she can make sure her work is true to her beliefs. Saunt is self-aware and this has made her career run more smoothly – she knows what she feels, how she wants to work and where she's heading and together this makes her an incredibly powerful force within modern architecture.

KNOWING AND IMPROVING THYSELF

'Know thyself, improve thyself, complement thyself,' says entrepreneur Anthony Tjan. If you are at a complete loss as to where to start, take a personality test. Flick to the endnotes (pp. 283–4) for details on the ones we recommend.

Personality tests are useful because they help unravel the knotted balls of how your mind actually works, giving us great insight into our behaviours and performance in the workplace.

These tests are by no means perfect but they encourage self-reflection, which is the key to self-awareness. They provide a useful starting point for learning more about yourself – which is not as scary as it sounds.

Once we know our personality traits, we can then begin to improve the traits that are holding us back. And one of the most useful feedback methods is learning from our past actions. Yup, there's a whole life back there, brimming with good times, stories and clues about who we are and how we tick. With this in mind, try our Feedback Analysis Workout. It's one of the oldest ways of learning and improving thyself.

WORKOUT Feedback Analysis

This isn't your average workout – think of it as more of a long-term investment strategy. A few minutes judicially invested in this exercise is proven to be deeply revealing of the components of Planet You.

(1 minute) Buy a diary.

(3 minutes) Whenever you make a key decision or take a key action, reflect on and then write down what you expect will happen.

(6 minutes) Twelve months later, compare the actual results with your expectations. Look for patterns. What results are you skilled at generating? What do you need to get better at to get the results you want? And what unproductive habits are preventing you from creating the outcomes of your dreams?

WORKOUT Feedback Analysis continued

> Ten minutes invested regularly on this will, over a period of a couple of years, reveal to you where your strengths lie.
>
> It will also show you where you aren't using your strengths most effectively AND crucially, what you aren't so hot at. You can use this as insight into what you need to work on, work with and improve.

COMPLEMENT THYSELF

No, this isn't an exercise in complimenting yourself on how clever/witty /loveable (delete as appropriate) you are, this is about complementing yourself in a work sense – in a strategic recruitment sense.

Unless you have autocratic career aspirations (hopefully you don't, by the way: autocrats never have the last laugh), then your success is not all down to you. To be able to reside in the splendour of your work utopia, you are going to need to surround yourself, or at least plan to surround yourself, with people – your team, your colleagues, your gang – who shine where you're a bit dusty.

The right colleagues are not a threat, they're an asset; utilise them properly, be aware of their needs, and you'll all fly. Put it like this, you can't make harmonies if you're singing alone. And the Nineties pop sensations All Saints continue to epitomise the notion of complementing yourself.

Cool chick and smooth singer Melanie Blatt and song-writing genius Shaznay Lewis got the All Saints ball rolling. Natalie and Nicole Appleton then joined and brought with them their pap-friendly, scandal-loving lives. Together, the All Saints were an incredible force. Their contrasting character traits and assorted capabilities combined to create booty-swinging songs that were the height of cool. The Spice Girls, of course, did a similar thing but with much less subtlety. You don't need a Sporty, Baby and Posh in your work department, but a blend of understated All Saints magic will make for a killer team – with a very successful lead singer (that's you).

Partnership is often at the heart of the most successful career stories. Another epic female partnership is that of Rose Gray and **Ruth Rogers**, co-founders of the River Café which opened on the River Thames in Hammersmith in 1987. The pair worked together as partners until Gray's untimely death from cancer in 2010, and their partnership, Rogers believes, is part of the reason that the River Café remains one of London's most highly regarded restaurants.

'I had no experience when we opened,' admits Rogers, who at nearly seventy years old is still in the kitchen on a daily basis. 'Rose knew a bit about cooking; but what was special, one of the greatest parts of my career, was having a female partner. We didn't need to explain anything to one another; there's a look in the eye and we both always knew what the other was thinking or wanted to do. We both treated the restaurant as we did our families – we gave everything. We led through hope rather than fear, and we always helped just as much as the waiters and kitchen staff. Everyone participates because we are a unified team.'

When we are able to get our River Café-style team groove on, we then need to open the gates of communication (we're planning ahead, see). A lack of communication was one of All Saints' failings (allegedly over finance, strategy and one particularly stylish jacket) and in the end the band collapsed. As a postscript, the band has now reformed, proving that communication troubles are a dead end. Conversely, at the River Café, there's always been communicative transparency.

'My team know that I am here to listen,' says Ruth. 'Leadership is about direction and listening; listening to what they have to say and being brave enough to sometimes say no. A restaurant is very much about the people who work there; if you invest in your staff and invest in the people it comes back to you in spades.'

As Rogers says, great teams require great listening skills. Feedback doesn't only come from within; it comes from those around us too. One way of discovering ourselves more fully is by chatting to those closest to us and seeing things (seeing ourselves) through their objective eyes.

When we set a precedent of regular discussion meetings (How am I doing? Was that what you were looking for?) we discover ourselves more fully and end up in teams that are open and communicative. With this in mind, talk to bosses, peers and juniors and try not to be too sensitive to anything negative that pops up. Criticism, as we know, can be as constructive as it can be crushing. Look around you at work. In particular, observe how other people approach tasks in a different way to you – especially when they are successful. By critiquing their traits and qualities, we learn something about ourselves and the way we work too.

HOW TO Emotions

Hopefully, you are now beginning to have a bit more clarity on your strengths and weaknesses. Now we want to give you codes to unlock and re-evaluate certain beliefs you have about yourself. We are all different and fundamentally we all have different personalities. You might be more extroverted than your boss, less anxious than the work experience and just a wallflower compared to the all-round entertainer you call your best friend.

Whatever your personality, you are neither more nor less likely to succeed. This is a good thing. It's not your type of personality but your ability to understand it that is key. We call this awareness.

And part of awareness of yourself is an awareness of your environment. You are good at your job, but do you like it? If your answer is yes, hold on tight, we are about to delve deeper into Planet You. Here's the thing: a woman of relative intellect could, research tells us, be good at pretty much any job with the right training. (Tightrope walker, anyone?)

But would she enjoy balancing on a piece of rope strung between two buildings? Probably not. Why? Because the likelihood is that she – you – are more suited to a job that is based on the ground. So we can all achieve relative success in most fields, but who wants a mediocre career? The way we take that relative success and make it unicorn-shaped is by adding in the magic of love. Enjoy your work and you will shine.

A woman who doesn't like communicating with new people is not going to enjoy a job in sales even if she could theoretically do it with her mouth closed. Likewise, a nurse who craves adrenalin and enjoys stress is not going to be fulfilled and happy working in palliative care. Accident and Emergency, that's where she needs to be.

Being happy at work, and being good at your job, is in some part dependent on finding an environment in which your personality can soar. Part of harnessing the power of Internal Influences is being aware and objective about where your personality sits at work and what makes you tick. We might all be able to (we've probably all had to) fake work enjoyment at some point, but for the long haul, we need to be truly happy and suited to our work to be able to meaningfully succeed.

Fortunately, this is very much something we have control over, because just like the nurse who needs to move to A&E, finding our own slice of career paradise doesn't have to mean looking for a new job.

Job crafting: two simple words that can open up an entirely new chapter in your career. It isn't always practical or attainable to be doing your dream job at this very moment in time, but your dream job should always be there in the plan. In the meantime, though, how can you take what you've got and make it better? You job craft.

Job crafting is the technical term for making a job that suits you. Successful women are very good at knowing who they are (self-awareness) and on top of that, they use this knowledge to make their roles suit their personalities. There are three simple ways to do this – task crafting (what we actually do), relational crafting (who we do it with) and cognitive crafting (how we think about what we do). Try this workout below and see how your humdrum job could become something enchanting.

WORKOUT Job Crafting

(3 minutes) Write down in bullet points what you know about yourself far split into four categories: your strengths, weaknesses, passions and things you like less.

(3 minutes) Now do the same for the different elements of your job. What do you have to do on a daily or weekly basis and what do you choose to do?

(4 minutes) Now review the lists and reflect, asking yourself the following questions in turn:

Where can you use more of your strengths and passions in the job list?

Where do your weaknesses coincide with tasks you have to do and is there any way to a) redesign the task or b) even better, offload it onto someone else and take on another responsibility more suited to you in return?

Where could your passions coincide with work? This may not be obvious. For example, a history teacher who is passionate about music could incorporate that into her job by bringing music into her curriculum, collaborating with the music teacher in the school and equating elements of her standing up in front of the class with a musical performance.

STARVE YOUR STRESS CAULDRON

Job crafting is all very well, but what if you can't see the wood for the trees? As we already know, a big issue at work is stress. We all deal with it but when we let stress become a bubbling cauldron of doom we lose control.

As we've already said, with a constant supply of new trigger ingredients, the cauldron heat will rise until bam, you turn into Stress Witch. She isn't one of those chic witches with the shiny black shoes – Stress Witch is all gnarly and grumpy and won't turn frogs into princes. You do not need to become that witch. In fact, you do not even need to invest in a cauldron because stress can be a positive force – we just need to know how to grab it, handle it and shoot it in the right direction.

Academics define stress as the state that is induced when the demands placed on us exceed our personal resources (and our ability to mobilise those resources). We all have an optimum level of stress, just as we all crave (often unknowingly) a degree of stress to keep us motivated, productive and happy.

It has been proven that when we are able to raise our stress tolerance and stress management levels, we become more likely to sashay northwards towards senior positions, fruitful entrepreneurships and multidimensional portfolio careers. What we're saying is don't fear stress. We all have to endure it, so the best plan of attack is to learn how to harbour its energy, so that stress can drive you forward. Better the devil you know, and all of that.

Women who conduct stress more effectively are more productive, happier and are also able to employ and implement more career strategies and find their jobs more challenging. It's a paradox, but when our work consumes us, we enjoy it more. We have less time to think about stress when we are positively challenged. Not just that, women with higher stress tolerance also find more support and encouragement from mentors, coaches and general industry networks.

If stress tolerance is such a game changer, then how the hell do we increase the darn thing? According to Cognitive Behavioural Therapy (CBT), when we are worried about something it affects our feelings and attitudes, and these feelings and attitudes then affect our behaviour: if the first cog (your thoughts) is turning the wrong (stressy) way, then the rest will follow.

When we are stressed or anxious, our behaviour influences what happens and this perpetuates our negative beliefs. You are worried about an upcoming interview for promotion. You can't stop thinking about the interview. The interview (and everything that could go wrong in the interview) accompanies you to the canteen, to the gym, it even rears its ugly head on date night. You worry so much about the interview (which, by the way, on paper you could smash in an instant) that you start to feel scared. Once fear takes hold inside your head, it releases another fatal blow – lack of confidence. And you end up brimming with irrational anxiety. You are a mess. You don't talk yourself up, you don't take risks, you apologise too often, and you give others credit for that project you nailed last week. You don't get the job.

Throw into the mix how difficult women find it to keep their worries in perspective, and you begin to see how damaging the cycle of stress can become. In the end, if you let the stress cogs keep turning the wrong way, your watch will eventually stop. When this happens, our lack of self-belief is reinforced. Stress is a vicious cycle of cogs. The good news is that this cycle of fear and failure is fuelled not by fact – but by our own perceptions. And perceptions are phonies. The trick to setting free your stress witch is to understand the cog cycle – and to then interrupt it.

CBT/STRESS COG

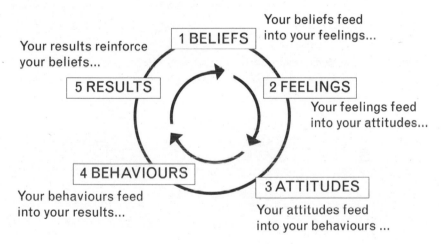

Your beliefs feed into your feelings...

1 BELIEFS

Your results reinforce your beliefs...

5 RESULTS

2 FEELINGS

Your feelings feed into your attitudes...

4 BEHAVIOURS

Your behaviours feed into your results...

3 ATTITUDES

Your attitudes feed into your behaviours ...

Next time you face an interview or have a big meeting in the diary, don't take your worries out to dinner. Process them rationally and accept them as perceptions (your own) rather than fact. By doing this, you will break the vicious cycle of doom and replace negative thoughts with positive ones. Once you let positive thoughts drive the cogs, your vicious cycle will be replaced by something virtuous.

Disclaimer: this shift is not going to happen overnight. CBT requires many hours, weeks, even months of a positive replacement of negative thoughts to truly break bad habits. Having said that, you need to start somewhere, and if you can breathe life back where there were only fears then you'll have started your cog realignment.

WORKOUT Positive Thoughts

Struggling to think positively? Thinking the CBT way doesn't always come naturally. It's about identifying your negative thought processes and stopping them in their tracks. Think of a current work dilemma then spend ten minutes answering each question in turn. We've used the example of a big work project to show you what we mean, but your example could be any source of stress at work.

Q. What are you worried about?
A. A big work project.

Q. What are you predicting?
A. Here, it's that I won't get it done in time or it won't be good enough.

Q. What's the evidence for your belief?
A. I am really busy and I don't think my boss likes me much anyway.

Q. What's the evidence against my prediction?
A. I have always had good reviews before even from this boss, previous projects have been decent; I have coped well with stress before.

Q. What's the worst that could happen?
A. I could get fired. But then I could find another job. Or my boss could criticise me. I could cope with that and maybe even take it constructively.

Q. What's the best that could happen?
A. I could knock it out of the park, my boss will be thrilled and it will impact bonus or promotion.

Q. What's the most likely outcome?
A. It will be fine and my boss will be happy or neutral.

Q. What are the consequences of worrying about this (i.e. what behaviours will come out of it)?
A. The stress will make me less able to do the job well.

WORKOUT **Positive Thoughts** continued

Q. What is a more helpful way to view the situation? What if it was a friend's problem (we tend to be kinder to friends than ourselves!)?

A. I have done this sort of thing before, so I can probably do it again. I am good at what I do, so I'll probably do a good job – it doesn't have to be absolutely perfect. I could tell my boss I am under a lot of pressure – they don't expect me to be a superhero. Other people's work is not as good as mine, and they don't get fired. I can be happy with just getting it in on time, and doing a good job – I don't also need my boss to praise me.

Q. What is a more balanced and helpful thought to replace my worry?

A. Worrying about this is unhelpful. I know I can do this job on time and well. All my past experiences show me that. I should remember that, rather than thinking the worst.

Outcome? You should have more perspective. Much of what you're stressed about is likely to be in your mind and isn't justified or even based on past events or fact. Perhaps just reading through these questions and answers has made you feel a little less stressed. The point of the exercise is to show you how worthwhile it is to employ new techniques to manage difficult situations.

CBT is a brilliant form of rehabilitation that should help make you feel freer from the negatives. We advise that you start by repeating this process as often as stressors arise because if you make it part of your coping mechanism, you'll find that gradually it becomes natural to rationalise worries in this way.

DRILL YOUR RESILIENCE ARMY

As long as we don't give stress the upper hand, we can harness its powers and use it as a valuable tool in our personal career climb. Stress makes us focus on a problem, as it is a part of our innate fight or flight reflex. When we are faced with danger, our body draws together an army of mental clarity and physical energy to stay safe.

This fight or flight reflex relies on adrenalin. Having your heart in your mouth is fine in emergencies, but not for background work issues. When you are presented with a challenge at work, or if there is something bubbling under the surface that you've been ignoring for months, focus on the opportunities that it presents. Because as we've said, stress, in its range of buzzy, flustered forms, can be your friend.

Let's take a background team disagreement as an example of how you can turn around an ongoing tricky situation so that it puts you in a stronger position. So your team isn't getting on: three out of your five team members are in cahoots and the other two have been completely shut out. You've known that things haven't been right for weeks, and all you've done is sit there and fed your cauldron. What you need to do is see the discord as an opportunity to become more strategic – and wield more power.

What should you do? You need to instigate a meeting and steer the team ship back into harmonious waters. By being the initiator, you are now the bearer of positive change in your team and when things are resolved you will feel more powerful because you *are* more powerful. You have stopped stressing and used that energy to make a difference. When you feel powerful, success is easier to achieve.

Another reason to manage stress is because it puts mental and physical strain on our bodies. Due to the way that we have evolved as humans, our bodies and our brains can only tolerate stress in short bursts. It's that fight or flight reflex again. We are brilliant when disaster strikes, but panic mode is not sustainable. Being shacked up with stress all day long is hazardous.

Stress really does put you at a higher risk of cardiovascular disease and it makes our blood pressure bolt too. Stress gives us acne and psoriasis (equally depressing). It offers backache (stress actually hurts) and kills our fertility levels. Stress can make us put on weight too.

Stress is not beautiful.

We cannot work and succeed when we are stressed. So be good to yourself and walk away from your desk from time to time. Many workplaces function in a state of chronic stress, but we don't need to be part of that gang: don't work through lunch, go outside and soak in the sunlight. Research tells us that people who walk outside in a natural setting experience more feelings of relaxation than those who walk indoors. If it's raining, book a yoga class, practise some meditation or pick up a book on mindfulness. What the hell, do a bit of online shopping, anything to break the cycle and give your mind a rest.

Stress can also affect your digestion, so watch what you eat and drink. The fight or flight response is fuelled by cortisol and when there is too much cortisol coursing through our bodies, we're more likely to overeat, make bad food choices and store fat.

In work terms, this means binning the break-time BLTs and bigging up your grain intake. Put apples and pears on your desk instead of bars of chocolate and cans of Coke (oops). Also avoid excess alcohol and caffeine, and try to eat little and often. Then, when you're at home, sleep as much as you can and refrain from incessant phone flicking. Phone abuse is a stress creator – all those images, they don't do good things to our brains, especially late at night.

Proper breaks between times of high stress help our bodies to recover and our minds relax again. This means regular breaks from the office environment and holidays in the diary. Stress really is a medical issue. These pointers are useful when you're suffering but coping; if you try these and you still feel excessively stressed see your GP and get referred on for help because no one's health is worth risking for the sake of their jobs.

BE A SPRIGHTLIER YOU

Tiredness is another strain on your Internal Influence health store. Sure, we all feel tired sometimes. But what if it's all the time? Tiredness, like stress, is as much a perception as it is a reality. Tiredness can be a physical state. But tiredness is usually a state of mind.

Successful women have more energy (real and perceived) than the norm. This means that they are able to cope with what the day throws at them – and some. They also complete tasks more efficiently and with greater lasting effect. Energy levels are very important when it comes to making your mark at work not least because no one promoted the woman who yawned her way through the year.

We've already covered some of the obvious energy boosters above – take time out of the office, think positively, inhabit a happier state of mind. All of these will help you *feel* less tired, even if they don't actually add extra hours to your sleep at night.

Feeling tired can become a negative cycle of self-perpetuating apathy. If you feel brighter, you'll be able to think clearer, work better and get ahead faster. Having energy is just as vital at your career planning stage as it is when you're lifting off. Like your perceptions of stress, if you can change the way you view yourself in terms of tiredness ('I was born tired' – no you weren't), you'll start winning the Battle of Sleepiness.

Rather predictably, our perpetual state of tiredness may have been formed in childhood. As people, we tend to have scripts that we carry through life about what sort of person we are. Your script, or schema as it is sometimes called, could include a paragraph on energy. It might also cover how sporty you are, your assertiveness levels or your competence with a roast chicken.

If you have always been the tired one in the family, change the rhetoric. This is simple but empowering stuff. Of course, you can't just decide to change. These schemas run deep, and if you find that you have real trouble in changing what's on the page perhaps consider some professional help.

First, though, make sure you try our CBT workout again. This time, think about the beliefs you hold around your energy levels and ability to get things done. Then use the question series to review the beliefs you hold about yourself – you're likely to find that the evidence is not that close to the truth.

UNDERWHELM YOUR OVERWHELM

You have a big presentation next week and you also have to make sure that the dog gets to the vet and your best friend cannot cope

with her impending professional exams and your boss wants
to schedule a (worryingly) short-notice meeting and your hair
needs a cut and the shower isn't working properly and your gym
membership hasn't been used for months and you were meant to
look into places to stay in Greece and get the Christmas shopping
done in advance this year and now your mother has just called to
tell you that she's going to put her house on the market and she
needs you to finally (after thirty years) empty your school books
out of the loft.

You. Are. Overwhelmed.

A major factor in low energy, particularly in women, is overwhelm. This
is the strong and often all-consuming feeling of not being able to cope
with all of the pressures and plates that you're simultaneously spinning.

Women are prone to feeling overwhelmed because of our
physiological ability to multitask. That is basically what it comes
down to. On top of that, we really do have more on our plates
than men because of our inability to shut the door on familial
responsibilities. And these responsibilities don't diminish as we rise
up the ladder.

Parents. Fitness. Clothes. Hair. Children. Dog. You get the picture …
Feeling overwhelmed is fair enough, but it should never restrict the
flight of your unicorn.

Brigid Schulte in her book *Overwhelmed* and Laura Vanderkam, who
studies how women spend their time (yup, she accounts for every
minute in the day), have some enlightening views on how to dilute
your overwhelm.

Schulte's view is brutal: a lot of important things are not going to
get done in your life. She says when you accept that you can't do
everything that you want to do then you'll stop trying, and feel less
overwhelmed.

This is her method.

Step One: Identify which, right now, are the most meaningful ways for you to spend your time.
Step Two: Schedule time for these things.
Step Three: There is no step three.

There is no step three because all the other things that you haven't identified as your most meaningful moments (and there will be plenty, and they will also seem important in their own ways) just won't get done.

Approach life like this, and a lot of unimportant things won't get done, but, crucially, a lot of important things won't get done either. It's radical, but this method is surprisingly effectual in reducing the dooms of overwhelm.

Certain friendships might get neglected, that holiday to the Big Sur won't be had, your regular trip to the farmers market will be no more and you won't eat as well, or exercise as regularly, as is advised in the Sunday supplements.

We live in a time of extreme busyness and Schulte believes the only conceivable way to live a meaningful life is to not do thousands of meaningful things. If you learn to say no, even to things you really want to, then you can do a handful of things that really matter. This way you are guaranteed to overcome your overwhelm.

Kirsty Young, BBC darling, presenter of *Desert Island Discs* and all-round female success story, is just as prone to overwhelm as the rest of us. And she is an advocate of the Schulte approach to calm.

'Not feeling stressed is an area of constant negotiation in my life; that idea of constantly reviewing when things feel out of balance and addressing it is a major part of my juggling. There are times that it does feel overwhelming, but I have learnt to accept that not everything has to be achieved and not everything has to be perfect either. It's unrealistic to think you can have it all. You have to prioritise. I've discussed this a lot with my friend Claudia [Winkleman]. She says that there's family life, social life and work life, and that you'd better choose two out of three if you want to be able to cope. I'd say my social life is the one that goes the quickest; when it's there I love it but it's the last thing on the list.'

Like Schulte an advocate of prioritisation, self-help guru (and author of *The Seven Habits of Highly Effective People*) Stephen Covey takes a more moderate view. He tells the story of a professor who tells his class that it is time for a quiz. He pulls out a jar and sets it on the table next to a platter covered with fist-sized rocks. 'How many of these rocks do you think we can get in the jar?' he asks the class. After the students have made their guesses, the seminar leader says, 'OK, let's find out.' He puts one rock in the jar, then another, then another – until no more rocks will fit. Then he asks, 'Is the jar full?'

Everyone can see that not one more of the rocks would fit, so they say, 'Yes.'

'Not so fast,' he cautions. From under the table he lifts out a bucket of gravel, pours it into the jar, and shakes it. The gravel slides into all the little spaces left by the big rocks. Grinning, the seminar leader asks once more, 'Is the jar full?'

A little wiser by now, the students respond, 'Probably not.' 'Good,' the teacher says. He reaches under the table to bring up a bucket of sand. He pours the sand in the jar. The sand fills in the little spaces left by the rocks and gravel. Once more he looks at the class and asks, 'Now, is the jar full?'

'No,' everyone replies. 'Good!' he says and pours a pitcher of water into the jar. 'Ladies and gentlemen,' he says, 'the jar is now full. Can anybody tell me the lesson you can learn from this? What's my point?'

An eager student speaks up: 'Well, there are gaps in your schedule. And if you really work at it, you can always fit more into your life.'

'No,' the professor says. 'That's not the point. The point is this: if I hadn't put those big rocks in first, I would never have gotten them in.'

Covey's point is that in our lives, we have big rocks, gravel, sand and water. The natural tendency seems to be to favour the latter three elements, leaving little space for the big rocks. In an effort to respond to the urgent, the important is sometimes set aside.

WORKOUT Covey's Rocks

Take three minutes to reflect on the 'big rocks' in your life. A large project? Promotion? Spending time with your family? Money? Personal development? Your dreams?

Now spend two minutes making a list of your big rocks.

The remaining five minutes are for planning. How can you ensure each of these big rocks is put first? Block out time in your schedule and allow the rest to fall in alongside.

Periodically reflect on how you're doing. Are you putting your big rocks first, or do gravel, sand and water dominate your life? If the big rocks aren't getting in, what will have to happen so that they do?

When you're planning your month, your week or your day, and even when you're making specific decisions during the day, refer back to your list of big rocks. Then, put those in your jar first.

Laura Vanderkam takes yet a different stance. She chips away at overwhelm with the axe of time. In her book I Know How She Does It, Vanderkam says the key is realising – and accepting – that you are not actually as busy as you think you are.

She proved this by taking a sample group of working women and getting them to diarise a working week. Her sample group were female high achievers: each had at least one child and a salary in excess of $100,000 a year.

Vanderkam asked each to log what she did for all 168 hours of her week. What she found was that although these women estimated that they worked very long hours, in reality they averaged a pretty typical forty-four-hour week. And although they felt tired, the sample group had actually slept, on average, a rather restful fifty-four hours per week – that's 7.7 hours per night, which meant that they had approximately seventy hours a week to do other things.

Just like our skewed perceptions of stress and tiredness, the rhetoric of business and overwork is just that – rhetoric. Most studies into how we spend our time ask us to estimate our routines first and inevitably these estimations are affected by our perceptions – we exaggerate.

When Vanderkam explained her findings to her group, the women reported feeling empowered by just knowing that they weren't as tired as they thought they were. This helped them change their own rhetoric. For many, it was a potent lesson. They found that just knowing they weren't as overwhelmed as they thought made them feel more content and able to take on new challenges.

The pressures and strains that we carry around within ourselves can be debilitating. But we are more able than we think to break through the seemingly impenetrable cloud of tiredness, stress or overwhelm. Work, like life, can feel like it has more control of you than you have of it but this isn't the case. Be a clearer, stronger, brighter you and don't conform to the harmful and damaging pressures that make brilliant women crumble.

WORKOUT Log Your Time

Fill out your own time diary. Split a piece of paper into 168 squares. One for each hour of each day, for seven days.

Spend ten minutes a day for one week completing the diary. Be specific. Reviewed sales project figures is better than 'worked'.

At the end of the week spend ten minutes reviewing your data. Highlight work in one colour, sleep in another. You can categorise other things too – exercise, hobbies, family – whatever's important to you.

Result: Notice you're less busy than you think you are. Feel relieved and empowered. (Go to www.lauravanderkam.com if you want a pre-created template for this.)

HOW TO Work Factors

BE OVER-FLOW-ING WITH HAPPINESS

Think of a hobby or sport you love. It could be swimming – imagine how the water feels as you glide through it, the power you feel as you kick your legs and propel yourself forwards. You come to a stop and simply float; you are free and it's wonderful. You are swimming. You are in flow.

Flow and happiness are business partners. They work in tandem.

Throughout our lives we are taught the mantra: be successful and then we will be happy. But this is a fallacy. Research into positive psychology (sort of like the science of happiness) shows us that happiness is the precursor to success, not the other way round. Happy successful people might have just been lucky. More likely, though, they have made deliberate choices that have led them to that joyous run down Mont Blanc.

Being happy at work relies on us doing something that we are truly passionate about – a job that makes us feel that we're in our element. This is often called flow. And being in flow when we work increases our work enjoyment – and in turn, our overall happiness.

Flow is the sensation that people feel when they act with total involvement. Flow feels great. Jessica Ennis is in flow when she's rocking through her heptathlon, just as young children are in flow when they're engrossed in play.

Flow is made up of three distinct elements: pure enjoyment, total absorption ('wow, time flies...') and intrinsic motivation – you're in, whatever the rewards or costs. If you're racking your brains for your Mont Blanc moment, the chances are you weren't aware of it, but that doesn't mean it didn't happen. Flow at work is surprisingly common. It relies on us doing a task that we enjoy with a clear goal within a manageable amount of challenge.

Flow most often happens when we are doing our favourite (non-work) activity. Organising your iPhoto account, cooking your favourite meal and planting bulbs in the garden are more flow friendly than sorting through your flooded inbox. So how to get the static flowing?

Let's start at the beginning – you need a job that interests you and that you can become passionate about. A senior lawyer in our *Step Up* study was fervid about justice and people. She was able to cope with the huge time demands and conflict in her role by focusing on the help she imparted to her clients and the personal impact she had on their business and lives. This state of satisfaction enabled her flow to flow. If you can find a job that incorporates your passions or, better yet, find things you are passionate about in the job you already do, then success will be much easier to achieve.

On paper, once you've found your work sweet spot, then flow should, well, flow. But things aren't always that simple. Here are our top three tips for getting your flow flowing.

|1| TAKE RISKS: Flow comes from focus, and focus comes when we are present. Rather unexpectedly, this often happens when we are taking risks or doing something new. The mind can't tell the difference between physical and social risks so both will have the same positive effect on flow. Speak up at a meeting when you normally wouldn't; share your creative ideas; send a direct tweet to someone in the public eye; approach a stranger or tell the truth when it feels awkward. These small acts might seem unrelated to your daily flow, but the more you try new things and take risks the more likely you'll be to find your flow.

|2| EXPERIMENT: The atmosphere around you can trigger flow. Make small changes to where and how you work. The idea is to get out of habits and routines. Move a meeting out of the office if you'd usually convene in the boardroom. Take advantage of working on a laptop and do an afternoon in a café, or at least, sitting on the other side of the office. Change is your friend where flow is concerned.

|3| USE YOUR SENSES: When you engage in sport you become acutely attuned to the world around you and the minutiae of your own body. Capture this and breathe it into your work. Try meditation or mindfulness. Both will engage your sensual awareness when you feel yourself going into autopilot and should perpetuate a state most ready for flow time.

PLANNING

Successful women not only have a plan, they are able to communicate that plan too. To be able to get your dreams in motion, you need to be able to organise a clear and strategic plan of attack – the training course that would benefit your choices, the right relationships to foster – so that you can organise your thoughts, time and energies. And then, once you've worked out where you need to scatter your energies, you have to stand up (figuratively speaking) and tell others about the designs you have for your career.

Plans are the hooks from which we hang our careers. And when we align them correctly, these hooks multiply and offer us more opportunities for success. Being meticulous about how we approach our careers is not exclusive to either sex – women and men both do better when they have a strategy. The problem is, that for reasons of confidence, integrity and (yes, again) our multifaceted definition of success – research tells us that women find it harder in the career-planning department. Even the youngest and most sprightly among us aren't particularly keen on sitting down and plotting their careers.

We also tend to stumble when it comes to vocalising our plans. And this is a problem, because when we let others – colleagues, mentors, friends – in on our career designs, it can be a joyous and enlightening experience, not to mention a strategic one too. Once your boss hears that you are aiming to lead your own team before the year's out, or when you tell a potential investor that your app will be rivalling Uber in a decade from now, you plant a seed that starts to grow.

In our *Step Up* law research, when it came to planning, partners repeatedly cited the differences between male and female juniors. When they were asked if they wanted to progress to partnership level (Law Holy Grail), the women usually said that they just wanted to become very good lawyers. As noble as this is, being very good lawyers didn't reveal a killer instinct to the bosses. In the main, the junior men were vocally focused on partnership from day one. In truth, these men were not all so single-minded about where they were heading, but they excelled at articulating something as a forward plan, even if it was only one of several possibilities.

Plans, like politics, are about what people believe to be the truth at that moment. It's great if your communicated plan and your actual plan are harmoniously in sync, but even if you don't exactly know where you're heading, you can have a persuasive retort. Now, we aren't suggesting or advocating deceit, what we're saying is that sometimes, at work, you need to learn the art of spin.

Let's take the case of a doctor who wants a career change. If she has aspirations of joining Médecins Sans Frontières and becoming a pioneering surgeon, then depending on whom she is speaking to she might want to reveal one or other of her plans. Ditto a promotion: never say no, even if it's a no for now. Think of your career as an A, B, C. Planning is all very well, but daily life can sometimes get in the way, so have a few options and make sure you articulate at least one (the most pertinent one) when you're speaking in the long term.

Changing from A to C is always possible, but changing what you've said to the CEO about not wanting a promotion will be a harder mountain to climb.

Having said all of this about planning, we're about to throw you a curve ball. Because while we know that goal-oriented behaviour drives success, some of us have a tendency to over-plan (it's all part of our desire to be perfect) and that can be just as toxic as ambling along with your eyes closed.

If you are a diligent over-planner you may feel beholden to put a tick in every plan box that you've set yourself and whilst you're busy working your way through your self-imposed list you might miss an opportunity that you hadn't foreseen. To avoid over-planning, keep To-Do lists to three- to five-year blocks of time; know where you are heading but make sure you leave space for spontaneity and the here and now.

Try periodically reviewing your goals and plans; make sure they are still relevant and then leave a little bit of space for luck. Because you never know what tomorrow will bring...

Kirsty Young is a self-confessed advocate of short-term goal setting and it hasn't exactly harmed where she ended up. 'I think I probably have had a lack of strategy in my career. Although I set goals (even the word "goals" sounds a bit strategic for my liking), they've tended to be very short-term. I've been highly opportunistic. When I started out, there wasn't a well-defined path and there were no predictable career consequences. In my work, you can be flavour of the month one day and forgotten the next. Perhaps less so now, but this was certainly the case when I was embarking. Things are always changing and I've had to be flexible.'

THOUGHTS

If you read between the lines of everything that we've covered in this chapter, you'll see that a constant across many of the obstacles wrapped up in your Internal Influences is the simple desire to be liked at work. Yes, we all want to be likeable cogs in the watch of work, but don't let approval drive your decisions. The aim of this chapter is to have a clear head, because when we sweep away the cobwebs of failure, fatigue, overwhelm and everything else, we become a sharper, more focused being, who just happens to be confident and empathetic to boot. These are the qualities that make you likeable, not being the Yes person, or the passive cog in the corner. Sometimes you will have to compete or take charge and not everyone will like it. But that's life, and accepting this fact should drive you forward and get you ahead at work.

——————— THE TIPS ———————

Devoured the chapter, mastered the workouts, now it's time to spend ten minutes a day implementing our tips into your daily work routine:

|1| Tap your resources

We've alluded to it but self-awareness crucially doesn't just come from within. Our workouts, personality tests and your boss aren't the only tools in your self-knowledge box. Identify those who know you best – peers, juniors, friends, your partner. Then seek out feedback and relish – rather than hide from – what you get back. If you're exhibiting a trait at work, the likelihood is it's following you home and those closest to you will be likelier to share it with you, especially once they know it will be taken in the right way.

|2| Make sure the shoe fits

> If your job doesn't make you sing and job crafting isn't the answer, consider your employer. Environment – and how that environment interacts with your personality – is crucial to work enjoyment. So before you ditch your career track completely, consider a change of scene.

> If the shoe still doesn't fit, then it's time to take the leap and change completely. We regularly coach women who think they are too old to make that change, but it's a fallacy. If Julia Child could take up cooking at thirty-six and Mary Wesley could publish her first novel aged seventy, then what is stopping you?

|3| And breathe

When it comes to stress, CBT is your friend. But so are your mind and body. Channelling that energy into some form of spiritual practice – whether that be mindfulness, meditation, yoga or simply regulated breathing – is proven to reduce the effects of stress, thereby increasing your resilience.

|4| Be ruthless

If in doubt, take it out. Streamlining will impact on your energy, time management, stress levels and – in terms of how much you can take on – planning too. Like the Hemsley sisters, Arianna Huffington famously says no to dinner in favour of an early night. Ditch the FOMO and the desire to be liked and practise saying 'N-O.'

|5| Shades of grey

Remember all decisions, all personality traits, all relationships come with both good and bad. In other words, everything is grey. Successful women know that there is always a rainbow after a thunderstorm and take the rough with the smooth. Remind yourself of this in any panic situation and watch your anxiety levels lower and your success star soar.

CHAPTER 4

Confidence

THE FACTS

When Billie Jean King accepted a challenge to play the former male tennis World Number One, Bobby Riggs, in 1973 she took a step into the unknown. Not only was she about to take on a challenge from a physically bigger and stronger opponent, she was also up against his atrocious opinion of women. 'Number one, the woman should stay in the bedroom. Number two, she should get to the kitchen. Number three, she should support the man.' It took confidence to even walk out onto the court that day, but King didn't just take the contest in her stride – she won in straight sets: 6–4, 6–3, 6–3.

'I thought it would set [women] back fifty years if I didn't win that match,' King later said. 'It would ruin the women's tour and affect all women's self-esteem.'

Confidence, self-esteem, poise, whatever you want to call it, King had it in spades that day; more than that though, she recognised and shouldered the fragility of her female peers. And by doing so, led them to a new place of bravado and belief. Confidence, like the Internal Influences we've already discussed, is a state of mind. We aren't born confident, it is something that evolves – a changing, fluid attitude that influences how we attack and shape our lives. In terms of work, confidence is crucial because it's the difference between our hopes and our achievements – it's the missing link.

Billie Jean King *believed* that she would beat Riggs that day in Texas. If she had walked out convinced of the other outcome, she would surely not have tasted victory. That is the power of confidence.

On paper, confidence is defined as a feeling or belief that you can succeed at something. Confidence is so crucial that unless you can get it playing the winning volleys for you too, you might as well give up on defining your success or any of the other themes to come in this book. Because confidence is the cornerstone on which we build our careers.

For the record, confidence isn't just feeling good and happy and walking into work with a spring in your step; confidence is multifaceted. And when you do not believe that you are important, able and worthy, you marginalise your success.

Having confidence is what enables us to turn our thoughts into action; without it we are unable to thrive. It's the difference between grabbing hold of an idea passing through your mind – that new position, or throwing it all in and becoming a yoga instructor – and sitting impassively at your desk resentful of the status quo. Confidence is wrapped up and stitched into every action you take at work; those awkward situations, scary eventualities, successes, failures, wins, losses, and everything in between, are each defined by how confident we were in that moment.

Low confidence can affect us all. Men, women, children, the elderly – we have a propensity to lack the stuff, it's human nature and it's what keeps us humble. But, when a lack of confidence dominates, we become inert. And the downward spiral of low confidence is a speedy and dangerous fairground ride: when you don't believe, you cannot do.

Because of the way most women's minds work (active, analytical, over-critical of ourselves) we suffer more greatly from deficiencies in the confidence department. We talk ourselves down, we think, we overthink, we allow weaknesses to creep in and infect our minds and then we stop taking risks or even speaking up at the weekly debrief.

We've seen it first-hand (heck, we've suffered it ourselves) in the many hundreds of women we work with. All of them are talented women – you are a talented woman – the problem is, we don't have faith in the truth. We put fear on a pedestal and when fear gets the upper hand, good stuff falls by the wayside. The more we trust that we can do it, the more we'll try and realise that we can.

Back when she was a BBC trainee, **Kirsty Young** relied on a confidence instilled within her from her mother. 'On a daily basis, I had an inexplicable inner confidence; well, it is explicable if you meet my mother. She didn't heap praise upon us, but there was a sense of an absolute belief that you held your place in the world and that you deserved your place in the world. From a young age, I could always get up in a room and speak. I remember giving a vote of thanks at the age of seven on behalf of the school and I just got up and did it. In fact, I quite enjoyed it. What also helped me was realising what the worst-case scenario was; for me, that would have been making a complete fool out of myself on national television. And if that happened, nobody will have died. It's about being objective and to a degree, living on your nerves. All of my first jobs, at BBC Scotland, at Channel 5, and then at ITV were exhilarating sausage factories. And as long as I delivered on a daily basis, my confidence remained intact.'

Kirsty Young is an example to us all. She makes mistakes, we all make mistakes, but she doesn't let them define her or bring her down. Women are more likely to have self-doubt about their job performance and careers as a whole than men do, and we rarely overestimate our abilities in the workplace. Our scrupulous desire to be accurate about what we can do actually leads us to undersell our abilities, especially in the areas of maths and science, which in turn means we are less likely to pursue lucrative STEM careers. Men, research says, overestimate their abilities, put their labs coats on and get stuck in.

As if you need to read more, it goes on. We know women are more likely to let this underestimating of our abilities hold us back from applying for the perfect job. And, crucially, we frequently misattribute our success and we repeatedly thank luck (sound familiar?) when something goes right at work. It wasn't luck, of course, you made that deal/design/website happen, you just weren't confident (or bold) enough to recognise your own ability.

As we explained in Chapter 1, women and men are very different beings. While, according to science, we are less predisposed to overconfidence from a very early age, we do tend to have self-awareness and a drive for self-improvement. And it is these that are your keys to change.

Like many women, Burmese opposition politician **Aung San Suu Kyi** is not naturally predisposed to confidence. But despite this she has proved that she has it in bucketloads. Despite her abysmal and unfair treatment by Burma's (mainly male) military leaders, she continues to rouse within herself unrivalled self-assurance and courage.

The irony is that her peaceful protestations have become more powerful than any amount of martial law. And without raising her voice or beating her chest, Suu Kyi has proved that she is in possession of more confidence than her opponents: 'In societies where men are truly confident of their own worth, women are not merely tolerated but valued.'

When we talk of confidence in world-scale proportions it seems too big to grab. Confidence, though, as we said at the start of this chapter, is a state of mind. Sadly, you cannot buy it over the counter. But we promise, with this book, to give you the secrets to strengthen your foundations. It's a jungle out there, and it's OK to accept a bit of guidance now and again.

Not only do we need to contend with the pesky voice in our own minds (number one low confidence culprit), we also need tools to manage the impact and feeling when those around us seem to brim with confidence, and thrive on acting all cool and together.

For the record, the dominant male might appear showy and peacock-like, but chances are he's no more talented than us peahens. Peacocks put on a good show (it's the iridescent feathers) – they make us believe that they are great at their jobs and because of this, we succumb to their charms. The truth is, their confidence is really just bravado and shimmer. We can't knock them, men are great at giving off strong, persuasive confidence vibes. What's more interesting, though, is that confidence is not a permanent state:

rather, it has a switch that you turn on when things are looking gloomy or dark.

And if the truth be told, the confidence landscape is rocky for both sexes — we all suffer insecurities. It's just that men don't doubt themselves so persistently, plus they're less likely to let it affect their work. The problem is, as we've already pointed out, in the face of all this showy male resolve, we tend to falter even further.

Confidence can be a seesaw between you and your colleagues, just as it's also a voice in your head, a physical performance, a state of mind and a deep belief. This is why we have given confidence its own chapter; it's a complex fiend, but it's one that you can own and use and it'll pay dividends when you get it onside. How do we know this? Because research says that success correlates with confidence almost as much as it does with aptitude. Confidence is a major player. And in this chapter we will show you how to get in the game.

LOSE YOUR INNER IMPOSTER

Just before we get to our big Ten-Point Confidence Action Plan, there are a couple of confidence skews that are worth knowing about. You may have read about imposter syndrome in the press recently; it's confidence's trendy arm mainly because celebs have jumped on its bandwagon. This is a good thing. When you know that others — successful others, others in the public eye who earn big bucks and wear slinky dresses and get their hair done every third day — also feel like frauds in their jobs, it should quieten the imposter voice.

Between them, Natalie Portman, Emma Watson, Jodie Foster, Tina Fey, Michelle Pfeiffer, Renee Zellweger, Kate Winslet and Maya Angelou share four Academy Awards, nine BAFTAs, thirteen Golden Globes, fifty honorary degrees, one Pulitzer Prize nomination, four Grammys and a dead weight in imposter syndrome. So what is this particular strain of career insecurity?

Imposter syndrome is a subset of low confidence — it's insecurity's first cousin and even Oscar-winning actresses aren't immune. What sets imposter syndrome apart from other forms of low confidence is the fear that the sufferer will get found out. That he or she will be publicly ousted as a fraud.

'Today I feel much like I did when I came to Harvard Yard as a freshman in 1999.' This is an extract from **Natalie Portman**'s 2015 Harvard Commencement Speech. 'I felt like there had been some mistake, that I wasn't smart enough to be in this company, and that every time I opened my mouth I would have to prove that I wasn't just a dumb actress.'

This is a quote from **Maya Angelou**. 'I have written eleven books, but each time I think, "Uh oh, they're going to find out now. I've run a game on everybody, and they're going to find me out."' If you've read I Know Why the Caged Bird Sings, or any of Maya Angelou's work, you'll appreciate how far she is from a literature fraud.

'I thought everybody would find out, and they'd take the Oscar back.' It's **Jodie Foster** talking this time. '[I thought] they'd come to my house, knocking on the door, "Excuse me, we meant to give that to someone else. That was going to Meryl Streep."'

Like many of confidence's relations, the feeling of secret incompetence, the sense that you are alone in a sea of high achievers, isn't uniquely feminine. There are plenty of male imposters out there too, it's just that in the main, men experience imposter syndrome less often and, importantly, they are less likely to let it impact what they do. The problem is that imposters, even Hollywood imposters, find it harder to thrive because they are strangulated by their own, misplaced, beliefs.

Thanks to Portman, Foster, **Tina Fey** ('I'm a fraud! Oh God, they're on to me! I'm a fraud!') et al., imposter syndrome is a hot topic. And if these women can acknowledge their weakness, then you can too. It might be worth taking a moment to consider this question: do you maintain a strong belief that you are not intelligent and do you convince yourself that you've fooled anyone who thinks otherwise?

If you've answered yes, keep reading. Any lucky No's out there, feel free to proceed to our Ten-Point Plan (although we'd encourage you to stay put, as although you might not be a sufferer, someone in your team, company or wider network could relish the information henceforward).

Imposter syndrome is the realisation of the devil inside your head. We all have one; it's how comfortable you make that devil feel that will determine how destructive she's allowed to be. Women with imposter syndrome tend to combat their feelings of fraudulence by working really *really* hard. To some extent this can work. 'As a woman in the architecture profession, you need the confidence that you can carry on and take new steps every time,' explained **Zaha Hadid**. 'So I believe in hard work; it gives you a layer of confidence.'

But hard work alone – and in particular overwork: putting in endless hours, keeping your head down and painstakingly dotting every proverbial i – won't rid most of us of our inner imposter. In fact, it might even make things worse: you graft, you don't get ahead and you end up feeling worse (cogs turning the wrong way...). Imposter syndrome thrives on insecurities.

Phoniness is another devilish division of imposter syndrome. Have you ever tried to gauge what, say, your boss thinks on a subject and delivered an opinion to support her stance (instead of supporting your own view) in a bid to ingratiate yourself to those at the top? This act of self-submission and acquiescence to another person's point of view is called phoniness and women suffering from imposter syndrome tend towards phoniness because they don't have confidence in their own opinion.

A subtler version of this is someone who stays silent in the face of a comment or discussion on which she disagrees. Being passive might feel easier in the moment (no one wants to rock the boat, right?), but being passive will make you feel like a fraud in the end.

We say, Rock. That. Boat.

Take hold of your career, grab it with both hands and be proud of your opinion. When you become a stronger, more powerful you, you will learn to accept that you haven't got to where you are today by luck. You are not a fraud – you have secured your own success. If you need to, defeat your imposter as part of a group, which is exactly what architect **Deborah Saunt** did.

'I didn't realise until I walked into the doors of my university that architecture was such a male-dominated vocation; it just didn't occur to me that there wouldn't be parity. I was shocked that none of my teachers were women; it was daunting and the best way I coped was by speaking to other women. When we qualified, we formed a Women in Architecture group, to try and work out what was going on within our culture. We were a very proactive bunch – to be honest we were an elite bunch as we had all been to Cambridge – but in life we noticed that, even as confident women, we'd ask ourselves if we were good enough. Through this sorority of fantastic friends, we have encouraged each other to never deselect ourselves from opportunities or experiences. I don't want to extinguish my vulnerability; I think women should be able to show their whole range of emotions and concerns, but I've learnt to focus on my strengths too.'

Imposter syndrome runs deep but, like many other facets of confidence, in small doses it keeps us modest and likeable. What you need to be able to do is cage the imposter devil when it roars and gnashes and takes over. Because if the devil's in situ, you'll be a less able, less respected and less satisfied member of the working world.

WORKOUT The Voice(s) of Reason

Sometimes the imposter voice is persistent. It sits on our shoulder, whispers in our ear and is hard to shake off. If you're struggling to shake the pesky blighter, it can be useful to harness the power of those you believe you have tricked.

WARNING: Best not do this on the bus, it may involve talking to yourself.

Take a couple of minutes to think of four people you believe you have fooled: your boss, your client, the agent who believed in your book (ahem). Now imagine you are facing each of them in turn.

WORKOUT The Voice(s) of Reason continued

Have a two-minute 'conversation' with each of them. In this fantasy, you tell them (out loud) how you have conned or tricked them. Then you imagine, again out loud (funny voices optional) how each of them would realistically respond.

Try it. The likelihood is that even in your head they won't agree with your point of view. 'I did not give you an award in English', says your teacher, 'because you charmed me. I do like you as a person but I honoured you for your outstanding work.' 'I'm angry that you think I'm so stupid that I can't judge a good book when I see it,' says the agent; or 'I don't like your negating me and my opinions,' answers your boss.

TEN-POINT PLAN TO RECLAIMING YOUR CONFIDENCE

Right, that is enough theory. Chances are we've all suffered with low confidence at some point in our lives and during our careers. As we've said before, while this book is pitched at working women, the contents within extend beyond the office into the many folds and seams of our rounded lives.

Though a lack of confidence can affect us deeply, like many other skills, it's something that we can conquer. To make this process as pain-free as possible, we've devised a unique plan of attack. So, get ready to stand taller, speak slower and unearth your gravitas.

1. FAKE IT TO MAKE IT – SEEM MORE CONFIDENT

When people *feel* confident they exhibit lots of verbal and non-verbal clues that give off an air of control, contentment and aplomb. Simon Cowell calls this the X Factor and we tend to agree with him. What you're aiming to achieve (or at least be able to fake) is an aura.

'I'm tough, I'm ambitious, and I know exactly what I want. If that makes me a bitch, OK.' **Madonna** has achieved an unprecedented level of power and control in the music industry. She has the aura. Now, we're not suggesting that you need a conical bra, but who can deny her seat at the summit of Mount Confidence? She's an example to us all, because talent-wise there are better women on the circuit, but Madonna, with her self-belief, grit and don't-give-a-damn nerve has trumped them all.

Her behaviours make us believe that she's a star, and that's the point. Once we start acting fearlessly, the negative beliefs we hold about ourselves begin to wane. **The Meringue Girls**, Stacey O'Gorman and Alex Hoffler, have been described as the punk princesses of baking and their rainbow-tastic creations have amassed over 100,000 followers on Instagram. When starting out, they worked on a fake it till you make it approach.

'We pretended we knew what the hell we were up to and that helped us get to a place where we could draw confidence and structure from our idea and business plans. Plus, a lot of our confidence built up as we overcame obstacles, and felt a sense of achievement in our new-found knowledge. Confidence is definitely a cumulative thing in life. We say, don't be afraid to put yourself out there, the worst that could happen is that someone else will say no. Our motto is you've gotta risk a shipwreck to find an island.'

The physical realisation of women with confidence, as we'll explain more fully further on, is that our body language becomes more expansive, we intervene earlier in conversations and we work with a calm, relaxed air. Even faking confidence can make us feel more self-assured. It's that old belief cycle again: feed the cogs' confident behaviours (fake or not) and in time they will spin into bona fide confident feelings. If it feels like a charade then that's because it is – and that's OK too. In time, these acts of confidence (speaking up in meetings, pitching an unexpected story to the editor) will become self-fulfilling.

WORKOUT Visualising the Confident You

When we have done something confidently – as we now know – we actually become more confident. But what if you could trick your mind into believing that was the case?

1. (2 minutes) Close your eyes and focus on what it is you'd like to do with confidence.

2. (1 minute) Focus on your breath: make it even, focusing on the outbreath to calm your body and inner voice.

3. (5 minutes) Now take five minutes to relax. Imagine the moment twenty seconds after having done what (before) you weren't self-confident enough to do. Imagine it in depth – what actually happened? What were the sounds and smells? What was said? Notice how easy and natural it felt. Now, notice how relaxed and serene you feel being confident in what you've achieved.

4. (2 minutes) Now press rewind. Practise replaying how it went, how calm and self-assured you were – as if you've just had that experience, 'remembering' in detail how you felt and what you 'said' and 'did'.

When it's time to do it for real, you will have tricked your brain. It will know the confident you – the one that is calm and relaxed in the face of a hurdle it has conquered before. Now you have acted, the circle of increased confidence can carry on.

2. BYE BYE PRAISE, BYE BYE CRITICISM

We want you to start turning the volume down on praise and criticism.

We know, praise is your friend and criticism your foe. This is mainly because when others tell us how great we are it makes us feel gooey and liked, just as when we receive condemnation it makes us want to curl up inside our coats and sob.

Let's start with praise and how it affects our confidence. We're going to be honest here, however nice it feels, praise can be a cunning swine that panders to our insecurities. It's a short-term high – that shot of tequila at the end of a very long night.

The majority of us became hooked on praise at around the same time that we became hooked on Cabbage Patch Kids and Barbie Dolls. This is thanks to a constant stream of 'Isn't she lovely?' and 'What a clever girl'. When we receive this much praise (misplaced or genuine) in childhood, it fuels our cravings later on in life. Yes, we are strong women. But many of us are also women reliant on praise and terrified of criticism and in terms of being a resilient, confident career woman, it's a lethal combination.

It isn't so much the receiving of praise that's the problem, rather the act of *seeking it out* that weakens us and becomes emblematic of our latent insecurities. The way praise holds us back is by being addictive: are you the type of person who comes to expect praise on a daily or weekly basis? If you are, how do you feel when it doesn't flow? You feel low. And feeling low is a slippery slope towards that pit called Self-Doubt.

When we are able to work in a way that does not require immediate approval or approbation, we become self-sufficient and that breeds confidence. Plus, anyway, in many cases, praise says as much about the person dishing it out as it does the recipient. Perhaps that person wants to be liked too and is only telling you that you're a whizz because he or she wants the reflected glory? Sounds familiar? If this is you, learn to work in ways that do not require immediate approval or approbation.

It's a similar story with criticism.

Criticism, when dished out by Sir Alan's chums in the interview round of *The Apprentice*, is criticism that has been made for TV. It's obnoxious and sensational and no one wants to be the target of that type of denigration. But criticism isn't as bad as it's cracked up to be. Like praise, it can reveal more about the person delivering the news, so don't look at criticism like an unwanted guest at a work party; rather, think of it as a valid call to improvement.

When you can become the person who doesn't let criticism sweep her into the gutter, you'll place another brick in your confidence foundation. Try thinking of praise and criticism as either side of an old-fashioned set of scales. What you're aiming for is equilibrium – you want to keep your emotions balanced and in control at work to reach your new confidence status.

Of course, as Deborah Saunt said, in the mix of cutting through the emotions, we must retain our vulnerability; managing praise and criticism isn't about becoming an impassive android, it's about taking the control within. Because constantly seeking commendation or being crushed by criticism hands your power to someone else, and that can leave you exposed and in free fall.

'If you set out to be liked,' said Margaret Thatcher (a woman who became very un-liked by some), 'you would be prepared to compromise on anything at any time, and you would achieve nothing.'

A good way to get a handle on praise and criticism is to take it, dissect it and dump it. When either arrives, try asking it these three questions.

Who gave you to me?
What is your purpose?
Why do I need you?

Just as praise may well be genuine, it's just as likely to be used as a social mechanism. People at work can use praise as a way of controlling others. On the criticism front, we know that the stuff that really sticks and hurts is the criticism that relates to insecurities we already hold about ourselves, whether that's our intelligence, gravitas or looks. This is emotional stuff, and as we said at the top of the chapter, confidence is a complex and sensitive subject. We know that this plan of attack isn't something you're just going to be able to achieve in a day. Rather, this is a guide to laying those stronger foundations, so that in time you're able recapture the confidence we took for granted as young children.

Having said all of that, there are times when we are all well and truly entitled to bask in praise's glory. It's OK if praise sometimes makes you feel like the Queen; just don't let feeling regal be your sole motivation – don't rely on praise. Think about why you are being praised: take on board the praise that is useful, discard the unhelpful stuff and be very careful not to let praise (or criticism for that matter) knock you off balance.

Remember, praise is an external factor that is completely unrelated to us achieving our goals. If you crave it, a clever way to replace that yearning is to find a more meaningful motivator: reaching your personal goals, delivering for a client, making money, giving back to others, honing your expertise. These are all solid incentives that have lasting worth and will make you feel more confident.

In terms of managing criticism, we need to let go of the unhelpful beliefs that we all hold about ourselves so that they can't fuel criticism's fire. If you need to, go back to the belief cycle in Chapter 3 and work on changing those demons inside your head. Because when we can dilute our negative beliefs, criticism loses its sting. And when criticism starts to lose its sting, we start to feel strong.

The moral of this tiny story is that once we can unfetter ourselves from praise and criticism, we become more confident.

WORKOUT Dare to Disagree

Part of unfettering yourself from the praise/criticism cycle is learning to disagree with that feedback. We are hardwired to agree with those in authority, to be pleasant, compliant girls. But what if that feedback is just plain wrong? Allowing yourself to disagree, getting in touch with Belligerent You, opens up the possibility of rejecting superfluous feedback.

Prepare: grab a taxi. Nowhere to go? Walk into your local artisan coffee shop. Anywhere an in-depth chat is on the menu. Best leave friends and work colleagues out of this one. You'll see why soon.

Take aim: strike up conversation. A ten-minute one of course. Lead the taxi driver/barista/innocent victim (delete as appropriate) into talking on a current issue or opinion. Russell Brand's politics, the migration debate, Chris Evans on *Top Gear*. The topic doesn't matter as long as they have a point of view.

WORKOUT Dare to Disagree continued

Fire: now for the hard part. Unleash your inner American and disagree. They want Greece out of the Eurozone? Your soapbox stance is keeping them in. Whatever they say, whatever your true feelings, take the opposite position. This is about getting comfortable with speaking out. And learning to disagree, even as an academic exercise, is a great place to start.

Rehearse and repeat. For a week, try engaging in debate at least once a day.

3. TRANSACTIONAL ANALYSIS

Transactional analysis (TA) is a psychological theory that examines the interactions within us and between people – when you understand the thinking behind TA, it should help you process and manage the relationships you have with other people at work. And good working relationships are another brick in the foundations.

TA splits people into three ego-states or ways of being:
PARENT
ADULT
CHILD

Within the parent state, there are two types:
NURTURING PARENT (concerned with caring, loving, helping)
CONTROLLING PARENT (criticising, censoring, punishing)

Within the child state, there are also two types:
NATURAL CHILD (spontaneous, energetic, curious, loving and uninhibited)
ADAPTED CHILD (guilt, fear, depression, anxiety, envy and pride)

To be clear, this model has nothing to do with actual family life. You certainly don't need to have a child or be a parent to be able to reap its benefits; this is a clever and insightful theory that will help expose in you underlying character traits that impact on how you work. Moreover, this is not about typecasting. You are not stuck in one specific state, rather your role will change depending on the situation.

The Adapted Child type is especially interesting and needs a little more explaining. An Adapted Child mindset is developed when one learns to change one's feelings and behaviours in response to the world around. The Adapted Child in you might be the part that tries to please everyone else, or wants to comply with all demands. This is especially true in the face of a Controlling Parent.

We'll leave the theory's complexities for another time, but what's important and useful here is the idea that in every interaction between you and others, you will adopt one of these states.

Perhaps you are a junior employee having a meeting with your boss. The boss might assume the role of a parent, either criticising or nurturing. And you could be a child, learning from the parent, or an Adapted Child rebelling. The aspiration in this employee-meets-boss situation is that both are adults, each respectfully listening and learning from what the other has to say.

Women often adopt the Adapted Child persona particularly in relation to a Controlling Parent. We take on board criticism as a child would from a parent. We believe it deeply and think we need to change. Clearly, this is a destructive interaction. What you should always aspire to is an adult-to-adult relationship, because those are most likely to be healthy and productive.

The TA theory illustrates how you have the power to dictate your next interaction. If you want to achieve the blessed adult-to-adult scenario, you need to take control, be straight-talking in your communication and regard the other person as your equal, whatever your respective business cards reveal.

This is the basis of assertive communication.

The key to breaking a pattern of the injurious unhelpful parent-to-child interaction is to consistently communicate from an adult ego state and to continually invite the other party to operate from their adult state too. Obviously, there is no guarantee that the other party will respond as an adult.

There is a consciousness to this process, but if you practise, it will become natural and you'll more often assume the adult role, and invite others to meet you there too. Be an adult by always reacting in an open, mature and direct way. Do not be subservient or slip into acquiescence. And keep inviting an adult response.

Often, those in a parent state, when faced with an adult, will naturally move towards an adult state themselves and the union will benefit all. If it helps, dress in a way that makes you feel confident, senior and equal. For example, if your nine o'clock meeting is 6 foot 6 tall, then wear a pair of heels. If you want to get the best out of work interactions, keep your conviction and assertion in yourself strong and present. Before a meeting with the Big Boss, try looking yourself in the mirror and affirming that you are an adult, your Big Boss's equal, and you will speak to them as such.

We can all choose which state we embody – and arriving at places as an adult is an instant confidence booster.

4. EMBRACE FAILURE

Failure. Who likes things going wrong? Not us. But there is a sliding scale of wrong, and really, again, it is our perception of situations, as much as the reality of what went wrong, that plays on our minds when we fail.

We all attempt things at work that we aren't able to pull off. We make mistakes. We take a wrong turn. Work is pitted with ups and downs, but failure needn't be a dirty word. What doesn't break you makes you stronger; it's a cliché but it's true. The reason that failure is so important to confidence is because one cannot happen without the other. Risk, the springboard to failure, necessitates confidence – and then there's the actual fail, if it happens, and what you can learn from it.

Knit one, purl one: risk and failure are interlinked loops on the same piece of knitting. A successful career woman needs to be able to look failure in the mouth and not be scared of a bite. Failing is a process: it's a journey from idea, via risk assessment, through action and eventually to the dreaded faux pas. Yes, you have failed; your ego is wounded, but you have grown a little stronger and more confident by just riding that wave.

Elizabeth Varley is the founder and CEO of TechHub, the global tech startup community. TechHub is home to over 1000 members in London, with other community spaces in six cities around the world. Elizabeth has been selected for Computer Weekly's UKtech50 top influencers, the Evening Standard's Silicon 60, the Debrett's 500, Vogue UK's Generation Tech and Cosmopolitan's Fierce 40 Under 40, among others. She also initiated the Startup Funeral, a celebration of failure.

'Failure is something we talk about a lot; we run an event called Startup Funeral, where the leader dresses up as a priest. We hold a proper ceremony, there are flowers and the "congregation" wear black. It sounds frivolous, but it's a serious meet up where we invite partners to get up and talk about what went wrong and really discuss the experience of failure – to accept that failure is part of starting up and that it's part of business. Failure is not the end, it's an opportunity to work out what's not working – to think of it as an end is not helpful. It's important to be able to say that things didn't work out. Again, it's about not trying to make the failure personal; yes it hurts when things don't work out the way you planned, but pretending that it doesn't isn't helpful either. Failure is part of business life. It doesn't mean you are a terrible person – it just means you had a go and nobody should be denigrated for that. Failure is a badge of honour.'

Treating failure as a positive goes against everything we've been conditioned to believe. But as Elizabeth points out, failure shouldn't need to shackle us on our ascent. Many of us, thanks to our perfectionist tendencies and deep-seated risk aversion, especially in situations where the risk of failure is greater than the risk of a slam-dunk success, shy away from having a go. But learning to fail and even, get ready for it, finding a positive in failure, is essential, liberating and confidence-boosting.

Because the truth is, when we survive failure once, we go on and play with jeopardy a little more often. And that breeds confidence (and plenty of other career success too). The new risk-friendly you will be a ballsier, more self-assured character, who isn't scared to fail.

The good news is that in today's energetic work landscape, we can fail fast.

Job. Done. Didn't. Work. Failed. Fast. Moved. On.

Fail Fast is a buzz term for modern entrepreneurs. In a world of tech startups, quick fails are important learning tools that allow companies to stay relevant and confidently churn out new ideas. Failing Fast is especially pertinent to women, because its speed helps us to lessen the perfectionist within and ultimately solidify our confidence.

As the tech world proves, failures are digestible when they arrive as small canapés. If you know you're risk and failure averse, start small and beat down those failure jitters one stride at a time. Remember, scared women are less likely to succeed. So listen to us now: it's OK to fail. Hear it, accept it, and keep on going.

If you need more convincing of the importance of failure, here's **JK Rowling**, from her 2008 Harvard Commencement Address, *The Fringe Benefits of Failure, and the Importance of Imagination.* 'You might never fail on the scale I did but it is impossible to live without failing at something, unless you live so cautiously that you might as well not have lived at all – in which case, you fail by default.'

WORKOUT Embrace Failure

The trick to embracing failure is to stop seeing any sort of failure at all. To do this, you need to change your goals. If you are able to view things as a learning experience then you won't have failed, but you will have learnt something new.

WORKOUT Embrace Failure continued

The best response to perceived failure is to ask oneself these three powerful questions:

1. What did I learn from this situation?
2. How can I grow as a person from this experience?
3. What are three positive things about this situation?

When you first attempt to list three positive things about the failure, your mind may be resistant. But if you stick with the exercise and do it as a default and on repeat, you'll start seeing new opportunities in things that went wrong.

5. PERFECTIONISM AND OVERTHINKING THINGS

In this war for female career empowerment, perfectionism is the enemy. It makes us risk averse, it kills our confidence and it congests the channels of production.

Not all women are fixated on being perfect, but it affects many. We take pride in doing things nicely and correctly (hardly killer adjectives there), and worse than that, we wallow in our past imperfections and prophesy them in the future too.

Before she had secured her book deal, **Stephenie Meyer**, author of the stellar Twilight series, wrote to fifteen literary agents. It was not the perfect response: nine rejections and five non-replies. She must have felt dejected, but Meyer kept her perfectionist tendencies in check – she didn't buckle in the face of adversity. The final agent signed her. In 2010, Forbes reported Meyer's annual earnings as $40 million.

Humans are imperfect. Millionaire authors are imperfect. Even those who are masters of sport, the arts, music and business make mistakes or get rejected. **Oprah Winfrey** was told she wasn't right for television. To get to the top of Mount Confidence, first you're going to have to tame that perfectionist voice. When we lower our self-imposed expectations, we set ourselves free.

Just as we are professors of multiple, cross-platform brain activity, we are also suckers for corrosive internal thoughts: we are champion self-belief assassinators.

What we need to do if we want to be truly confident is to pick up those negative, intrusive thoughts ('I'm not good enough', 'I'm too old to learn', 'I am weak') and put them behind a heavy locked door inside our heads. Better still, actually write them down on a piece of paper (yes, go and get a notepad), and then take immense pleasure in tearing up the list of misplaced negative beliefs, and dumping it in the bin. By the way, this act is surprisingly effective at banishing mental pessimism.

What you're aiming to do is to unbridle your brain from poisonous thoughts so that's it's free to be strategic, sparky and, yes you've guessed it, confident again. If you're really struggling, try some creative visualisation. Instead of wasting time thinking about all the possible bad outcomes, flip the coin. If you're going to overthink, at least do it with a smile on your face, because things can go well too, you know …Your brain is a supercharged organ; the least you can do is to make it your friend.

6. ASSERT YOUR ASSERTIVENESS

Most of what we've covered so far has been about adapting your thoughts. Now it's time for a bit of behavioural therapy. Because confidence also comes from actions: and number one on the list today is assertiveness.

When 'assertive', 'woman' and 'work' are used in the same sentence the implication is often unfavourable. But don't let that put you off. Being an assertive woman is not about being a tyrant bitch boss. It is something subtler than that. When you have the resolve to pursue a goal, if you know that goal is right for your project, team or company, you are being assertive. Assertive women can be quiet women. They can be screechy types too – although screechy sometimes gags the point. Assertive women stand up, absorb criticism and keep going. Assertive women drip with external confidence.

Being assertive and realising your objectives can be a major endorphin hit. You feel great! But assertive women aren't always liked. To make sure you keep everyone onside, while you harness your inner assertiveness, massage in some of your natural female style. Whatever our position in terms of pay brackets, confidence and equality, women have a trump card in their purse: empathy. The trick here is to use this empathy to round the edges of assertive's sharp tongue so that you can power forward, act all confident and become the self-assured woman you were always destined to be.

When you aren't assertive, the opposite becomes true: you know what you want, you don't have the courage to grab it, you end up fulfilling your negative self-beliefs and you spin in a negative cycle of doom. Your self-esteem swoops out of sight, you put others' needs before your own and before long, you've morphed into that Transactional Analysis child.

Assertiveness, like optimism and efficiency, can be learnt. Try the small steps route that we covered in handling criticism above. If you finesse assertion when you're in the comfort of your home surroundings, you'll slowly train yourself to make it part of your everyday stash of confidence weapons.

If you're still not convinced, think of it like this: assertiveness needn't be a permanent state, rather, it's a place you can advance to when needs be. Don't be daunted. You can become a strong, assertive woman, but strong assertive women take time to grow.

WORKOUT The Faces of Confidence

If possible, nab three friends for this. But it can be done alone (ideally, again, not in public – jumping around the different chairs might look suspect to casual observers).

Prepare. Person One sits in the middle of the room on a chair. The others sit around them. Each of you will embody a different face of confidence: the first assertive, the next aggressive, the last passive.

WORKOUT The Faces of Confidence continued

(6 minutes) For two minutes each, the 'faces' take it in turn to try to persuade Person One to give up their chair – in the relevant aggressive, assertive or passive persona, of course. Observe the difference in each aspect of behaviour, voice and stance.

(1 minute) Person One feeds back the impact of each behaviour style on them (if you're alone, notice the differences). How did they feel? To whom are they going to give their chair?

(3 minutes) Each 'face' describes how their behaviour made them feel.

The end result is that the chair is usually relinquished to the assertive person. And you can situate assertiveness between passivity and aggression as a positive, confident way to behave.

7. LUCK ISN'T LUCKY ANY MORE

So much of confidence is control. Which is why crediting luck rather than genuine know-how for our achievements is such a fatal mistake. We make our own luck in life. This is received wisdom – and it is true. When it comes to work, though, women aren't able to recognise their own prowess and the upshot of this is that we give luck (arbitrary, dropped-from-the-sky kind of luck) the credit when things go well.

'Oh, I've just been lucky in my career.' 'Right place, right time.' 'The new job? Oh, it was a fluke.' If any of these sound like they could have sprung from your own lips then you are not alone. Because of our generally lower confidence levels, not to mention our strong imposter tendencies, many of us give luck the upper hand.

Men, as a useful comparison, tend to do the opposite – and rather frustratingly, it pays dividends. They, in the main, attribute their successes to skill. So while women, when they bag a promotion, say, rarely brag about it (controlled bragging is no bad thing, by the way) because they wrongly believe they just got lucky, a man will feel he earned the promotion – and guess what, that's worth bragging about.

Yes, the winds of luck might have blown your career boat in the right direction, but that same wind will have benefited others too. Luck isn't worth dwelling on, because luck is democratic. We all get it; we all love it. Your intelligence and aptitude, your don't-give-a-damn resolve and your killer networking prowess, that's what has got you where you are today. When you are able to accept and communicate these facts, your confidence – and career – will glide elegantly northwards.

Repeat after us: I'm not lucky, I'm awesome. I'm not lucky, I'm awesome.

To be able to truly accept your brilliance (and we all have brilliance within us), it's worth taking a moment every week or month to step back and be objective about your recent achievements and how they came into being. This is a good moment to flip through your positive belief record.

Another way of finding some kind of impartiality about your career is to imagine how your best friend would describe your career trajectory. Go on, do it, imagine what she'd say, because we're pretty sure she wouldn't say you've been lucky.

If you're really struggling to give luck the heave-ho, rope in actual Best Friend and run through your career successes together. Hopefully, this simple exercise will help kick-start some real belief in yourself – there's just one rule to this game: no one is allowed to mention the L word.

8. GET GRAVITAS

Gravitas is a state; it is a way of being that infers authority. Politicians have gravitas because they need to be able to persuade the electorate to their points of view. Many doctors have gravitas. Royalty are gravitas experts. Michelle Obama, Anna Wintour and Beyoncé each possess their own brand of gravitas, their own kind of presence, their own vibe that is applicable to their work and their lives. Gravitas isn't about what you think or say, it's about how you say it.

Confident people have gravitas and gravitas comes with confidence. The two are intrinsically entwined, both playing into the base ability to be able to stand up, be counted and have people take note. Gravitas can present in many forms: poise under pressure, absolute decisiveness, an indisputable power of persuasion. Happily, gravitas can also be a bit of an act. Sure, what we're aiming for in the long run is a constant and natural state of gravitas, but in the meantime faking it will do, because sometimes careers are about show, and that's OK.

So how do you feign this kind of noticeable, potent influence?

Trained actress, top impact coach and author of *Gravitas: Communicate with Confidence, Influence and Authority*, **Caroline Goyder** believes it's a question of freeing your mind. 'The number one blocker to gravitas for many women is overthinking. In a meeting, you need to follow the advice given to actors that you should be clear on delivery – that means you just deliver and don't analyse as you speak. But what a lot of women do is have a critical voice in their head as they are speaking and that is a real gravitas blocker. So the first thing I do with clients is help them silence that inner ticker tape.'

Caroline's advice is simple: 'Practise really listening to what's in the room when you are in a meeting. The same if you are presenting. Before you present, you need to just really listen to the other speakers. I believe the voice is adrenal. So it gets worse when we are nervous. I tell clients to get grounded before they present anything. Go for a run, do some yoga, breathe – take fifteen minutes to get into your body. You can even do this on the tube. Don't frantically check emails. Multitasking is very anti-gravitas. What that means is that when you get to the meeting you are present to what is in the room. That is an instant gravitas booster. We have all experienced the very calm, grounded presence of extremely senior people. I worked with a FTSE 250 CEO who had a million things going on. But when we went into the meeting she was calm. She was completely there. She gave you her full attention and that was powerful.'

9. BODY LANGUAGE

Non-verbal communication is another powerful player in the sport of confidence. Just the way you position your body will influence how confident you feel and how others perceive you too.

In her study on body language, social scientist and author, Amy Cuddy, analysed a set of nervous interview candidates and the impact of body language on their confidence levels. What she found was that when an interviewee adopted a more powerful stance for two minutes before entering the interview (shoulders back, arms stretched out to the sides, chest raised) it significantly increased their testosterone, lowered their cortisol levels and increased his or her chance of securing the job. Yup, just the mere act of emboldening their body language actually raised the interviewee's confidence – and that confidence got them hired.

Positive non-verbal communication also makes us more liked. We know this because, as another clever research study proves, we draw our conclusions on others before they speak a syllable. A sample group of students were shown very short film clips (between two and ten seconds each) of potential new college lecturers. The brevity of the clips meant that body language became the only discernible tool for communication.

Whether those in the sample group liked the lecturer, even after such a short amount of time, was used to predict how the lecturer's actual students rated that teacher. The results were simple. The more positive and likeable the lecturers' body language to the sample, the better their ratings overall. In short, good body language pleases everyone.

Confident body language feeds into gravitas, and gravitas lets others see you as a natural success story – a leader, even. Try this workout to see how simple this shift can be.

WORKOUT Power Posing

(1 minute) Take a minute to scroll through this week's schedule. Find a situation that requires confidence. Nothing too high stakes – you don't want to experiment on an interview for your dream job, but maybe a team meeting or networking event.

(2 minutes) Before the event, go somewhere private. Adopt a low power pose – hunched over, arms hugging your sides, perhaps staring down at your smartphone: the typical pre-interview stance in fact – as you await your fate.

WORKOUT Power Posing continued

(2 minutes) Now see how the event goes. Stress reactive? Check. Underconfident? Check.

(1 minute) Now find another event or meeting. This one can be higher stakes – we're so confident this will work.

(2 minutes) Find your private place again. Adopt a high power pose. Sitting or standing, your arms should be wide and you should take up space. Chin up. Chest out.

(2 minutes) Check how you feel. Dominant? Check. Powerful? Check. Research has shown that adopting a power pose before a big event increases testosterone and lowers cortisol, making you more confident, less anxious and more likely to get ahead.

10. VOICE CONTROL

Body language and voice control are two peas in the same confidence pod. British actress **Imelda Staunton** has spent so many hours training her voice that today it can just as easily be heavy with emotion, gush with humour, twitter like a bird, sob, sing, cackle, whisper and do everything else in between. Whatever state her voice is in, it is always convincing.

Interestingly, though, Staunton didn't always have this level of voice control. When she was training at RADA, her then director told her to take some voice lessons because at the time, as she recalls it, her voice was too shrill. 'Those sessions changed my voice forever. They centred it and lowered it.'

Now we're not suggesting you suddenly drop three registers and come over all Morgan Freeman. But it is a fact that we are conditioned to find lower voices more powerful; and yes, it's all strung up in those unconscious biases towards men being leaders.

So what, you ask, can you do about your high-pitched tone? Well, all of this is more about tone than pitch and there's a subtle but crucial distinction between the two. When we speak in a shrill voice, one that rings in your ear, it suggests anxiety rather than confidence and the same goes for speaking very quickly.

We think our voices are stuck in their ways, but when we're conscious about not just what we say, but how we say it, we feed confidence – and that's the aim of the game. Try, not just for a complete departure of screech, but a slow, even pace in the lower end of your own register. A steady (pause) deliberate (pause) voice (pause) conveys total (pause) confidence.

Actually, when we reduce the tempo we end up with more control over our voices. Speaking slowly relaxes the vocal cords and that makes everything run more smoothly in the vocal cord department. Another tip to speaking with gravitas and confidence is to turn the volume down. This might seem counterintuitive (don't loud people command attention?), but when you force people to strain to catch what you're saying it encourages them to value your thoughts.

FINAL THOUGHTS

The cycle of confidence is powerful and self-perpetuating. The more you start doing and achieving the more confident you will feel. We know that sometimes your confidence cogs need oiling and that they might slow down and take some time to get going and gain momentum. Once they're spinning though, confidence can take you up many gears at work.

Countless women feel paralysed by a lack of confidence. We think of confidence as this slinky, sharp woman who struts and winks and knows all the answers. Confidence can look like Jessica Rabbit, but confidence can look like you too. Small steps, that's what you need to keep in your head.

Try at some point this week or this month to push yourself out of your comfort zone: speak up in that meeting, be bold when it comes to new ideas, strike up a conversation with a stranger at rush hour. So much of fear is heightened inside our head and fear is a destructive beast. Plus, as Kirsty Young says, 'What's the worst that can happen?'

———— THE TIPS ————

|1| Smile smile smile

We've covered body language and voice but what about your face?
Perhaps the oldest tip in the book (literally), plastering a smile on your
face – even when you're crying with fear inside – is proven to make you
feel more positive. So if you have something scary coming up at work
and Confident You is playing hide and seek, smile. You'll immediately feel
happier to take the plunge.

|2| Don't believe the hype

Overconfident people can have us believing they're something
special. By extension, we feel we're not. Social media is guilty too. Our
confidence takes a battering both in person and online from the hype we
believe about others' success. Don't buy into it. Overnight success is a
myth. The Hemsley sisters, for example, told us how they had worked as
chefs for years before hitting the media bigtime. And most people don't
air their doubts, or dirty laundry, on Instagram. Stopping the cycle of
comparison is key to building up Confident You. If you're getting bogged
down, take a hype (and social media) holiday.

|3| Be your own best friend

If imposter syndrome and self-doubt are still refusing to stay in their
box, you need to take action. First step: become your own best friend.
What would you do if your real-life best friend told you she felt less than
capable? You'd talk her up. Studies show both that positive thinking
improves confidence and that we are more likely to accept this from
someone else. So don't treat yourself less well than you would her.
Tell yourself you're worth it, because you are.

|4| Accentuate the positives

Therapy was always about moving from low to neutral. But positive
psychology has bucked that trend. It focuses on moving us from just
OK to plus ten. Which is where we're aiming for with your confidence
too. Like us, positive psychology is also a big fan of the notebook and
pen. This week, write down three things every day that you have done
well. Three things to use as ammunition against self-doubt. Starting to

feel better? Continue. After two weeks, you will feel more confident and, better yet, six months down the line the benefits should still be there.

|5| Target the right strengths

Reliable. Organised. Keeps her head down. If these adjectives could have been lifted from your annual review, Confident You needs to come to the party. Confidence isn't just a goal in itself, it also impacts on how others perceive you. When you embrace confidence, you should be able to shift the narrative around your strengths to those that matter in terms of progression at work. Strategic. Effective. Strong. They're what you're going for. Use your emerging confidence to target these attributes and the reaction you'll get will feed your confidence right back. It's a beautiful circle.

CHAPTER 5

The Influence of Others

THE SETTING

Lena Dunham talks about her late mentor, the American screenwriter, novelist and director, Nora Ephron, in fluid terms. 'Over the course of our year-and-a-half-long friendship, Nora introduced me to, in no particular order: several ear, nose, and throat doctors; the concept of eating lunch at Barneys; self-respect. She explained how to interact with a film composer ("Just say what you're hearing and what you want to hear") and what to do if someone screamed at you on the telephone ("Just nod, hang up, and decide you will never allow anyone to speak to you that way again"). She called bullshit on a whole host of things, too: donuts served in fancy restaurants; photo shoots in which female directors are asked to all stand in a cluster wearing moustaches; the idea that one's writing isn't fiction if it borrows from one's life.'

Lena and Nora's relationship was a profound meeting of minds. They may not have become acquainted on a work mentoring scheme and presumably there was no formal exchange of contracts. Nonetheless, they formed a powerful – and pivotal – bond. 'Her advice was unparalleled,' Dunham wrote in the New York Times after Ephron's untimely death. Though it was short-lived, the pair's relationship neatly encompasses the notion of modern mentoring: two talented, visionary and productive women from different generations who nourished each other's careers, opinions and lives by the simple act of becoming friends and respecting one another.

In this chapter we will discuss the concept and potency of mentoring, sponsorship and role models. What are their functions?

In what way are they different from each other? And just how the hell do you nab one anyway? Many of us struggle with the idea of forming specific work relationships (ones with buzzword names like those above) because we think they are somehow unusual and daunting.

So let us set one thing straight from the off: mentors, sponsors and role models (referred to here for ease under the umbrella term mentors) are just fancy words for friendships and associations that centre on work. Of course, they are friendships with function, but they are friendships nonetheless and, in the case of role models, a face-to-face acquaintance need not even materialise.

However daunting they sound, this trinity of External Influencers represent purposeful work relationships that will buoy, guide and enhance your unique breed of success. And if hotshot, multitalented types like Lena Dunham are open to advice and mentoring, then you should be too.

The strategic bonds that we build during our careers can be absolute game-changers. We might deny it, and women especially are professional deniers on this front, but talent and hard work only get us so far in our unicorn pursuit. Because it is specific working relationships, the ones we build with people who have influence in places that our position won't yet reach, the ones who have trodden our paths and survived the battlefield, even with the people we never meet but whose careers and vision inspire us to greater heights, that can really supersize our careers.

Nora Ephron was one of a gaggle of inspirers who picked up Lena Dunham and delivered her to the stars. It is worth mentioning here that mentors and sponsors don't just work in hallowed New York creative circles; in whichever industry you inhabit and at whatever level you currently reside, a mentor will, almost without exception, improve your prospects.

The human race is built on meaningful relationships with other people. Money doesn't make the world go round, friendships do;

talking, sharing, laughing and learning from one another is how we progress in life. And the same is true at work.

What you'll notice, as you read through this chapter, is that while we start with and give more space to mentoring, we affirm the importance of the sponsor or champion as most crucial to your success. The reason for this is that sponsors are a subset of mentoring and as such, many of the tools and knacks for finding and building these relationships cross from one sphere to the other. And since we're acutely aware that all of us are time pressed, and no one wants to read the same advice twice, we've consolidated for ease.

Role models are crucial too, but unlike mentors and sponsors, this is a relationship that can be built from afar. Put shortly, you can find a role model without her – or him – even having any say in the matter. Many very useful role models are in the public eye; we see and admire their achievements and it inspires us towards greater things.

Before we go hell for leather on the mentoring front, here's a little External Influences overview: this is how your triumvirate of support can open our eyes and careers to new opportunities, work fulfilment, fun, money, power, unicorns and everything in between.

MENTOR, CHAMPION, ROLE MODEL: The Definitions

A mentor: '*Had there not been you, there never would have been me.*' Oprah to her mentor Barbara Walters.

Mentors offer advice and provide guidance. A useful analogy for a mentor is your work parent: he or she has walked in your shoes and possesses the kind of experience that will provide you with confidence and insider knowledge. A mentor is a trusted friend with whom you enjoy spending time – and crucially, a mentor wants to see you succeed.

A sponsor or champion: '*Larry Summers offered to advise my senior thesis, gave me my first job out of college, and has been an important part of my life ever since.*' Sheryl Sandberg thanking Larry Summers in *Lean In*.

Champions promote you at work – they push you forward and endorse your cause. A champion uses their influence to get you promotions, plum projects and powerful introductions. It's all in the signalling: respected champions let others know you're worth backing too.

A role model: '*I don't think she realises how what she has done has made what I am doing partially possible. She is a role model for me in so many ways.*' Michelle Obama on Hillary Clinton.

Role models are people we hope to emulate – a work exemplar. You don't actually need to know your role model for them to have a positive influence on your career. Role models can be in the public eye, or prominent within your industry. Role models inspire us to work towards their success. They often remind us of ourselves; seeing their success gives us hope and guidance.

ABOUT Mentors

When work feels like a tundra of loneliness, a mentor is there for support and to watch our backs. In fact, a mentor will be waiting in the wings whatever is going on front of stage, because mentors are first and foremost dependable. They are also sounding boards, counsellors, friends and guides.

If you're one for historical references, the concept of mentoring originates in ancient Greek mythology. In Homer's *Odyssey*, Odysseus fights in the Trojan War and when he is away, he entrusts the care of his household to Mentor, who serves as a teacher to Odysseus's son, Telemachus. And just as back with Mentor himself, trust remains a main ingredient today.

A great mentoring relationship feels like any other great friendship. As Nora and Lena prove, being part of a mentoring marriage isn't about sitting at two ends of an empty boardroom and tweaking the CV every so often. Rather, it's an effortless, healthy and enjoyable cross-pollination of supportive thoughts and ideas, although as a postscript, it might not feel like this at the very start. Mentoring relationships take time.

Amy Cole, Instagram's Head of Brand Development for Europe, Middle East and Africa, has moved roles and geographies many times in her career. But wherever she is in the world, her mentors are unwavering in their help and encouragement.

'I think it's incredibly important to have support; to have people who inspire you and from whom you can learn. I have changed industries and countries so often that I need certain people to ground me. I look to my mentors for advice on leading my team and carrying myself within the industry. More importantly, though, they are my support network; startups can be incredibly tough and lonely when you're going through the process of getting new ideas off the ground. For me, having mentors there to call and lean on when times are tough is crucial.'

As Amy attests, mentors provide advice and guidance and once the relationship has fully cemented (more of how to get there shortly), they'll be the ones who'll take a call from you when you don't know where to turn. Mentors, in theory, help us process all types of work highs and lows.

But theory and mentoring don't always go hand in hand. That's perhaps one of the reasons that some of us find the concept baffling: how can you have a rulebook for a friendship? Of course, you cannot. In a purely work capacity, mentors are friends with benefit. And just as with our different friendships beyond our careers, mentors come in all shapes and all sizes.

Cole is lucky enough to have a whole gang of career supporters and that's crucial to the modern career too. Gone are the days of a mentor for life; what you're aiming for is an array of influencers who can fulfil different needs at different points in time. But what never fluctuates is their impact on our success: we do better at work and enjoy it more when we have a mentor and that is a fact. Mentors give us the tools, strength and information we need to flourish.

Mentors also increase our work resilience, something many of us struggle with. Resilience, as we said in the previous chapter, helps us to march forward and remain unwavering in the face of career adversity.

You see, mentors (if you find it easier, you can refer to them as strategic friends) have incredible power. Not power in a scary, shouty kind of way; rather they imbue us with inner strength, and that, in success-finding terms, is nothing short of magic.

Their view from the top helps with office politics too. Why did so-and-so get the job? Who is looking to invest at the moment? The right mentor (and we'll explain how to identify the perfect match shortly) will make introductions, pass on crucial contacts and generally be your eyes and ears further up the tree. On top of this, mentors share with their mentees (that's you) their breadth of knowledge, they give an objective viewpoint and are generally just wise and helpful beings.

'I don't have one mentor,' says **Kirsty Young**, 'but earlier in my career I had women and men who were brilliantly encouraging; they helped give me confidence. Today, I have a great agent; she's unwaveringly supportive and emboldens me to turn down work if it's not right – and that's a very empowering feeling. Think about the marathon, she says, not the sprint.'

What Young's agent advises in terms of picking and choosing her career choices is especially pertinent against today's complex professional landscape. As statistics currently stand, we are all likely to have chewed our way through at least ten jobs by the age of forty. If you consider that many of us don't get our careers off the ground until our early twenties, that's an extremely speedy turnover rate. Careers have evolved from the predictable, linear blueprint of old (a job for life) into something wavier and more mercurial. And movement on this scale requires reinforcements.

Part of the reason that this chapter is such an important one is that many women struggle to build weighty work relationships. Our lower confidence (hopefully we're starting to win that battle now), a knack for over-analysis, imperfect networks (as we'll see in Chapter 7) and a host of other issues stand in our way. But as we've acknowledged, purposeful career progression can be a slow burn.

We aren't expecting you to arrive at work tomorrow, proceed directly to the desk of the CFO and announce to her or him a set of mentoring intentions. Things don't play out like that. Have it in your mind though that mentors bring with them success. With support in the wings, you'll be a more capable, reinforced and better-connected version of your former self.

HOW TO Create Your Mentor Circle

So where do mentors hang out? Well, we're pretty sure there isn't some kind of exclusive mentoring club out there. If you're lucky enough to work somewhere progressive, where the bosses realise the benefit of strong mentoring relationships, you might be able to join the work scheme or buy into the established mentoring culture.

Many companies have active and established programmes in place that establish channels between departments and across strict hierarchy streams. Formal arrangements like these usually ensure that the mentors involved are focused and understand the rules of the game.

Those who don't have a mentoring programme at the office are going to need to blaze their own trail. In the nicest way possible, when there isn't a precedent of established mentoring bonds, the buck kind of stops with you. Even those who are the lucky targets of a formal regime will benefit from adding to their mentor menu with some choice selections from further afield.

As daunting as this might sound, being forced to unearth our own mentors can be a serious advantage. In fact, the mentoring relationships that build organically over time are often the most profound. Think about that person you've always had a soft spot for; not in a romantic sense, rather in an I-love-the-way-you-work kind of way. Those are your mentor targets, because when you have a backdrop of established respect (hopefully mutual) and admiration, the rest will inevitably follow.

Obviously, we're unable to tell each of you which stones need turning to reveal your ideal aides. What we can do is inspire you to think broadly and deeply about the people you already know who could step up to the mentoring mantle. And someone you like and respect is a great place to start.

It goes without saying (although we say it anyway) that when we're identifying our mentor, we must remember not to discount men. Don't get us wrong, we're all for sisterhoods and female fist punches, but men offer a different mentoring flavour.

It is also worth pointing out that while mentors don't necessarily need to be older, someone who's been around the racetrack a few more times offers experience, and experience is a vital tenet of mentoring. A stumbling block for some women, when identifying older mentors, is that we can be reticent when it comes to building relationships beyond our immediate circle of colleagues and peers. But when we shy away from speaking to our elders, we restrict our valuable mentoring pool.

Work, remember, is an ageless society; so never feel inferior just because you are the youngest on the roster. Instead, take pride in your own opinions, use your youth to your advantage and don't be shy to look up for support.

As much as we might think that mentoring is a one-sided relationship there's an inevitable reciprocity. That sharp young mind, that Periscope and SnapChat know-how is crucial to someone who's perhaps out of touch with social media. Everyone benefits when we build worthwhile and supportive working relationships across career generations, so take your youth and springboard it northwards.

The Michelin-starred chef **Ruth Rogers MBE** is an unequivocal female success story and over the course of her career she has learnt the value of being a mentor. Among many others, Jamie Oliver, April Bloomfield and Hugh Fearnley-Whittingstall all turn to Rogers when they need that unique type of mentoring support.

'Being a mentor is one of the greatest compliments in life. I often think about what April Bloomfield and Jamie have achieved, and it gives me an immense sense of success when they talk about what they learnt at the River Café. Being at their side at the start of their careers means I have done something more than just design nice recipes and provide good food.'

Rogers has mentored some greats, but even at nearly seventy years old, she still has her own mentors to turn to. 'I have a very strong group of people around me; I turn to my friends who run companies when there's a problem at the restaurant that I can't sort – it might be a question of equity for example. And my greatest advisor is my husband Richard. But most of the time, if I need advice, I turn to the people I work with.'

Don't assume that your mentoring relationships need to be a formal arrangement; instead, look for specific qualities in others that provide the type of support you require at that time. And remember, our mentors don't even need to work in the same industry; as long as you share an easy rapport with a person and they inspire you too, then your mentoring stars should be aligned.

But wait. 'This is all very well,' we hear you say, 'but I just can't get into my head how I actually get a mentor.' To us, the starting point is identifying the mentors you already have – the ones who support you, but who you haven't necessarily labelled as a bona fide mentor. We think this exercise is crucial because it shows us that we are already in possession of mentors, and that's empowering in the search for more. Having said that, we don't all think in the same way, so if you're just desperate for the nitty gritty How to Ask bit, skip down a section for some practical advice.

As we were saying, a good way to break down the concept and focus on a potential future mentor is to look back at the past. The very act of acknowledging that we've all had — still have, most probably — mentors in one capacity or another throughout our lives (thanks Dad) should bring a bit of perspective on the matter. So here's a little workout to get the memory juices flowing.

WORKOUT Past Mentors

Chances are you've had mentors in the past and possibly didn't realise it at the time. Here we look back on our lives to identify past mentors. What characteristics did each person possess that helped establish a mentoring relationship? What did we do to make the mentoring stick?

Spend five minutes thinking back on various stages of your life and remember those individuals who had a unique and important impact on your life. One question you can ask yourself to help you focus is: 'If I hadn't met X, how would I have learnt Y?' Some 'types' of people to think about are: teachers, coaches, counsellors, friends, relatives, supervisors and co-workers.

Now draw a table and spend five minutes completing it. The table has the following columns: Mentor's name, How the mentor helped me, What characteristics the mentor had that helped me grow, What I did in return.

Result: We now have a better idea of how our personal development has been enhanced by mentors, whether or not the relationship was officially recognised as mentoring. You might even find you have some mentors now you didn't even realise you have. Understanding how these relationships have worked in the past empowers you to create more for the future.

Mentors, in whatever form they present themselves, are the looms against which we weave the fabric of our careers. It might sound as though we're overstating their value, but really, when we become part of fruitful and productive mentoring relationships, ones that are based on spirited dialogues that lead to enduring friendships, we are able to reach places that we could never have arrived at alone.

At Bow & Arrow, a central London agency that specialises in developing modern, creative and strategic growth strategies for businesses such as Google, O2, Barclays and the BBC, Co-Founder and Creative Partner **Natasha Chetiyawardana** has installed a very modern take on the mentoring (or as she calls it, coaching) notion.

'We are all coaches; coaching is our way of feeding back to one another. We have unique feedback sessions after every meeting to work out what we could have done better. It helps us comprehensively understand each other, our clients and the business. We mentor up, down and laterally, so that we can all work together better. We might say things to our clients that they don't want to hear, but it ends up strengthening the relationship. There isn't a weird formality to all of this, we just ensure that we're a really collaborative and communicative place to work.'

The best mentors provide caring and altruistic advice; in Bow & Arrow's case, this presents as fluid and constant advice across the entire business. It might not sound like it, but as long as we are listening and guiding others then we become part of fruitful mentoring relationships. Bow & Arrow isn't rigid when it comes to the concept of mentoring, and you shouldn't be either. To be a mentor and to be mentored are not mutually exclusive concepts and neither requires a formal contract to have value and purpose.

So now we're clear that within our mentoring circle there will be many different relationships. There is no right way, but what is certain is that you need more than one. This diagram neatly illustrates mentoring and all its different permutations. If you are struggling to structure your external support network, it can be useful to target someone in each of these quadrants for the different goals you have. What you might find when looking at the issue through this lens is that you already have an informal mentor but didn't realise – now it's time to make the most of that relationship.

Highly structured

Formality of relationship

Highly structured, short term/Coach or trainer
The relationship is formally established for a short period of time, often to meet specific objectives or to help achieve a particular ambition.

Highly structured, long term/Sponsor or mentor
Often used for succession planning, prepping someone to take over a departing person's position or master a craft.

Informal, short term
This type of mentoring ranges from spontaneous advice to as-needed counseling. There may be no ongoing relationship.

Informal, long term
Often referred to as 'friendship mentoring' it consists of being there to dicuss problems, to listen or share knowledge.

Virtually no structure

Short term Spontaneous

Long term Even for life

Length of intervention

HOW TO Ask

Careers are a series of risks and challenges, and finding a mentor is no different. Not only do you need to choose your mentor, but in true mentoring relationships the mentor also has to – perhaps unconsciously – choose you. There are many ways to do this of course; piquing an old boss's interest again is pretty straightforward. A simple email, a phone call, a suggestion to meet for coffee; these are all obvious ways of rekindling a relationship and taking it to the next level. It may take several months, a year even, to reach the point where you feel comfortable broaching the subjects most playing on your career mind. These things don't happen overnight and the very act of just touching base again or lighting the spark on a new career relationship should increase your confidence and give you some kind of renewed support.

So, next awkward question: how do you know that someone has become your mentor? Well, when did you last ask a guy to 'go steady'?

Exactly. Explicitness tends to be the enemy of mentoring too. Outside of formal schemes, mentors are most usefully picked up by stealth. Go up to someone and just ask him or her to be your mentor and the point has been missed. Remember, if you repeatedly ask for advice from a mentor target, they give that advice and you get on well, then by default that person has become your mentor, whether she or he realises it or not.

Having said that, it's an honour to be someone's mentor, and however clumsy it feels to make the suggestion, it usually pays dividends. Because as your official mentor, that person will likely feel a responsibility towards you that will present as renewed support and unexpected opportunities.

HOW TO Be the Best Mentee

As we've already touched on, mutually beneficial mentoring relationships, just like mutually enjoyable friendships, don't just happen. We need to work at them and give what we expect to receive in return. For one, be honest. Your mentor can't help you if you hold stuff back. Similarly, they wouldn't be much of a mentor if they didn't tell you the truth either. Honesty is a crucial ingredient in your mentoring main course.

It is OK (right, even) to show your mentor your insecurities and fears: we are all fallible, and your mentor is there to support and develop you. If you are struggling with something at work, communicate this – tell them how shitty you feel. The chances are, they've felt shitty about something similar in the past too and will be able to guide you back to contentment.

NOTE: The same does not apply to sponsors. See below for why showing a potential sponsor your fluffy centre may not be so good for your career.

Beware of being too honest and open though. Telling the whole truth, opening up your entire heart, is useful sometimes; when this isn't the case, employ some strategic softening. Crying is not a good look at work, especially when it's about your boyfriend/dog/mother (delete as appropriate). Remember, keep things professional. Women can have a tendency to over-share; it's part of our rapport-building make-up.

In the workplace, over-sharing can be viewed as unprofessional and can put off even the most dedicated mentor.

Respect is another key area of mentoring. Never undervalue the time your mentor is putting in; to this end, make preparation key before each of your meet ups.

WORKOUT Make the Most of Your Mentor

Your mentor is likely, by definition, to be busy. That means you need to be careful with his or her time. You want them to feel useful, as well as feeling you've made the most of that slot. Spending forty-five minutes of your hour-long coffee debating the realism of last night's episode of *Scandal* does not count.

Before your next meeting with a mentor, sponsor or potential supporter, spend ten minutes working out what you want to discuss and writing down three bullet points you want to cover during the meeting.

Depending on the purpose of that particular relationship, consider one or more of the following questions:

DEVELOPMENT: Read back over your last performance evaluation; were there areas in which it was felt you needed more development and expertise?

PROMOTION: Read five descriptions for positions you aspire to hold in the next five years. What skills do you have already? What skills/ experiences do you need to develop to be qualified for these positions? How can you develop these?

ADVICE: Brainstorm how you feel about life and work. What basic needs do you have – less stress, more responsibility, challenge or respect? How can these be achieved?

OPPORTUNITIES: What opportunity, role, institution are you trying to access? What contacts do you need to make to get you closer to your goal?

Thinking generally around your current situation and future goals and then collating that into a meaningful agenda ensures you both get the most bang for your buck.

HOWTO Mentor Laterally

As you are probably realising, mentoring is a complex fabric that can be produced in many different colours and prints. We've covered the concept of mentoring, how to find one and the ways to conduct ourselves when a Slam Dunk Mentor is on our side. But what about situations where the mentor and the mentee are at the same level? Mentoring laterally is a modern twist on this ancient type of support and **Candice Fragis**, Buying Director at Farfetch.com, one of fashion's few billion-dollar retailers, pulls her encouragement from her peers.

'For the past few years I kept hearing the word mentor thrown around like it's the key to success – and often I felt left out of the club. How do you get a mentor? Why don't I have a mentor? It frustrated me. Especially when I was trying to make the next steps in my career or when coming up against challenges that only someone in my industry could truly understand. More and more I now believe that mentoring is far more useful from a forum or group of like-minded women who can inspire, share and motivate each other. Because a group of brains and experience is more valuable than just one.'

Our peers have a unique and insightful perspective on our personal challenges. They really understand the pitfalls and perks of our job and, usually, they'll have experienced first-hand our work style and will know where we're heading too. A lateral mentor may not be able to impart the kind of experience and wisdom as a unicorn-riding success story, but they'll be quick smart on the everyday, objective stuff.

HOWTO Pay it Forward

Now we want to explore the prospect of being the mentor. We've covered everything from the other side of the coin, but what about when we pay it forward and become that font of wisdom?

Almost without exception, we will have someone who is more junior than us at work. This person might be in a different department, she could be the unpaid work experience, the point is that when we become the mentor, like Ruth Rogers has done to many of the country's best chefs, we enrich our own skill set, and in turn, our career potential.

Here is a pretty convincing list of mentor benefits:

|1| Mentors earn more money.
|2| Mentors have better career prospects.
|3| Mentors are more satisfied because they fulfil a need for authenticity (Kaleidoscope model, Chapter 2).
|4| Mentors are more confident because they have someone to value their experience and advice; this boosts self-esteem.
|5| Mentors make better leaders; mentoring helps hone leadership skills and lets others view us in a leadership capacity.
|6| Female mentors with male mentees make positive impacts on workplace parity. These men have a better understanding of the hurdles women face and often become advocates of workplace equality.

If only for point 6 alone, we should all aspire to take on aspirant mentees in the near future. It's a proven fact that the only way to break down gender barriers at work is through educating men. This is true in all facets of career progression; when it comes to mentoring though, women can have a direct impact on the education of the opposite sex and that is potentially ground-breaking.

It's persuasive stuff, but mentoring doesn't always come naturally. It takes confidence, self-awareness and humility (all the things required of a mentee themselves) and then so much more on top of that too. In order to become effective and gracious mentors, we need to conquer a specific set of managerial-type skills.

SKILL ONE: LISTENING AND OPEN QUESTIONING

The ability to empower those below us is an essential slant of mentoring, and being a manager for that matter. One of the best ways to do this is by helping our mentees to help themselves. It's a cliché but when we probe and goad others towards the right solution, we empower. Swooping in and solving their problems for them does our mentee a disservice.

Plus, when we learn not to default micro-manage, it'll lead to a team (led by you, of course) with autonomy among the ranks. After all, no one wants employees who drop every small issue back onto your own plate.

Here's how you improve your knack for listening.

WORKOUT Active Listening

Find your willing partner. One of you is the speaker. The speaker should talk about something comfortable (an award, a special event, etc.). The listener must somehow get the speaker to continue talking for five minutes without saying much – no more than three statements. After the five minutes, switch and spend another five minutes in the opposing roles.

Now consider the following questions:

How did the speaker feel when the person just listened and did not exchange information?

How did non-verbal signals encourage the speaker?

How uncomfortable was any silence?

How did it feel to just listen without having the pressure to contribute?

How did the speaker feel having the freedom to say whatever she felt?

Result: experience the power of active listening. And the effect of being actually listened to. Learn to enhance your listening style.

SKILL TWO: FEEDBACK

There is an art to delivering feedback. When we learn to give appropriate comment and advice (rather than just liberally applying praise) we constructively nurture our mentee. This feels good, because we have been *useful*. And when we feel useful, we become more confident. By mentoring someone else, we are in a sense mentoring ourselves too: it's a positive cycle of support.

WORKOUT Feedback Time

Giving effective feedback is essential as both a mentor and mentee. Unfortunately it is one of the hardest things to do well. Take five minutes to read (and imagine) this scenario:

Imagine you are taking part in a skipping contest. Three judges are chosen to rate the quality of skipping on a scale of one to ten. You are a competitor and, naturally, you want to excel. You have one practice trial where you get feedback and then you do it for real.

Scenario One: You come into the room and prepare for your practice trial. You skip around the room as enthusiastically as you can for the required thirty seconds. Then you stop. The judges confer and then hand out their scores. The first gives you a six, the next a four, the last a six. You exit stage left to spend three minutes preparing for the real performance.

Scenario Two: You enter the room and again skip around for thirty seconds. The judges confer and respond as follows. 'I wasn't keen on the fast pace. The whole performance felt flat,' states the first judge. 'And your knees went much too high,' says the second. Judge 3 just shakes her head. 'Far too bouncy.' You earn two sixes and a four. You leave the room to prepare.

Scenario Three: You enter the room (again) and skip wildly for thirty seconds. The judges confer. 'The best skipping performance for me', explains the first judge, 'is one that builds. I prefer it when the performer starts slow, getting faster and faster. Your pace was perfect for the finale, but it would have had more impact if you created some contrast between the beginning and end.' The second judge nods. 'You could also have varied the weight of your steps by treading lightly to start and gradually letting your feet land with more force. I thought the skipping at the end was particularly good.' 'You are also looking for more movement. You stayed in one place but could have made use of the whole stage. That would really have taken your performance to the next level,' said the third judge. You earn two sixes and a four and go to prepare for your final performance.

Now we have five minutes to consider which scenario would really help us to shine.

WORKOUT Feedback Time continued

In Scenario One, we've received feedback – your marks – but with no idea what they're based on. We know we need to change something. But what? Without more information, we're equally likely to change for the worse as change for the better.

In Scenario Two, we've been told what not to do, but we don't know what the goal is. It's now easy to avoid what the judges don't like, but we are no more enlightened as to what they do. Importantly, if the judges had given only positive feedback rather than negative, the same issue would apply. You would know what you had done right to receive mediocre marks but not the extra that is needed to shine.

Scenario Three is the most useful. We are told both what we should eliminate, what we should keep and what we should improve. We are even given ideas for behaviours or techniques we may not have thought about. Which feedback do you think you would need to help you do your best?

SKILL THREE: STRATEGIC THINKING

A wise mentor is a methodical mentor. When we find ourselves in a position of influence, it's up to us to keep the relationship energised. You can do this by setting clear goals and parameters. Mentoring relationships run out of steam when we fritter away our time together discussing the what ifs. Whether it's a monthly phone catch-up, or a quarterly lunch date, mentoring relationships benefit from a plan that both sides stick to.

Being able to cut through the workload with methodical attack plans is a great discipline, especially as we get more senior and busier too. All three of these skills are useful at all times, but as our mentees develop and our mentoring styles change and evolve it's worth revisiting these strategies to keep things appropriate.

Really, we can't overstate enough the importance of becoming part of a valuable mentoring relationship. We encourage you to search out your own mentor, or better still mentors, and to keep the relationships fun and fresh as you pass through your career. Other people have a different perspective on things; it pays to share our knowledge and be proactive when it comes to building and maintaining pivotal career friendships. Mentoring is the realisation of the hackneyed (but relevant) notion that we are stronger together.

ABOUT Sponsors

While a mentor prepares you to succeed at work, a sponsor makes it happen. To put it succinctly, a sponsor is your number one External Influencer for bagging the next plum job.

When it comes to the similarities between mentors and sponsors, there's certainly crossover in terms of how to get hold of the darn things. The crucial difference though is that while a mentor supports us in the wings, a sponsor, also known as a champion, is our personal PR machine: she or he talks us up and pushes us forward.

A sponsor is our conduit to the loftier parts of our careers and industry. And when we have this conduit bridge to the right (senior) people, especially to the ones who will tell everyone else how bloody wonderful we are, big doors into influential networks open. And we earn more and progress more quickly.

If a mentor talks *to* you, then a sponsor talks *about* you.

MD of Get the Gloss, **Gemma Bellman** experienced the power of sponsorship first-hand when launching her app. 'Someone who's been a great support to me in recent years is Millie Kendall MBE, founder of Ruby & Millie and BeautyMART. I was introduced to Millie by a friend of a friend and she didn't know me at all at that time,' Gemma explains, 'but she kindly invited me into her offices to talk about BeautySpotter shortly ahead of the upcoming launch. We spent about an hour and a half going through the app, the progress so far and the route to market strategy. Millie then invited her colleague [and former beauty director at British *Vogue*] Anna-Marie Solowij over for a second opinion. At the end of the meeting Millie simply said, "You need to now speak to these people, I'm going to forward this on to my key contacts in the industry and, by the way, would you like to launch the app at our press day next month?" Ever since then I've gone back to Millie for help and advice. She's become a kind of impromptu mentor to me, for which I am hugely grateful. Especially as she didn't know me from Adam when I turned up on her doorstep!'

Millie didn't limit herself to giving Gemma advice. She actively promoted her both to industry insiders and to the press, giving relative newbie Gemma a platform that she could never have accessed on her own. The power of this sponsorship is twofold. Gemma was not only given access to the right people, but the right people also knew – through Millie's endorsement – that she was worthy of their efforts.

Sponsors, research says, are also crucial when it comes to improving gender equality in the workplace. First, because when we have senior sponsors, we (women) are more likely to hear about the jobs at the top. Second, once we know about these openings (a parallel could be winning the right investment for your startup, or being put in touch with the top editor at your dream publication), with a sponsor behind them, women become more likely to get the promotion. And parity will only come when we can put more women in positions of influence, because in the main, we employ in our own image. Happily, sponsors help to cut through this stalemate.

In very corporate environments, it's a boys' club at the top. This, of course, is the antithesis of gender equality. But when club members endorse women, the balance starts to shift. Deutsche Bank is a sparkly example to the corporate world. There, leaders are using sponsorship to realign the corporate gender imbalance, and their process affirms the centrality of sponsorship to reaching our goals.

After recent internal research revealed that female managing directors were leaving the firm to work for competitors because they'd been offered bigger jobs externally than the ones they had been considered for within the bank, senior members of staff realised that something needed to change.

Deutsche responded by creating a sponsorship programme aimed at assigning more women to critical posts. It paired young female employees with executive committee members in a bid to increase the female talent pool's exposure to the committee and ensure that women in the bank had influential advocates for promotion. A year on, and one-third of the female participants are already in larger roles and another third are deemed ready by senior management and HR to take on broader responsibilities.

Well done Deutsche Bank.

Not only has it set the cogs turning for improved female representation at the top level, the bank also proved the power of positive sponsorship programmes.

However, even if you are lucky enough to work for the Deutsches of this world, you shouldn't sit back. In part, it is the voluntary support of an influential person that affords sponsorship its power. It sends a signal to others in power that this person believes you are someone to back. Pursue organic sponsorship and you will have behind you a strong indicator that you are someone worth watching.

HOW TO Secure Your Supporter

A sponsor sees something special in us, they believe in us and want other leaders and ace industry types to sit up and take notice too. We can't buy this type of accreditation. What we can do, however, is promote ourselves in the right direction.

Men are useful targets in sponsorship spheres, because like it or not, they generally wield more power. More than that though, the male/female sponsor combination is the deadliest on the block. Perhaps it's the relative rarity of this killer combo, perhaps because to get the most powerful sponsor (still, in many industries, frequently a man) we have to deliver more than our male peers, but research tells us that women with senior male sponsors earn even more than men with senior male sponsors. Yup, that *Step Up* ideal of blending the best from each gender really plays out in sponsorship.

The problem is that unlike mentoring relationships, as we've referred to above, sponsorship is a high-risk career pastime. After all, the sponsor is putting her or his neck and name on the line for us and when reputations are at stake, intensity and expectations rise exponentially. Gemma received the sponsorship of a beauty industry heavyweight because of the strength of her work product. Her sponsor saw not only potential, but also something she personally would be happy to use and proud to promote. As much as we need to create the opportunity to have that relationship, to get a powerful sponsor, we also have to deliver something that makes us a worthy cause.

While they can happen spontaneously or through a more formal scheme, sponsorships often grow from deep mentoring relationships. Which means we need to be extra good to our mentors! When we are able to periodically (and subtly) remind them of our brilliance, share ideas together, and discuss key people higher up the tree that we'd like to be introduced to, it sets a tone for a new, improved – sponsor-style – relationship. In short, our mentors are key candidates to push us forward at work.

'I also have my investors in BeautySpotter,' Gemma goes on, 'all of whom are experts in their fields. Aside from their investment, having them on board means I can make informed decisions about things I haven't been through myself yet. It's like being able to fast forward through levels of experience that it would otherwise take many years to acquire. If you have someone sitting next to you who already has that insight, it helps hugely in getting the job done right the first time around.'

Not only can mentors morph into sponsors, but (as for Gemma) sponsors – people who have backed us to succeed – can also turn into valuable mentors. Nurture these relationships and who knows where they will lead?

When we can't, for any reason, use the mentoring slip road to get on Sponsorship Highway, look for other routes. For one, try searching out sponsors who got their big break in the same way as you: unconscious bias should draw them close thanks to a shared story, and this helps us to get noticed.

Another good way to get the attention of sponsors is to suggest improvements in the way things are being done. When we do this, we prove our ability as a critical thinker and as a potential change agent. As with so much of career enhancement strategy, you need to learn to challenge the status quo. Technology, for example, is an area where junior employees can be more up to date than their bosses – if this is you, get tweeting to the right people.

When it comes to sponsorship, we need to employ a long-term strategy. It helps, for longevity, to identify, say, the job that only one person can help you get. Once you've made that link, devise a solid business plan or strategy case as to why you are the right person for the job. Then go and get the job, prove them right and you'll bag yourself a sponsor for life.

But sponsors aren't just about getting the job; their contacts and reputation can have an immense impact on our careers. We can't tell someone to be our sponsor, but we can sure as hell show them how good we are.

ABOUT Role Models

Perhaps, like us, your adolescent role model was the curly-haired, cutesy-faced Charlene from Neighbours. She had the perm. She had the guy. She had it all.

The fact that Charlene went on to become Kylie is a graceful and telling postscript to the story. Twenty-odd years after she fell in love with Jason, Kylie remains a valid role model: she rose to greatness from humble beginnings, she has worldwide record sales in excess of 70 million and she also, very publicly, beat breast cancer. If Kylie is your role model, then you're on to a good thing.

Role models come in many different forms, and like mentors and sponsors, we're perfectly entitled to juggle as many as we fancy. Role models inspire us; they show us that someone who behaves in a way that we can relate to and that we admire has achieved the type of success that we aspire to. Role models give us confidence without even knowing that they're on our radar.

Role models come in all forms: and one who sits a million miles away in the public eye can be just as useful as one who sits at the end of your office corridor.

For those of us who struggle with confidence and assertiveness (two characteristics tightly woven into mentoring and sponsorship), having a role model is a good place to start in External Influence terms. However we'd counter that by saying that they also probably have the least sway and power over our careers; so while role models represent a useful element in our trilogy of supporters, their purpose doesn't stretch much further than inspiration and hope.

When **Emma Stone** received an MTV Trailblazer in 2012, she rattled off a long list of role models in her acceptance speech. 'People like Gilda Radner and Bill Murray and John Candy and Charlie Chaplin and the Beatles and JD Salinger and Lorne Michaels...' She was not following in their footsteps, she said. No, these role models help her be her own original. 'They make me want to be more myself.'

Women do, in the main, look to other women as role models; this makes sense, as we need to be able to see ourselves in them. Having said that, don't discount the men. Male role models, in comparison, can be incredibly valuable because they have different ways of doing things. While we aren't advocates of leaving our femininity at work's revolving door, we are strong believers that there are plenty of amazing men out there, and that a cross-pollination of skills and ideas makes for the sharpest knife in the career drawer.

HOW TO Reel in a Role Model

Really, there are two types of role models: the Kylies, and the Tangibles. And what you're after is a few from each side of the net.

The question of tangible male role models is an interesting one. As part of *Step Up*'s body of research among successful female lawyers, we tried to better understand who and why we choose who we do to inspire us. What we found was that, as we mentioned above, our women instinctively looked to other women as role models. But what happens when there are no women present?

Our interviewees reported that in law (and many corporate professions) there just aren't a high number of senior female success stories.

So what did our women, the ones who felt that there were no suitable female role models, do? They looked to senior men instead. And in the main, these men did pretty well at providing healthy doses of inspiration, especially in the sphere of client-focused relationships and technical skills. Often, like Emma, they were able to create a composite – a bit of John's networking style, a bit of client management from Bill – that combined to create an image of the lawyer they hoped to be.

What male role models lacked, however, was an ability to demonstrate and manage the stresses of dual focus and responsibility that many of us contend with daily. It's tricky; role models don't need to come from within our industry, or even from our working lives. The most important thing about role modelling is their capacity to inspire. When we find and hold dear a person who encourages us to higher achievements, enhanced balance and a healthier, more holistic approach to our careers, the rest is irrelevant.

Choosing a role model is as instinctive as it is personal. All we can do is point out their importance: in our careers we need to be able to look ahead, and often, we find it easiest to do that in terms of other people's lives – in terms of our role models' successes.

The art of picking a role model is seeing in different people the aspects of ourselves that we want to upgrade. It's worth remembering, of course, that role models don't need to be perfect success stories. A person who has battled through – who is still battling through – but got there anyway, may offer a spirited alternative to the CEO.

WORKOUT Rolestorming

There are many places to find a role model. Or models out of whom you form your composite whole. But what do you do once you find them? Modelling our behaviours directly can be incredibly useful, particularly for skills we find tricky. But equally useful can be applying the benefit of those skills we admire to solve our own issues.

Step 1: Identify your role models (see above for help) and pick five for this exercise. A mix of people you know and well-known leaders (think historical, political, even fictional) is ideal.

Step 2: Identify a thorny issue you are struggling to solve or skill you know you need to acquire.

Step 3: Spend two minutes as each leader. As that leader, how would you approach the problem? How do you embody that skill? As you inhabit the mind of that person and brainstorm their response, you are able to model your own approach on them.

TIPS

|1| Sponsors don't need to be role models

The sponsor is someone who advocates on our behalf. We should not confuse that with a role model or someone we admire. So make sure to identify the right person for the right job:

> 'I want to be like her' – there's your role model;
> 'She understands and supports me' – mentor, right there;
> 'She has the power to push me to the fore' – this is the sponsor you need.

|2| Neglect the detail

Keeping the various influencers separate in our mind is one thing. But don't sweat the small stuff so much that you shut down to the possibilities of the work relationships in your life. The categories we offer are not designed to restrict. Be clear on why you are approaching someone but instead of filing them in the mental drawer marked mentor/sponsor/boss [delete as appropriate] and leaving them there, keep your mindset open. Mentors might, over time, become sponsors. Who knows where each relationship might lead?

|3| Mentor for the future

We have the power to drive the future of gender equality. That's a central *Step Up* tenet. Mentoring is the foundation of that aspiration. As we are mentored we progress our careers. We in turn mentor and bring on the next generation of women. Embrace your duties in this regard and when your daughters are older, we will see the benefits in their lives.

|4| Get personal

The personal connection is key to any successful relationship and no less so with a mentor. The next time you meet yours, pay attention to their interests, glean facts about their lives and remember them the next time you meet to show your investment in them as a person. Equally important: share something of yourself. Yes, we need to be professional, but we need to be human too. Sharing details of your life creates rapport. It also opens up the possibility that you might get powerful support – for example from a fellow working mother – in that area too.

|5| Nurture the skills

The skills of successful mentorship or coaching – listening, giving feedback, motivating, garnering support – are not just essential to these relationships, they are crucial to our entire careers. Spend time nurturing these skills and watch your abilities as a leader, negotiator and creator of opportunity rise in equal measure.

CHAPTER 6

Self-Promotion and Negotiation

THE FACTS Our Grafter and Our Messenger

'In my experience, women – I include myself as the poster child – can be supremely rubbish at being their own cheerleader,' this, from British national treasure and BBC *Newsnight* presenter **Emily Maitlis**. 'We tend to think that if we work hard, do a good job, create impact then we will be noticed and promoted. That's rarely true. The people who get promoted, generally, are the ones who demand stuff and sulk if they're denied. This is a truly depressing thing to discover – but a useful one. Whilst I find it hard to advocate the sulk (if you do this as a woman you will get asked if it's PMT) I do find that having the courage to simply ask for things is an excellent way to start.'

It took Maitlis years, she admits, to work out that blokes in her office got the best stories because they spotted a news opportunity several years in the future and volunteered themselves to write them before the stories were even relevant. Yes, spotting a chance on a story is a particular journalistic quirk. But this pinpointed strategy, vision and nerve is applicable across all industries. Of course, this self-promotional trinity is not unique to men, but for reasons we'll go on to explain, the guys just seem to find it easier to publicise themselves at work. For Maitlis, things are still a work in progress.

'Sometimes the testosterone kicks in and I start demanding things because I want parity, even if I don't really want the thing at all. I remember kicking up a fuss and demanding to cover the Tory party conference the first year the Conservatives were in power. My boss turned round and said, "Fine, you can do all of them then!" I was knackered after a month of conferences but couldn't say so.'

It is a fact that women who publicly talk up their achievements and ask for what they want experience less discrimination and obtain more promotions than the majority who don't. In fact, one recent study has gone as far as to say that making our achievements visible is the only behaviour directly correlated with pay growth for women.

Self-promotion is a nebulous term because it encompasses many elements of career progression; indeed, it wouldn't be hard to uncover self-promotional threads in every one of our chapters. We just can't succeed at work if we don't put ourselves forward.

Often, as Maitlis points out, self-promotion is a simple case of being vocal about our intentions: Tory party conference, a work trip, pay rise, bonus or transfer overseas. For entrepreneurs, being self-promotional means seeking out support, uncovering solid investment leads and getting the company out on the circuit. Self-promotion is not keeping our head down and working hard (although this should never be overlooked) – it's successfully building and continually oiling our personal PR machines.

Some approach self-promotion as a game – a series of perfectly played, tactical manoeuvres that get us the real-life equivalent of £200 every time we pass Go. As American Presidential election campaigns illustrate, self-promotion isn't always about rolling a double six. Yes, the candidates hold serious rallies and present a cool demeanour when the moment requires it; they also get out on the street and mingle with real folk; they laugh, they take selfies and they prove that self-promotion can mean a different thing every day of the week.

Rather predictably, most men are natural self-promoters. Maitlis bears witness to this, and most likely, you will too. The reason they are so good at putting themselves out there goes back to childhood. If we've said it once, we've said it a gazillion times: when they were little boys during those precious first few years at school, our male colleagues were encouraged to be brave, tough, self-promotional little guys. Whilst they boasted their way around the playground, we played quietly under the shade of large trees. We were rewarded for calm, group-focused work and under no circumstances were we encouraged to be boastful or self-centred.

No, instead of standing up in the girlie circle and telling it as it was ('why are the boys having so much more fun?' might have been a good start...), we collectively bit our lips and absorbed ourselves into the group. As young girls, most of us were conditioned to passively un-promote – and now as working women we don't know how to be career lionesses.

This is a major problem.

Self-promotion is the link between the work we do on a daily basis and our overall career progression. It can take the form of small conversations, intimidating requests or just regular work banter. The point is, when we aren't able to talk up our achievements, we work in a vacuum.

When we aren't existing in a void, work tends to be a blend of the internal and the external. Much of what goes on in our lives does so in our heads in the form of thoughts, fears and new ideas. Even if we're lucky enough to enjoy lively office interactions, there'll still be the side of us that needs to work alone to get the job done. Let's call this side of our brains the Grafter. She is practical and she is necessary.

Alongside the Grafter is our other voice: the Messenger. She is the one who takes the essence of our graft and delivers it to the right people in the right places. The Messenger is our self-promoter and to successfully complete her side of the bargain, the Messenger requires confidence, strategy and guts – three concepts that challenge many women.

Good girls don't boast, or that's what we've been brought up to believe, and yet to successfully self-promote – and make positive career headway – sometimes we need to step out from behind Good Girl's shadow and learn to bask in our own glory.

This act of personal deliverance is part of the self-promotional battle; we need to make ourselves visible in the workplace, or new opportunities will go elsewhere. While the female Grafter sits at her desk and waits for a pay rise to fall in her lap (it won't, by the way), the blokes are jumping in, having a go and getting exactly what they want out of their careers.

THE FACTS Self-Promotional Insecurities

There are two broad reasons why women struggle in this arena: we fear a backlash against wilful self-promotion and we're riddled with self-doubt.

Of course, you're now screaming CONFIDENCE really loudly at the book, and you are right. Confidence is a powerful player when it comes to getting yourself noticed. This misplaced 'Good Girl' childhood conditioning complicates our stutterings around self-promotion; modesty and showing off aren't, we were taught, particularly feminine ways of behaving and even today, we still can't break the mould.

When it comes to self-promotion, many women struggle because they fear a showing-off backlash. Imagine what they'd say, we think, if I stood up and shouted about how great I am. I wouldn't be able to live it down. Except, standing up and shouting about ourselves (figuratively speaking anyway) is the perfect place to start. We have to learn to manage our backlash fears. Because really, what's the worst that can happen?

There are two parts to this feared backlash: the act and the lash. As we've already mentioned, one of the reasons women stumble in self-promotional circles is we've been brought up to believe that nice girls aren't grabby and boastful. We just don't act that way. We stay quiet and wait for success to find us in the corner office – after all, we couldn't risk being thought of as cocky and conceited.

The academics call this the Backlash Avoidance Model. We don't do it, because we worry about what might happen. We consciously or unconsciously draw the curtain on our achievements to avoid any kind of work uprising against a mutant, ballsy female – you.

Researchers have proved this a thousand times over. You're probably nodding your head right now in agreement, but if you need more convincing, then the study on university students who were asked to predict their future grades should convince you. The group – half male, half female – wasn't atypical in its aptitude or outlook, all the students were of a similar standard, and yet the females consistently underestimated their future grades, while men tended to significantly overestimate their performance. This is interesting because the findings were compounded by the fact that women were more prone to underestimation when they knew that their guesses would be publicly discussed. Basically, they didn't want anyone thinking they were being a bragger.

On top of this skewed view of what other people are thinking is what we think about ourselves. If we know that we aren't experts at talking up our achievements, then the last thing we're going to want to do is try it, fail and look like a fool. No, better to just avoid self-promotion altogether. The experts call this tactic Stereotype Threat Theory: we are stereotypically poor at boasting, so we avoid self-promotion for fear of confirming that stereotype.

Yup, you got it: the root of all of this is that we worry too much about what everyone thinks of us. We know this from our Internal Influences chapter, and it's just as true here. But trust us, too much self-analysis is detrimental.

What happens is that these self-effacing tendencies are spreading forest fires inside our minds: once the match is lit we are less likely to overrate our abilities, less likely to credit ourselves for our successes, more willing (expecting, even) to receive blame and, quite unbelievably, we start giving negative estimations of our general intelligence too. Better not to talk things up, eh?

Clearly, women are just as capable as our male peers: in fact, we leave university with better degrees and graduate pipeline employment is equal across the sexes. The problem is, childhood conditioning affects how we consider ourselves, and nowhere highlights this more acutely than in the competitive world of careers.

In terms of the aforementioned backlash, according to research, when women self-promote unchecked using the classically masculine tools of aggression and force, we head into troubled waters. As we've already touched on in the book, the successful female – in whatever industry she resides – is not the woman who chameleons herself into a man: no, that makes her unauthentic. The most successful woman can borrow his traits and weave them across her naturally feminine demeanour and this applies to self-promotion too.

When a woman simply borrows from the boys rather than tries to emulate them, when she pirates a few of his tricks, takes the odd step in his path and does this while retaining her female grace and poise, this woman transforms herself into a powerful self-promoter. This woman is the office firecracker, for the simple fact that she's stepped out from behind the expectation that Good Girls Keep Quiet.

'If you don't go after that thing you want at work, then you're missing out on a possible opportunity,' says TechHub CEO and founder **Elizabeth Varley**. 'If you don't ask or try you'll never know. And of course, hearing no can be painful, but it's not that big of a deal. I don't take things personally because I don't think of others in those terms either. If someone comes to me with an idea and I turn it down, I don't think they were silly for asking. I just didn't agree and I moved on. When you separate your personal and professional mindsets, you can be more daring – it's easier to be more audacious in your ask. Plus, it's easier for me as a boss; I'm not in the habit of trying to personally crush people – no one likes that.'

While we can theorise and endlessly converse on self-promotion's fundamentals, when push comes to shove, it will mean something different to all of us. Pushing ourselves forward, negotiating more money, announcing to the world how great we are so that we can secure that promotion is all exposing and scary. But it is also necessary.

So how do we get there? Well, we say with a comprehensive military plan to defeat the uneasy enemy within.

HOWTO Build Brand Me

BUILD BRAND ME

One sure-fire way to de-personalise our promotional odyssey is to build Brand Me. The way brand consultants go about constructing seductive offerings is by breaking down the product or service into its many parts and then rebuilding the pieces into something catchy and memorable.

When we are able to be objective about ourselves and assemble a sellable 'product' (that's you), it makes the process of self-promotion feel less prickly and daunting. Personal branding – as with all branding – is a force that can make us a more bankable commodity. What we're all after is a point of difference – make yourself the rustic bloomer on the trendy stoneware plinth, not the average sliced white.

None of us is immune to branding – it's natural to be tempted by the fancy bread (that's you again) just as it's natural to be impressed by the person at work who metaphorically wraps themselves in the most persuasive characteristics, achievements and know-how.

Of course, personal branding in the workspace isn't about fancy packaging and organic, hand-milled flour. It's subtler than that; for us to be able to professionally sell ourselves to others, we need to focus on our unique selling points and then fold them up into something intriguing. Is it that you have extra training, you're a woman and you're young? Or perhaps your brand is built on technical knowledge (spotlight on your niche), contacts and a devilish sense of humour?

When we dissect the sum of our parts and then link them together into three or four unique facets of our personality and work persona, we end up with a 'brand' that is ready to be imparted at a moment's notice. Perhaps you work in communications and your success lies in getting the right people knowing about the right new design labels? You might be an entrepreneur with a great service who is creating awesome, business-changing concepts that help your clients to earn more money or maybe you're just starting out and are brimming with ideas and energy ... When we can see the value in what we do and are able to get excited about our everyday achievements, it makes the whole self-promotion exercise feel less daunting, less personal even, and more genuine.

'If you can say, "This is me, rather than this is the company I work for," then you might just get ahead of your peers,' says **Gemma Godfrey**, the media finance expert and former Head of Investment Strategy who recently founded her own online wealth manager, Moo.la.com. During the first half of her career, Godfrey progressed quickly by making strategic moves between companies and having the perspective to know where to go next. 'I hate crudely promoting myself, but I understood that if I wanted to progress then I needed to leverage on my strengths, be vocal and keep my face and profile visible. Clients now come to me, rather than the other way around.'

Godfrey's brand is well known in the business and beyond. She achieved this by making herself just as recognisable in the boardroom as across external social media platforms. Gemma's brand is one part female, one part youth and two parts knowledge and grit. Together, and topped off with her distinguishable curls and bubbly persona, it's a powerful offering that is uniquely Gemma.

For **Lisa Armstrong**, Fashion Director at the UK's Daily Telegraph newspaper, her profession required her to build a brand early on. She got her name in the public domain by having chutzpah and never being too grand.

'I remember ringing up Helena Bonham Carter, who I loved. I lied and told her that I had secured a space for an interview with her in the Telegraph Magazine. I was a proper slimy journalist; then I called up the magazine and told them I'd secured this interview with Bonham

Carter, and boom, I was in. I remember an American friend said to me, "Lisa, you don't work it. You've got to be a bit more *Here I Am*." She was right, of course. Presentation is very important; you've got to act the part, not at the expense of doing the sodding part of course. Get your product right and your marketing right, and people will remember who you are.'

WORKOUT Understand Your Brand

Personal branding isn't just about getting any old message out there. It's about conveying the *right* message. Real-life brands spend months perfecting this idea before they advertise it to the market. You might not have months, but you shouldn't neglect the basic groundwork either.

What are you trying to promote yourself as? Which qualities do you want to highlight? Which work do you need to publicise to achieve your goals?

If you've been diligently doing your workouts, you should already have a good idea of your strengths and how they play to your goals. Now distil that down into five core strengths you believe you display.

Now test your theory.

(5 minutes) In person, by email or on social media, ask some people close to you (family, friends and colleagues) what they think sets you apart. It's important the message you choose allows honest answers (we've even had clients set up their own anonymous online survey). Then compare those answers to your self-assessment. If there is dissonance, try to understand why.

(5 minutes) Finalise the list of five. Do they get you to your end goal? Is something missing? If so, what? How can you build it? Be clear about your brand and where it will get you. Now you're ready to tell the world.

HOW TO Reframe the Proposition

When we know what we've achieved, it tells other people that we're self-aware, savvy and straightforward. This is the crux of fruitful self-promotion. Most of us, if we were pushed, could trip through our career highlights. But convey these highs to someone else? That's a whole different matter and it's where the majority struggle. If this is you, try reframing the proposition.

As we've already said, self-promotion is crucial but it doesn't need to be referred to in those terms. Not least because it has a faint whiff of *The Apprentice* about it, which is never something to aspire to. For those of us who struggle with the concept of self-promoting, a good first step is to drop the phrase altogether. The act of making ourselves more visible at work is simply raising awareness of our achievements to others — it's *telling a story*.

Sure, within that tale, you will need to point with pride at what you've achieved. But the simple act of calling this endeavour a story-telling rather than self-promotion will trick your brain into feeling less daunted.

Take it from us; it's worth the struggle. Because when we become expert self-biographers we impart our positive messages of success to the right people (remember, bite-sized). We also increase our visibility within our team and once that's sorted, it has a knock-on effect to how we are regarded and perceived across the company as a whole, and beyond.

Self-promotion also helps us to access the right networks and we already appreciate the upbeat momentum these deliver in terms of pay increases, promotions and overall job satisfaction.

WORKOUT The Evidence

Knowing your brand isn't enough. You need actual achievements to share. Seeing these written down will also help with reframing the whole self-promotion thing.

(5 minutes) In the diary you hopefully now already have, spend five minutes a month collating positive feedback you've received — both email and in person. Nothing is more powerful than evidence in getting your point across and what better evidence than colleagues and clients who've been impacted by your achievements.

WORKOUT The Evidence continued

(5 minutes) The same amount of time should be spent documenting (in the same place) your achievements. Some of these will be obvious – you will hardly forget delivering a massive project or submitting that big feature. But small wins are just as important to track as evidence of consistent performance.

Read these before a feedback meeting, interview or just when you need a little self-promotion boost.

HOW TO Know Who to Promote to

So, we need to do it, that's non-negotiable; but who the hell do we self-promote to anyway? A simple rule of thumb is anyone who is more senior than us is worth delivering those bite-size info packs to. Sure, it doesn't need to be the CEO every time, but managers and other influencers should be regular go-tos when it comes to raising our brand awareness. It is also worth self-promoting in the direction of our lateral peers, because if nothing else, this acts as good practice, and helps make self-promotion (story-telling) a skill that's part of our everyday.

Caroline Kuhnert, who runs the Ultra High Net Worth Clients business within Global Emerging Markets at UBS Wealth Management, discovered this early on in her career. 'It is so important to find out who is important to your success. You need to know who all these people are at the right levels. You can't say, if I just sit in my corner, then people will notice me. During a hard period in my career, I was invited to a women's network. I turned up to find 200 women in the room. That was amazing, because I had thought I was alone. The coach stood up at the front and said you can't sit alone and assume others will know what you do. If you assume you don't need to self-promote, that is arrogant. That was a turning point in my career. I realised I needed not only to engage positively in networks but also make sure my voice was heard.'

Caroline was fortunate to find like-minded, supportive women in the room. Be aware though, it isn't always in everyone's interests to bolster us up. We're not saying that you have the kind of manager or boss who wants to keep a lid on your progress, but there are situations where someone above us – someone who perhaps feels threatened by our abilities – may not pass on our strategic self-promotion.

Work politics as with all politics are complex and cloudy: if you're doing brilliantly at work, then your manager may struggle and your self-promotion could fall on deaf ears. So make sure your boss isn't an umbrella that blocks your sunlight. If you think this is happening to you, identify other people in the industry who could benefit from knowing how smoothly you wrapped up your latest project. Potential clients, investors, Twitter allies and many others in between are important landing strips on our long-haul self-promotional (unicorn-shaped) flight.

WORKOUT Define Your Audience

We should all spend some time every month mapping things out. Focus on who you want to highlight your achievements to or share your message with.

(3 minutes) Remind yourself of your goals. Now revise your brand. Put the two together and you should have the perfect road map of who needs to know what.

(4 minutes) Brainstorm. Who can help you achieve each goal? These might be people internally, in the industry, clients or peers. What about external people you should be talking to – the media, industry bodies?

(3 minutes) Strategise. Quickly look through each target and think about what they would be interested in knowing. What achievement this year can you use as a hook to have a quick chat? Some will be appropriate to talk to more regularly, others will just be a once-a-year check-in. Just make sure you're getting your message out there to the people who need to know.

When self-promotion is a considered part of your overall game plan it becomes an easier pill to swallow. It's a bit like identifying the need to boost your network; once you've had the realisation, you can easily slot dates and events into your schedule. Now put this plan into action.

As a postscript to this section, if you're having trouble identifying who needs to hear from you and why, then refer to our networking chapter, coming up next.

HOW TO Promote for the Future

So we've established that we need to be vocal about our achievements, however nauseated that makes us feel. But what about how great we want to *be*?

Just as important as talking about what we've done is telling others where we are heading. Most employees, and not just the female ones, assume it is obvious to everyone in their open-plan office that they're chomping at the bit for the next plum assignment. Emily Maitlis, for example, thought her editor knew that she was as keen as the guys on the newsroom floor to front the next big story. But actually, research tells us that if we don't speak up about where we want to go (or even what we want to do on a monthly or quarterly basis) then our bosses will wrongly assume that we are happy with our lot.

Aspirations. Aspirations. Aspirations.

Say it like a mantra.

Thanks to unconscious bias, it isn't uncommon for some managers to make assumptions about gender roles that result in us missing out on key opportunities, especially when it comes to business travel, relocation or assignments that involve tough clients and even tougher deadlines. To counter this, we need to use our voices and foresight to positively self-promote for the future. If you are a junior doctor with ambitions towards cardiology (for the record, less than 1 per cent of the UK's consultant cardiologists are women) then for heaven's sake tell someone about your plan.

Once we have in our mind exactly where we want to go, start spreading the word. Sing it from the rooftops! Network like a demon! Call up your boss from a decade ago, email the person you sat next to at that dreary work dinner, or just arrange a drink with someone more senior in the office. When we put ourselves out there, hear what others have to say about the industry and make secure contacts, it brings our career goals into view.

Networking is key to career progression and it represents the missing link where self-promotion is concerned. Because once we've identified our career achievements to date, pinpointed where we want to go and finessed our unique Brand Me, then we need to get out and tell the right parts of the world.

HOW TO Take the Credit

But before you start elegantly shouting about yourself, you need to nail credit-taking. You originated the project. You cared for it through every up and down. You delivered it safely over the line. But you don't want to come off as a show-off, so you dilute the responsibility. 'We did it together,' you say, chewing the top of your ballpoint pen. This is a common but fatal mistake in self-promotion circles, and research tells us that women are repeat offenders.

'My mother calls this the broken cookie syndrome,' says law firm partner and gender diversity champion **Tamara Box**. 'Women are socialised to take the broken cookie. We believe we need to look after others, to sacrifice to make sure everyone else is happy. This behaviour often allows other people to steal our thunder and take our accomplishments from us; we may perform admirably, but then we conform to society's expectations by standing back and taking second place, so we're just banging our heads against a wall. And it's painful and it's hard to get to a position of strength. Which is why it is so critical to talk to women about shining – but shining in an authentic and comfortable way.'

Just as Tamara learnt from her mother, at work, the power of 'I' over 'we' is immense. We only need to say the two words out loud to realise how much stronger we feel and how much more definitive we sound when we talk in the first person.

To this end, make sure you take charge of sending out your own work, and use presentations or office conversations to highlight exactly what you've achieved. When we talk about ourselves, we need to be confident, speak in concrete outcomes and short, matter-of-fact sentences.

Do not do that thing, where stuff gets a bit much, and you, er, stutter, and, er, sob a little and wave your hands in front of your face to stop your red cheeks from blinding your boss. No one said that talking about ourselves is easy; nearly all of us feel sick at the thought of blowing our own trumpets, but nothing is gained when nothing is ventured. Work can be hard. Not just the nitty gritty of clearing our inbox at the end of each week and getting all those reports out on time; work is hard because sometimes it requires us to lay ourselves on the line.

Pummel through the fears though and great things happen. Just the very act of putting ourselves in awkward, exposing positions will win you Brownie points – because you look brave. Whilst there will be many *many* times when it is important, right even, to recognise the whole team, we also need to learn the skill of taking sole credit, when sole credit is due.

Remember, if your boss knows that you worked alone on a certain project or alongside a particular client but you give the whole team the credit during your weekly debrief, there's a good chance your boss will negatively question your confidence.

Disclaimer: When things go wrong, stand up and shoulder the responsibility alone too. Everyone makes mistakes, but what will set you apart is if you're straight up, and you don't try to falsely distribute blame. That makes you credible, and bosses dig that kind of thing.

HOW TO Feed the Feedback

'If you have a reason to see someone, go see them. Don't drop papers off when they're not there, or rely on email, but actually make them see you, visually see you. It works. I've been in rooms discussing lists of candidates for top promotions and it is those whose faces are known – who have made a face-to-face impact – that the sponsors will talk about most confidently and positively and ultimately promote,' says top law firm Linklaters' former Global HR Director, **Jill King**.

In general, bosses report that while male employees regularly beat down the door to get their faces seen, women rarely ask for unsolicited feedback. Best not to bother the big guns, we think. But when we put off going in for a face-to-face, we do ourselves a huge disservice: reviews are as much a chance for us to list our achievements as they are for us to find out how we're doing.

Media finance expert **Gemma Godfrey** is a demon in the feedback department. And it's paid dividends. 'I'm always the one asking for the most number of progress reports. And when I move jobs, I make sure I ask for everything. Headhunters laughed at me when I said I wanted to be a director. They said come back when you're sixty. Well, a year after I started at my previous employer, Brooks Macdonald, I was sitting on the board – and I was the youngest one there by at least twenty years.'

Yes, it can feel awkward asking for a review, or even just a fifteen-minute catch-up, but the moments that we get alone with the right people in our organisation or industry are game changers. In an age of complete technological bombardment, popping our head around the door – yes, actually going to see someone and sitting in their office – will, if nothing else, be a pleasant respite from the computer screen. At the end of the day, or at any point during the day, a face is so much more memorable than an email address.

A good way to justify these meetings is to plot them into a broader career plan. This doesn't need to be a big, five-year deal, but as we've said already, we all need to exist and work within some kind of self-imposed career strategy that provides focus and regular excuses to go and see the boss.

If you're trying to get promoted, say, work out who the stakeholders and decision makers are in that process and then make sure they see you and your good work. Or, if you have a product to sell and you know a hefty proportion of your potential customers are convening at a certain work drinks party, get yourself there and get talking. Remember, feedback meetings aren't just for City corporates and they don't have to play out inside offices either.

What we're politely nudging you towards is a mindset where you don't just rely on annual reviews or the industry conference to get speaking to the Big Guns. All of us need to be getting in front of the right people regularly, so that they can see how we're doing and what we're up to. The good thing about regular contact is that it works both ways: we learn as much as we give when we speak to the right people. Strategic meetings (even ones across two Martinis) give both sides the opportunity to discuss where their heads are at, their achievements and the future.

A word of warning: nothing says 'out of touch' like an appraisal or catch-up plonked slap bang in the middle of the quarterly rent review period. It's wise and considerate – shrewd, even – to be aware of busy schedules.

As a ballpark figure, we'd suggest that these types of meetings should happen four times a year. That way, you'll have plenty to talk about and you should have a couple of prize proofs of progress to throw around too. If quarterly isn't possible, then aim for a review meeting at least every four to six months.

Communication with influencers is essential.

Yes, we just used the underline function there, and we don't employ that often. This is vital to your career progression; because when we don't engage in purposeful conversations we fall back into that career vacuum, and there aren't any unicorns flying there.

HOW TO Manage Complications

Maternity leave, yup here's a complication in the plan. Rather predictably, time off work feeds the need to actively self-promote. For women returning from maternity leave, research tells us that the level of communication we have with our manager upon return is the number one predictor of how successful our reintegration will be.

One of the most common fears from our *Step Up* clients is office politics – and academic research supports our findings. But the fact is, where there are people vying for positions of power we get politics. It is completely unavoidable and that means that we all have to engage in it from time to time. Politics isn't a dirty word, it's just being smart and it's a necessary part of work life.

HOW TO Get Out in the Jungle

Self-promotion internally keeps our careers ticking over. Self-promotion beyond the office revolving door though, out in the wider jungle, makes magic happen.

Clients, External Influencers and career types who inhabit completely different spheres of influence to us are vital self-promotion targets. Yes it's scary to cold call, spontaneously book in a catch-up or offer an unsolicited pitch, but when fear holds us back we stall. Yup, we're back into confidence territory again now, and it's true that self-promotion requires poise and determination. A good way to beef the bravado is to tag along when others are cutting their way through the overgrowth. For example, insist that you get taken along to significant meetings or make yourself a plus one at a speed-networking night. Whatever it takes, we must deliver those bite-sized bits of self-promotional information to an awaiting wider world.

Think of it like this; if you work in a male-dominated industry, just your presence as a woman might be enough. We are aware of several situations where diversity (or a lack of it) became the deciding factor in proceedings. At one FTSE 100 company, the board turned away a set of consultants who had just pitched to them, for the simple fact that as a group of white, middle-aged men, they were completely unrepresentative of the business.

Clients are increasingly demanding diversity from the companies they use, so if your advances get the push back, use your gender to your advantage. As we said at the start of this chapter, self-promotion comes in many forms. As important as writing and telling your story is possessing sensitive antennae to potential self-promotional situations, especially beyond the office. When we have these, the rest can be learnt.

HOW TO Know Our Story

Being vocal isn't just about explaining our role within our corporation, it's saying this is me; this is what I do differently and this is how I can help drive the success of the business. When advising her mentees on how to speak eloquently about their careers, HR director **Jill King** actually makes them write their own work storybook. See, story-telling again.

'You need to create a career narrative. You need a story that you've worked up that you are able to tell proactively and with confidence. You need to make it interesting to people and to have your own CV on the tip of your tongue at all times. I tended to be a typically self-effacing, conscientious person and my coach persuaded me to actually write my own CV even though I wasn't looking for a job. I wrote down what I had achieved and talked about it with her to get me used to talking confidently on the subject of me. This exercise put the right things at the front of my mind ready for when I needed to promote myself.' Genius.

When you write a convincing Once Upon A Time about why you in particular are so valuable to your organisation, then you strengthen your position and set yourself apart. Another of **Gemma Godfrey**'s USPs is her non-stop chatter and now she's made this trait part of her overall career offering. 'I was out one night and someone told me that I was a good communicator, that I'd be good on television. I was already trying to raise my profile so I got a show reel together, sent it to a producer at CNBC, and quite unexpectedly, she liked it and took a risk on me. I'm basically building on my strengths as a chatterbox.'

We aren't suggesting that we all go out and get a presenting gig. The point is, Gemma had the guts and voice to get herself noticed. She didn't, as many of us do, sit behind her desk and wonder whether she was good enough or if perhaps she'd be wasting the producer's time. No, Gemma spoke up and got booked.

HOW TO   Weave in Confidence

In situations when guts remain elusive, refer back to our confidence workouts. This book is intended as a healthy manual that shouldn't be read once and then abandoned on the top shelf. The advice in each of our chapters is part of a patchwork quilt of theory and advice. Don't feel bad flicking back as well as forward; career progression is a complex beast and no one is expected to tame it first go. With the workouts, and this is particularly relevant here while we're talking about self-promotion, keep on practising.

We already know that as women, what goes on (and on ... and on... and on) in our minds can be destructive. We overthink outcomes. We overthink slip-ups. Some (many) of us are so caught up in what we think might happen, we never get around to just jumping in and having a go.

If all else fails, and it shouldn't because there is plenty in this book to buoy even the most timid of ships, then trick the mind. A group of researchers carried out a test in which half of the candidates were randomly chosen to be told information about a (fake) subliminal noise generator in the room that might cause discomfort, and half were told nothing about the generator. All of them were then asked to write their own scholarship application.

Interestingly, those who believed that there was a fake generator in the room, who could misattribute their discomfort to the sound they thought they were experiencing, rather than their own internal discomfort, reported increased interest, adopted fewer performance-avoidance behaviours, perceived their own work to be of higher quality, and produced higher quality work. This shows that when a situation helps women to escape the discomfort of defying her modesty norms, she feels happier self-promoting and she's actually better at it too.

So why are we telling you about a subliminal generator?

Well, what this study proves is that when we are feeling uncomfortable about something (in this case, shamelessly self-promoting) a good tactic is tricking our minds so that we plonk all our awkwardness associated with self-promotion into a completely different bucket. One way to do this is through exercise, because physical exertion has a similar physical impact on the body as anxiety.

So, for example, if we're on our way to a big meeting and we know there will be people there who may sit up and take notice if we passionately riff about our own achievements, then instead of spending the ten minutes before the meeting getting sweaty with nerves, get sweaty by doing some exercise. A brisk walk, say, raises our adrenalin and our heart rate too, which just happen to be the same symptoms we might get from nervously thinking about self-promotion. Once we're hot under the collar because of exercise rather than nerves, we can then attribute any anxious heart-pumping to that, rather than the impending act of self-promotion.

We promise, the result is simpler than the explanation. Exercise, don't fret and you will feel more relaxed.

WORKOUT Best Friends

Another form of misattribution is removing the personal element. In another recent study, job candidates were asked to supply two résumés: one they had written themselves and one written by a close friend. It won't surprise you to know that independent researchers repeatedly ranked the friend-written résumé higher than the personal one, proving again that us women are foolishly hard on ourselves.

WORKOUT **Best Friends** continued

Whilst you probably can't take your best friend to work with you (alas), you can still harness the power of her support. And here's how you do it:

Find a comfy sofa, prepare yourselves a nice drink (approx. 1 minute).

Take a deep breath and then in three minutes, talk your friend through your career, focusing on what you have achieved in your current role and where you hope to be in five years' time (3 minutes plus one breath).

Give her a couple of minutes to process what you've talked about and then get her to tell you your career story back as she has heard it (4 minutes).

Listen to what she said, process it and then repeat the story, as told to you, back to your obliging friend (2 minutes).

This exercise will teach you two important lessons. One: you've probably achieved more than you thought you had, right? And two: your career as a story – a narrative – is much more compelling than a one-page résumé.

Now, when you're at work or out networking, harness that perspective and enjoy talking people through your story as if you were talking about someone else.

Remember, the best way we human beings connect to each other is through simple stories. Make yours a bestseller.

HOW TO Negotiate

We opened this book with some stirring words from Hollywood actress Jennifer Lawrence on pay inequality, and it seems fitting to pick up more of the story here. If you missed it (see Chapter 1) her controversial essay talked to the world about discovering, through the Sony hack, that her *American Hustle* male co-stars earned a load more money than her – despite her being an Oscar winner and a proven box-office draw.

In the wake of the essay's publication, Lawrence spoke at a news conference in Hollywood on the subject of unequal pay – a topic that affects almost all women in all walks of life. That it is endemic in one of the world's most well-known and high-profile industries is no more significant than if you are earning less than your male colleague. But it's certainly telling. Why should women suffer financial discrimination? Lawrence has a simple answer.

'They're not going to give somebody more money if they don't ask for it.'

Although the majority of us feel we are underpaid at work, less than half of us have ever dusted ourselves down and gone in to ask for a rise. Jennifer Lawrence didn't feel comfortable asking for more money when her *American Hustle* contract was put before her, and most probably you didn't either before you signed on the dotted line.

In the United Kingdom, the gender pay gap remains at 20 per cent. That means for every £1 that a man earns, on average, a woman with the same job gets just 80 pence. These figures are about the same in the United States and Australia too. There are many reasons for this disparity – and with this explanation we are not letting managers off the hook – but again and again we hear that the crucial point of difference between men and women, in terms of pay, is willingness to negotiate. Many of us (wrongly) think that we don't deserve the top rates – and because of this, we settle for less.

And it isn't just our salaries that make us feel uncomfortable. We loathe the process of discussing money so acutely that in a study into people buying new cars, women were willing to forgo as much as $1353 off the market price to avoid the pain of brokering a deal. For men, if you want the comparison, the amount was somewhere nearer $600.

Vogue contributing editor and *Daily Telegraph* Fashion Director **Lisa Armstrong** is as icky about sitting down and chatting through her salary as the next woman. She disliked it when she was young and poor at *Vogue* and she loathes it just the same today, despite being one of the country's most accomplished journalists. But

Armstrong has learnt to advance through the ick, although it has taken a while.

'I wasn't always rational and open to money discussions. I remember distinctly an early conversation I had with Alexandra Shulman, my editor at *Vogue*, where I said, "It's not about the money..." But of course it was. I was underpaid. But like so many women I thought it would look bad to ask for more.'

When she went to the *Telegraph* in 2011, she took a more direct approach.

'I thought this is my last shot to broker a big deal. I was really very happy at *The Times*, so I knew they were going to have to really make it worth my while. After I went in for my first meeting at the *Telegraph*, I called up my good friend Anne Robinson. I said to her, "You are the woman I think has the best way with money, what should I do?" She guided me [so the moral of this story is get yourself a mentor]. First of all she told me to go in really prepared. So I did, and they were impressed. I arrived with lots of ideas, and I had figures on how the advertising spend had gone up under my editorship at *The Times*. As advised by Anne, I was completely unemotional and very strategic; these weren't pie in the sky numbers for what I wanted to earn, it was all planned out.'

Guess what? Lisa got exactly what she asked for.

But Lisa is an exception; this cultural difference in how men and women ask for new salaries is so deep-rooted that it actually impacts on what we're offered to start with. As shocking as it sounds, research tells us that today many women earn less for the simple but galling fact that the employer knew she wouldn't negotiate so tried their luck and offered less than they would a man.

In another study, over 150 managers were asked to allocate a fixed pool of money for raises among equally skilled employees. When they were told that their employees could not negotiate, the managers gave male and female employees equal raises. But, more interestingly, when they were told that they might have to explain the raise to their employees and negotiate, the managers gave salary increases nearly 2.5 times larger to the men than to the women.

As Lisa's story shows, women are just as capable at securing the big bucks, or even just the equal bucks, as long as we are able to handle the negotiation period. A good first step to becoming a salary shrew is to accept this plain fact: we all feel uncomfortable talking about money and selling ourselves as a bankable product. Yes, at first it might feel immodest and gluttonous, but when we don't ask we don't get.

Award-winning cake maker and founder of online baking school Pretty Witty Cakes, which just happens to have an enormous worldwide customer base, **Suzi Witt** quickly learnt the power of tough negotiation when she started her business. 'For any woman now starting a business,' she advises, 'I would say put on your hard hat and be prepared to fight some battles so people know they cannot walk all over you from day one. There will be a presumption you are too "nice" to negotiate. You need to wipe any prejudices away from the beginning and ensure you create the image that you want and need for them to take you seriously.'

Both Suzi and Lisa have exercised their demanding side. It takes guts, but we all deserve to earn what's fair, so here is our *Step Up* guide to getting the right money:

| 1 | Be a peaceful negotiator. Remember the aggression backlash that we mentioned earlier on, well, it's applicable here too. When cutting a deal be sure to use direct language – plain, non-emotional talking always works best. This isn't enough though; once we have that simple mode of speech we need to coat it in something smooth and feminine. It's been proven many times over that the straight-talking feminine is the most persuasive in the pack.

| 2 | Expect more. Yes, we have to truly believe we are worth it before we can feel comfortable asking for a raise, or securing that big financial move. Again, confidence is key here. If it helps, rely on cold hard facts: it's always worth investigating salaries for our role in our industry and valuing ourselves near the top of the range. When women believe that we are worth the same as men, we are just as likely to negotiate. And once women ask, as Lisa did, then we're just as likely to get what we want.

|3| Don't just talk numbers. Talking money is fine, but you know we're big on authenticity. So if you feel uncomfortable chatting straight cash, cool things down with a complete package. When we approach every aspect of a deal in a negotiation, rather than just homing in on the bottom line, it feels like less of a battle with a win or lose outcome. If we are able to put everything on the table – the pension, the pay, the bonus scheme, even the hours – then we have options to play with. A classic negotiation tactic is to include some elements that we feel very strongly about and others that are less important as this allows us to give little gains to the employer while keeping the big win back for ourselves.

WORKOUT Ask for More

Still finding it trickier to ask for more? Research shows that women find it easier to negotiate when we're acting on behalf of someone else. Here's how to do it for yourself.

(2 minutes) Identify your goals. What do you want? What's a must have? What would be the icing on the cake?

(4 minutes) Imagine you were asking for all of this on behalf of your best friend. How would you feel if she were being under-offered by her boss? Why, outraged of course. And determined to set things straight. Now put that imagination to work. List out the reasons why she (you) deserves what you're asking for.

(4 minutes) Now practise the conversation with a friend, preferably one who can impersonate a tough boss.

Tomorrow, take your plan to work. Floor your boss. Get that raise.

THE TIPS

|1| Stick to your limits

Self-promotion is essential for everyone but not everyone will do it the same way. As with everything, it's important to stay authentic. So if something feels too uncomfortable to talk about or shouting about a promotion on social media doesn't sit well with you, take that into account. For naturally quiet types, there's nothing wrong with having a subtler and more targeted approach. As long as we do it and the right people hear, make self-promotion work your way.

|2| Don't forget to listen

> When we self-promote, we communicate about ourselves. And as with all communication, listening is a crucial part of self-promotion success. Most self-promoters look for an opening. They search for opportunities to sell their brand or fit their achievement into the conversation. Sometimes this is valid – in a performance review for example – but it's not always the most effective way.

> Instead of pitching whenever possible, spend some time listening for people's problems. When we discover what they are struggling with – what is missing from the team or project perhaps – then we can work out how we can offer a solution to that problem. And who doesn't love having a problem solved?

|3| Remember to take the credit

Reviews and formal meetings aren't the only time to self-promote; we need to incorporate it into the day-to-day too. The next time someone bigs up something you've done, make sure you take the credit. 'Thanks, I worked really hard on it,' beats 'aw, it was nothing' every time.

|4| Share the spotlight

Taking the credit is important but so is sharing the glory. When we can bring the team along with us in our boastings, we'll not only look like a great leader but it will win useful allies along the way. The trick is all in the pitch. Emphasise both your involvement and the support the team gave. Just like love, there is enough credit to go around – just make sure you are taking your fair share.

|5| Sell yourself

We've said it before, but we'll say it again. Once we get the confidence to self-promote and we get visible, we need to know what to say. Hone your ability to talk about work you've done in a positive way and, for ten minutes every so often, practise. Whether it's at drinks with your team or in one of those reviews we've now scheduled (right?!), the more we pitch ourselves, the more natural it will feel.

CHAPTER 7

Networks

NETWORKING The Facts

Y ou were born into a network. You have parents. You may also
have a sibling or two. Moving outwards, there's possibly also a
series of uncles, aunts and cousins. This is your birth network.
Of course, birth networks are likely to have little bearing on our future
career development, but the point remains that from the day we are
born, we are all absorbed into strong groups of connected individuals.

Of course, as we move through childhood towards our working
lives, our birth networks extend. Today, you will have a colourful grid
of contacts that, if you plotted each within its sphere of influence,
would resemble some kind of decorative Venn diagram. We all have
overlapping groups of connections that encompass education, work,
hobbies, friends and social media.

This is our network and our network (it need not be divided by our
personal and professional lives) opens doors. Of course, it's not just the
size of our network that matters, but how we employ it to our advantage.

Before we really get started, here's our chapter disclaimer: henceforth,
as we unpick the workings of networks and everything that surrounds
them, it is inevitable that we'll have to engage in a fair amount of
gender comparisons. In the main, women and men fall into two
networking camps that expose our character differences and how we
cope in social situations. It's useful to see networking from both sides,
because in the end, as with so much of *Step Up*'s career advice, when
we are able to cross-pollinate tactics, we put ourselves in pole position.

Around 75 per cent of new jobs are found through networks (whether
it's internally at work or externally through referrals) and the majority

of new business comes via word of mouth too. For small businesses, networks produce around 83 per cent of new profitable fruit.

And not just that, though: when we have access to influential people, it actually makes us more powerful ourselves – just as having more influence (a bigger network) has the same reciprocal benefit. The wider our networks stretch, the more likely we are to be talked about, and reputation is a defining element of career success.

You see; networks are ace.

While our parents may have had a job for life, the chances are we'll be moving and shaking our way to the top. These days, career journeys are faster paced and less obviously linear. Generally we have more dynamic ambitions and ways of working; many of us will twist and turn our way through all number of career changes, multi-jobbing and retraining as we head towards a complex and redesigned future. All of this means one simple thing: we've never needed to be able to network, and build a stonking one too, more than we do today.

For **Natasha Chetiyawardana**, Co-Founder and Creative Director of growth agency Bow & Arrow, networking has been an absolute necessity from day one.

'Why did I become good at networking? Because I moved to London from Birmingham and I didn't know anyone at all. I was moving into a field that I knew nothing about and I needed to make contacts quickly. I literally accosted different people in the classrooms at Central Saint Martins and gave them no option but to become my friend. I knew nothing about the design industry, so I decided to just write to people I admired, which I suppose in a sense was networking too. I pulled together a group of four or five contacts and grew my network from there.'

Natasha is a fearless and avid networker and the success of her business is a direct result of her gutsy approach. OK, Natasha's introductory letters may have been replaced by direct social media conversations, but the essence remains the same. Having said that, today, we absolutely cannot ignore the infinite possibilities of the internet and social media – it's a gift to networking, and it's one we must all master.

It's no wonder that many of us stare wide-eyed into networking's gigantic abyss: meeting new people can feel like an added, unwanted pressure when we've already got our day jobs to consider. Plus, being a woman can complicate matters even further. Our tussles with confidence, assertion and self-promotion don't exactly provide a strong footing on which we can lay the bricks of our network empire. But here's the thing, networking is as much a state of mind as it is small talk over a tapenade crostini. And this chapter will show you how.

The best way to start breaking down the networking nut is by simply writing down as many contacts as you can bring to mind. Don't just include the people at work – be more creative than that. Think about your hobbies, parents' friends, their children, extended families and the friends you made when you travelled around Australia. When we mine our pasts we begin to see how we're a better networker than we might have thought. Here is a workout to help.

WORKOUT Start Your Network

So you've listed your network (we know we may have exceeded our allotted 10 minutes on this one but it's vital so bear with us). Focus (for now) on the ones most obviously relevant to work.

(5 minutes) Now look at the list, considering each of these questions in turn:

> Where are they from: your team, your industry, somewhere else?
> What benefits do each of them give you?
> How energising are those interactions?

The last question is an important one. Energisers bring out the best in everyone around them, and research shows that having them in your network is a strong predictor of success. These are the people who always see opportunities, even in challenging situations, and create room for you to meaningfully contribute. De-energisers are the opposite: negative,

WORKOUT **Start Your Network** continued

inflexible and quick to critique. You need to ditch these. Roughly 90 per cent of anxiety at work is created by 5 per cent of one's network – the people who sap energy.

(5 minutes) Next, classify each contact by the benefits they provide. There are six basic categories: information, support with work politics and influence, personal development, personal support and energy, a sense of purpose or worth, and work/life balance. We need representatives from each in your network. Categorising your relationships will give you a clearer idea of whether your network is extending your abilities or keeping you stuck. You'll see where you have holes and redundancies and which people you depend on too much – or not enough.

Now you're ready to extend this thinking to the rest of your network and see where they might be able to fill the gaps or where you'll need to go out and network.

This list is the start of your new network. Each of these people (there will be more, you just need time for them to filter through) is a potential work opportunity waiting in the wings of your web. Your list will be a good start; as we've said though, a network is a living organism; it needs tending to and feeding for it to thrive and grow.

So why are networks – and the art of networking – particularly important to women? Well, the truth is they aren't – both sexes rely on networking in equal measure. What is different is the importance we place on networking, their accessibility, our networking style and the way we build our web of contacts.

NETWORKING Accessibility

Work networks are less accessible to women. Fact. Thanks to old-fashioned company and industry social structures, which are designed in a way that inadvertently favours men, women are often sidelined from powerful networking circles. Of course, the degree to which this happens shifts depending on the industry, our pecking order and how aggressively we self-promote. In the main though, team-building rugby matches and corporate boxing tickets give man-to-man networking the upper hand.

Put bluntly, classic networking – as well as team-building development – doesn't always suit who we are or how we work. There's an expectation that women should just join in and do it, but half-hearted participation is an imperfect starting point.

Things will change, of course. We know this because by 2028, experts expect women to be controlling close to 75 per cent of discretionary worldwide spending. By then, big global companies will have to sit up and take note of the female voice and how it likes to chat. In the meantime though, while many of us feel marginalised from the macho stuff, it's really up to us to hone our skills and dive in feet first, regardless of what's expected or who else is involved.

Another accessibility problem centres on children. Obviously, not all women are mothers and not all mothers are the ones to put their children to bed every night. Those that do, though, enjoy another spanner in the works, because the majority of career chin-wagging takes place in the evening. That 7pm cocktail, or a quick dinner before the last train home; these seem like user-friendly networking opportunities until you have a toddler at home who's begging for a bedtime story. While the men and that small percentage of career-centric women (more of which in our balance chapter) are drinking, cracking jokes and brokering their next pay rise, many women are at home managing the final tantrum of the day.

Labour MP, former Cabinet Minister – she was the first woman to serve as Chief Secretary to the Treasury – and mother of three, **Yvette Cooper**, acknowledges this barrier. 'A lot of things would happen in the evening over dinner or drinks or, alternatively, breakfast meetings. I took the approach that I would never do breakfast meetings unless I absolutely had to and also avoid dinners if I possibly could, especially when my kids were small. So I think I did a lot less networking than most politicians would do. That has made it harder for me. For me it was not possible to do the job, spend time with the kids and do that morning and evening networking as well.'

Of course, women don't have to have children, to bear the brunt of a more demanding and less networking friendly out-of-work schedule. We've already mentioned how our perfectionist traits and desire to achieve in all areas of our work and social lives mean that we have more on our plates. And that is why footloose and fancy-free male camaraderie remains the backdrop of most successful work connections.

So before we even explore how some of these characteristics can diminish our innate networking superpower, women are already up against it on the accessibility front. Of course, this antiquated boys club mentality is at its most extreme in the most traditionally male-dominated industries – step forward engineering, property and much of the City – and there are many sectors that feel more female-friendly on the networking front. But even in these circumstances, women don't always take advantage of what's on offer.

NETWORKING Our Webs

THIS IS HOW MEN BUILD A NETWORK

Like a spider, the male networker stretches his sticky web far and wide. When a fly or a bug gets caught in his network, the male spider engages quickly, sends the requisite follow-up email, but does not linger long with each catch. The minibeasts in his web are not his friends; they are merely useful garden acquaintances that he hopes will assist him as he marches towards success.

THIS IS HOW WOMEN BUILD A NETWORK

Like a Queen Bee, the female networker surrounds herself with like-minded bumblebees. She feels most comfortable inside the hive, and likes to spend the majority of her time protected from the outside world. She knows the other bees very well, but isn't too bothered about the moths and butterflies beyond. Queen Bee is most secure ensconced within her bee friends – despite her bee friends really only knowing about honey.

Whether we like honey or not, if we're a Queen Bee surrounded by like-minded buzzers, then our network is doing us very few favours. What we're saying is that in terms of fashioning and building networks, we need to spider things out a bit. Yes, a woman's beehive will always be highly valuable, there's no debating that (we'll see why later on) – but our beehive isn't enough. Sprawling networks that reach across the entire garden of our industry (and beyond) propel us skywards. Each person in our web, each bug, fly and wasp, is an opportunity waiting to happen, and the more we know, the further we'll soar.

For balance's sake, it is important that we include a small body of research that wholly disagrees with our bug/web analogy. It says that actually, while men will be rewarded for having bigger networks, women are only rewarded for what we have done – our past performances – and not who we know. The controversial findings have led some people (wrongly, we believe) to advise women to stop wasting their energies on networking altogether.

We think these findings and the subsequent advice is spurious – not least because they are based on a single study, into the single job type of stock analysts. As you've probably worked out by now, *Step Up* is a big believer in women having the freedom and right to stay true to their femininity, and sometimes, if and when the situation requires it, to do things completely differently to our male counterparts.

However, this – networking – is not one of those times. Yes, men and women tend to build and utilise their networks in wildly opposing fashions, but the truth of the matter is that both sexes can benefit from learning to blend our disparate techniques. To have the best network on the block, all of us should aim to combine a woman's beehive with the flimsier but more wide-ranging spider labyrinth. The way we get there though is dependent on our personalities.

Staying true to her priorities when it comes to networking has benefited Labour MP **Yvette Cooper**. 'I don't think the answer for that is for women to feel that they just have to network the same way men do,' she continues, 'or they just have to go along to those male events to get on. Because in the end that isn't going to work for a lot of women and why should women have to limit themselves to networking in that way? We need to recognise that you might do things at different times of day, not just morning and evening because everyone else does it then. And also consciously challenge traditional networks and traditional ways of doing things. I would encourage women to have the confidence to do things the way that works for them.'

In short, unless we are already very senior or work in a female-dominated industry (and there aren't many of those, especially at the top), a network that is small and created in our own image will just not include all of the contacts that we need to be speaking to.

Here is a visual explanation of how things stand at the moment.

	Men	**Women**
Size	Large	Small
Tie strength	Weak	Strong
Diversity	Diverse	Homogenous
Power	More influential	Less influential

NETWORKING Introvert versus Extrovert

Before we work through the nuts and bolts of strategic hive expansion, it's useful to consider how comfortable we are with the basic notion of networking. It's all very well talking about what we should and should not build; but the details are irrelevant if our networking comfort level is nil. Well, actually that's not entirely true. Even in circumstances of complete networking turmoil, there's a way to continue adding new connections and we do that by functioning within our safety zones. One size definitely does not fit all when it comes to networking.

So where do you sit on networking's rainbow? If striding across a sterile bar to start a convo with a very senior stranger sounds like a thrill, then chances are you're an extrovert. Prefer a deep and meaningful discussion with your colleague (female) on the adjacent desk? You're most likely more introverted. For the record, introverts don't shun human contact, just as extroverts aren't required to dance on table tops. What's relevant in a networking context is recognising how our personality type affects our networking prowess.

WORKOUT Introvert/Extrovert

(10 minutes) To find out where you fall on the introvert–extrovert spectrum, answer each question True or False, choosing the one that applies to you more often than not.

1. _____ I prefer one-on-one conversations to group activities.
2. _____ I often prefer to express myself in writing.
3. _____ I enjoy solitude.
4. _____ I seem to care about wealth, fame and status less than my peers.
5. _____ I dislike small talk, but I enjoy talking in depth about topics that matter to me.
6. _____ People tell me that I'm a good listener.
7. _____ I'm not a big risk taker.
8. _____ I enjoy work that allows me to 'dive in' with few interruptions.
9. _____ I like to celebrate birthdays on a small scale, with only one or two close friends or family members.
10. _____ People describe me as 'soft-spoken' or 'mellow'.
11. _____ I prefer not to show or discuss my work with others until it's finished.
12. _____ I dislike conflict.
13. _____ I do my best work on my own.
14. _____ I tend to think before I speak.
15. _____ I feel drained after being out and about, even if I've enjoyed myself.
16. _____ I often let calls go through to voice mail.
17. _____ If I had to choose, I'd prefer a weekend with absolutely nothing to do to one with too many things scheduled.
18. _____ I don't enjoy multitasking.
19. _____ I can concentrate easily.
20. _____ In classroom situations, I prefer lectures to seminars.

The more often you answered True, the more introverted you are. Now read on to discover what that means for you.

To summarise, introverted people are more introspective and attentive to internal thoughts, while extroverts thrive on new sights and sounds. Somewhere in the middle there are ambiverts, who present aspects of both character types. Here are the details.

EXTROVERTS

In the context of networking, extroverts find things fairly easy. They enjoy the ride, the new people and the sights; everything about classic networking events feeds their extroverted vigour. Extroverts don't struggle with spontaneous networking; in the main, they're happy to put in the effort, reach out and instigate a conversation. Busy networking events and social gatherings are their natural habitat. If this is you, go forth and connect.

As long as extroverts remember to expand their reach beyond the default female parameters of close friends (also female) and peers, then they should breeze the building stage.

INTROVERTS AND AMBIVERTS

Those of us on the other end of the scale, or somewhere in the middle (the majority), will inevitably find networking trickier. It is never impossible of course, but these types might require more resolve and Dutch courage. It's a fact that success won't come if we opt out of meeting new people. With this in mind, it isn't a case of closing networking's lid; rather it's about finding a way to do it that suits the more introverted personality.

As Susan Cain points out in her global bestseller, *Quiet: The Power of Introverts in a World That Can't Stop Talking*, introverts most likely spend much of their working life already conforming to an extrovert ideal of career success. For introverts, she says, big meetings, brainstorming sessions and group away days represent a series of confronting challenges that need to be conquered. These situations are daunting and fail to bring the best out of introverts.

Being an introvert working in an extroverted world is not dissimilar to being a woman who operates in a man's world. Introverted females, to give all of us some perspective, cope with a double whammy of torment. Instead of fighting it, what introverts must do, to allow for solid networking (and many other requisites of success), is appreciate their preference for the internal. Really, all introverts require is an introvert-friendly battle plan.

Here's how we think introverts should attack key networking expectations.

THE BIG OCCASION: Large business events that require introverts to engage with lots of people in a short amount of time can feel hellish. The way to handle these types of situation is to see past the crowd – tackle them one person at a time. When introverts give themselves achievable goals, say, two new connections per night, then the event is easier to manage. More time with fewer people is appropriate to how introverts best function. Yes, they may have to attend more events to really get their network going, but that's certainly more doable when introverts feel less anxious.

INTRODUCTIONS: Being a CEO, being a celebrity even, does not exclude introverts from introversion if that's their inclination. When we acknowledge that everyone in the room could be feeling as uncomfortable as we do, then making introductions suddenly seems easier. When introverts learn to smile and offer a hand – when they make the first move, however scary it feels – they take control of the conversation. Not only is this empowering, it usually also means that they can dictate what's discussed – and crucially, when they want to duck out.

PREPARATIONS: To some introverts and ambiverts, networking can induce the same palpitations as a large-scale public speaking ordeal. If this is you, fight fire with groundwork. Networking is most effective when we're prepared: write down a few leading questions, find out who else is attending and have some prepared subjects to discuss. When we can engage others in their favourite subject (usually themselves) then things get off to a good start. Especially if we ask leading questions we know they'll have an opinion on.

SCHEDULING: Introverts don't enjoy too many social gatherings and they need to bear this in mind when they're planning what to attend: there's no point being gung-ho if that means three back-to-back networking events before the day is out. Because introverts draw their energy from within, rather than from external influences, they aren't their best when they're wired or tired. Introverts especially, although really this applies to us all, should always remember to make time to re-energise. A short walk between appointments or a half an hour stopgap in a bookshop gives us time to reset. And when we're fresh, networking always feels less intimidating.

HOW TO Build Our Network

Hopefully, we've now gone some way to alleviating your networking fears. Better yet, we may have rekindled in you the thrill of the chat. Either way, now it's time to learn how to landscape your networking garden.

HOW TO BUILD

How many friends do you have on Facebook? 100? 300? We know what you're thinking, you're thinking, yes I have lots of Facebook friends, but they aren't *real* friends. They're old friends. Friends you picked up on long-forgotten summer holidays. They're friends who lived next door when you were nine years old.

Part of the reason women struggle is that we find it hard to accept the simple definition of a network. You don't need to speak to all the people in your sphere, and that includes your Facebook friends and the ones you're loosely connected to via your school alumni association, for them to be a valid dot on your networking diagram. If you have access to someone (and these days, we have access to nearly everyone), then they are a valid connection who may have the capacity to inch you a step nearer to your success unicorn.

Because many women are too narrow in how they define their network ('Is she a friend?'), we tend to wrongly think we have fewer connections than is the case. Men, on the other hand, are usually more brazen in how they view their networks. They'll quite happily suck anyone they've ever met into their webs and then boast about them as loudly as they can. OK, so that's a huge generalisation; the point though is valid. The first step to building that super network is to shift your point of view: and you can do that by appreciating what you've already got.

The best way to do that is to take the list from the beginning of this chapter, hold it tight, and then spend some time flicking through other contact lists. Start at work but also look at your social media connections, contacts from the past, friends, friends of friends, and so on.

Once we have reframed how we define a contact and worked out who we're actually connected to, we begin to realise how big our network already is. If you're struggling, think of those people you know whom you may have met only once or twice but who would be happy to receive an email from you. These, as well as the members of your Saturday morning netball team and the ones you chat to at the local coffee house, are all dots on the networking chart.

And when we plot each of these individuals into different mental plans (or actual spreadsheets – see the 'Start Your Network' workout above for guidance) our network starts to have structure. It will take some time to organise your network, so try not to rush this stage.

When you've got this organised, it's time to expand that web. And one way to get things going is with a hit list in tow. Think strategically now: who in your industry and beyond could help with investment, promotions, advertising, sales or leasing that property on file that just won't budge? Networking isn't as easy as writing lists and sending LinkedIn requests, but when we plan a route we don't get lost. See, you now have a plan of attack and you haven't even picked up the phone: whey hey, you've just extended your potential reach and influence.

HOW TO Expand Our Network

We have our beehive in check. We've even compiled a register of people we want to connect with. But what about uncovering others in the ether that we don't even know exist?

Well, the obvious place to start is at work. You might not be the social type, but why not set yourself a networking challenge: for one month, try to be as open and exploratory as you can. Look for work sports teams, attend professional conferences and volunteer at the charity bake sale. Yes we know, this all sounds a bit noble and worthy, and we're also aware that your time is limited; but don't forget the end goal – networks lead to success. Yes, be judicious but make sure you're bold too.

Once your month is up (count new connections as you go) set yourself a new ongoing plan. Decide how many events you are going to attend each month and then find things that you really enjoy and that fit in to your schedule. For example, if you decide to volunteer for a cause that you care about and which also aligns neatly with your new business, it won't feel like networking at all. Next: stick to the plan.

We also suggest proceeding down the friend-of-a-friend route. An effective way to build your network is to ask your inner circle, your trusted contacts, for referrals. Unlike the bake sales, or any type of modern speed networking, this method is based on introductions and requires far less bravado. After all, you're practically friends already, all you're doing is joining the dots.

Don't feel embarrassed asking for favours from someone you value. When we are network building, we need to be bold and confident. If a trusted friend makes an introduction and the recipient doesn't take the bait, it's hardly a life-over situation. Some dots will connect and others won't; all that matters though is that we keep marching forward. Remember, most of us feel flattered to be thought of as worth meeting.

Another good resource is our college or university. Try contacting the careers service there, because most have a rich database of alumni. This is simple, strategic work that will pay dividends. Universities may not advertise this resource, but for those of us who are savvy enough to ask, it will be there and it will be a goldmine of ready-made (senior) contacts waiting to be tapped.

And then there is social media – the new networking dawn. Twitter, Instagram, Facebook and LinkedIn, social media's four biggest career-focused players, offer a whole realm of new contacts and connections. *Step Up* is a big advocate of riding this crazy wave, because the internet is an unlocked door to pretty much everyone on the planet. It's mindboggling stuff, and when we get it right, the results can be diamond-studded.

The trick is to choose the platform that best suits your business or industry. **Nicola Eyre** is the owner of Cissy Wears (55k social media followers), a small, south-east London children's boutique. She launched in 2012, and today, the shop has a global customer base – despite barely any footfall – and is a recognised innovator and market leader. How did she do it? Instagram.

'The impact that Instagram has had on my annual sales has floored me; they went up 150 per cent over the course of a couple of months at the back end of 2013. There isn't a business in my shop if I just rely on local trade; I'm not here to survive as a standalone business. I knew that I needed to embrace the digital age, and Instagram works for us, because its visual representation can showcase the products artfully and in the context of the home too. Thanks to Instagram, I now have customers flying over from New York or Asia, arriving at Gatwick airport and catching a taxi straight to the shop. It blows my mind; there are people who live in the vicinity who don't even know that we're here and then there are these husbands with their shopping lists, who pull up in flash cars after travelling halfway around the globe to shop. We're probably one of the best-known children's retailers out there – and Instagram is everything to me.'

On the other end of the business social media spectrum sits our friend **Gemma Godfrey** (54k Twitter followers): FinTech Founder and CEO, board advisor, broadcaster and quantum physicist. For Gemma, work life revolves around Twitter. 'I've found Twitter vital to my career. It has enabled me to build my own brand, push forward my message and reach a seemingly endless new audience. When I have a service I want to launch, say, I go and talk to people via Twitter. Through social media, I've met some of the world's leading lights; more than that though, I understand what my clients want and what they are thinking about.'

Social media has broken a dam of information, contacts and inspiration. It isn't all plain sailing online, though. Godfrey is still honing her skills six years after joining the Twitter rally. 'There is a certain responsibility that comes with having lots of followers. I've realised I need to be more thoughtful about what I'm putting out there, as it can be really motivating to others; it's a total misconception that social media is silly. We all need to change the mindset. This isn't a case of just having space for some online musings; when you have followers, you're changing people's minds and causing new actions to take place in business. And all of this from your phone. It's crazy that I have the capability to enact change in the world from the palm of my hand.'

What Gemma is saying is veering into the sphere of leadership, and we'll cover that in Chapter 9. It's pertinent here too though, because her position illustrates the world's commitment to, and depth of feeling for, conscientious social media networking. Gemma, Nicola and many others have worked out for themselves the good, bad and ugly of connecting in this way. To make things easier for you, we've obtained the lowdown from senior women at our three favourite social media platforms. But before this, the ultimate social media #HowTo, a few words on working your web.

HOW TO Flex Your Web

So once we have all these new dots on the plan, how do we make the most of our new-look webs? As we've already said, the way most women network is not wrong; it's just not expansive enough. Our friendship-building skills are unrivalled but we fall short when it comes to making occasional contact with larger numbers of people.

Here is a mildly irritating gender reveal: not only are men super network builders, they're also demons at network utilisation. And they do this by being transactional in their approach. When a man requires something, he tends to think of who he knows that has what he needs – whether that's a job, investment tip or introduction. Then, he goes and asks for it. Simple. He also knows that when a contact reaches out to him (when things are the other way around) he gives back too. Transactions are about give and take, just not always at the same time.

Women have a more complex approach. We're driven not by what we need, but by what we can give in return. And really, that's the wrong way around. Because while emotional/strategic/career-enhancing generosity will lead to long-lasting, deep relationships based on trust and mutual appreciation (friendships with leverage), these types of associations, in networking spheres, take up too much time. Time that also needs to be spent being transactional.

If this still sounds tough, learn from a master. Lawyer **Tamara Box** cites networking as one of her greatest skills, describing how her husband jokes that 'there really isn't a social situation I can't turn into work and there isn't a work situation I can't make social. And that's really true. I love the people I work with; I have fun with them. And I never go into a social situation without thinking, "Hedge funds, really? Well, let me tell you what we do in that space." I can't help it. It's just who I am. So I can integrate my life in that way. If I had to pick one thing that, frankly, has augured success in my life, it would be that. I honestly don't notice when I'm working and when I'm socialising. Remember with your network that when you are asking for something – an introduction, a meeting, whatever – you are also giving an opportunity; and remember, most women like to give. If you are asking a man, then most men like to be flattered. So you just have to figure out how that ask goes. Most of us are very uncomfortable with the "I'll scratch your back, you scratch mine" perfect transaction. So with most of my female contacts it's almost always an asymmetric ask with the knowledge that the next one will go the other way. Or it will go in a circle.'

When we embrace our female network style and learn to incorporate a less emotional, more masculine air, we create a network with light and shade. Don't discount good friends, just learn to add in potential contacts (the ones you listed above) and set a new precedent in how to build those relationships. It might take a bit of trial and error and that's OK; over time you will find a new adaptable groove. And that groove absorbs the realisation that we don't need to be sugar and nice all the darn time.

HOW TO Use Collaborations

Collaborations are enormously beneficial because they help us to perform better and make us more visual. As a member of a high-performing team, or one half of a killer duo, our successes are more obvious to others and when there is greater awareness of our achievements we automatically become absorbed into new networks, whether we know it or not. And what facilitates these collaborations? Networks.

Collaboration, as opposed to merely dishing out help, also builds trust-based relationships. You worked with Miss X on the editorial for that new fashion website. The site rocked. You and Miss X both looked great internally. You now love Miss X. Miss X now loves you. Miss X told a few people in her network about the site. Your network grew. Miss X's network is now part of your network. Sales on the site are booming. Everyone is talking about you. Other people (senior Miss Xs) now want to work with you too... And so the positive collaboration effect goes on.

Collaboration is an under-celebrated facet of networking, but it's one that we wholeheartedly endorse.

HOW TO Know Your Goals

Do your career goals trip off your tongue? If you're squirming in your seat and finding it hard to call to mind where you want to be in five years' time, then you're not in a position to positively network.

A cornerstone of networking will always be the exchange of aspirations – goal sharing. Some women don't talk about their goals because they don't know what their goals even are. Hopefully, you are not that woman. You have methodically worked your way through this book and you have your goals up your sleeve (and in your handbag too). And while we're at it, you're also not the woman who doesn't want to talk about her career aims for fear of appearing too ambitious or boastful.

Yes, we all fear failure and we all worry about putting our objectives on the line in case we don't fulfil them. But the opposite is way more detrimental to our success: if we restrict expectations about ourselves we lessen our impact on others and we slow our ascent. Communicating our career goals is a proven tactic for getting the most out of our networks; learn to be bold and to be upfront about your dream career move.

HOW TO Vie with Anxieties

Many women are deeply uncomfortable about being ego-centred. We don't enjoy talking about ourselves and we worry that others will find us boring. The thing is, anxieties don't sit neatly in networking formulas.

Here's the thing: networking is just talking. It's conversations with the right people. Here's the other thing: women are brilliant at talking.

What's missing in this happy story about talking is self-assurance and a clear mind. Women often lose their nerve, because it feels as though there is so much at stake when we actively network. And we aren't just referring to organised events here; women also tend to struggle in impromptu networking situations, when we don't make the most of bumping into potential contacts when we're in the park, say. Instead, our instinct says run and hide. So how can we learn to take our first-rate chatting skills and use them to extend our networks?

By having a purpose.

The best networkers go into each interaction (chat) with a goal. Yes, this sounds contrived, but when we can set ourselves loose objectives (meet someone new; find out how to tweet more effectively; chat through latest business plan to a relevant PR), then we make proper career headway. Plus, having something concrete to fall back on if the conversation dries up (unlikely) is a confidence boost. When we have a purpose it makes networking more efficient and easier too.

Plus plus, it shifts anxieties away from the personal 'Do they like me?' scenario, to something more external and useful, like, 'Am I achieving my goal?' We know that when you have a goal in mind, you will feel more powerful, more strategic and less emotionally attached to each person you meet.

Here's another thought: if you really want to push the boat out, organise your own (fun) networking event. For this type of thing the theme can be as wacky as takes your fancy; garland making, cocktail shaking, supper club – these events are bang on trend and offer bountiful networking opportunities. Go in with a friend, and each commit to inviting five, or even ten contacts, you'll be swimming in new work connections before you can say, 'Pass the hydrangea.' Boutique networking (especially in your favourite local bar or florist) is enjoyable and effective because there's less pressure – and you can't hide behind the mushroom vol-au-vents.

WORKOUT Conversations with a Purpose

Disclaimer: For this workout you will need other people. That's the thing about networking – we can't do it alone.

This workout needs ten minutes of your time at your next networking event. Tonight you have three missions (three minutes each).

1. Start small. Approach one person you already know but find out one new thing about them.
2. Get bolder. Find someone you only know vaguely or haven't seen in a while and reconnect. Then tell them one development for you since you last spoke.
3. Now the deep end. Reach out to one completely new person and get their deets.

Finally, take a minute to seal the deal by sending each a follow-up email securing recontact. Networking 101 done.

HOW TO Follow Up

It doesn't matter what your character type, where you meet your new contacts or how successfully you engaged them in conversation, when you don't follow up, you haven't networked at all.

Our ultimate career networks are not made up of people we've chatted to once at a party. Meeting is just the first step. To cement the relationship, we need to get ourselves to second base. This usually just involves a 'nice to meet you' email or a quick telephone call. The point is, when we follow up, especially with an interesting offer, invite or introduction, we tell that person that we were engaged in the conversation and value the connection.

The post-chat email also keeps that lead warm. And warm contacts result in shiny white unicorns.

WORKOUT The Art of the Follow-Up

The art of the follow-up is in actually doing it. And adding the personal touch.

(1 minute) Find three business cards you've collected in the past week from your heightened networking activities.

(2 minutes each) Craft an email to each of them. Make it brief. Say you enjoyed meeting them. Include a detail about them you remember – their son's exam, an upcoming holiday – to show you listened. Then if you want a follow-up ask for that too. Remember though immediate follow-up isn't always your goal. Cementing that contact is the key.

(1 minute each) Now add each contact into your New Contact Filing System. This is either a Rolodex – remember those – spreadsheet or app where you keep track of who you've met. Include the little details that will make reaching out again seem natural and the date you spoke. The contact you make today might not be of use now but you don't want to be racking your brains for their details (lost somewhere at the bottom of your spare handbag) when you really need them.

(Optional) Set a reminder to contact them again in, say, three months' time. A quick catch-up email now and then keeps things fresh.

HOW TO Be a Girl Online

The power of social media is in its ability to deliver us to anyone and everyone: customers, celebrities, potential clients, old employees, new employees, politicians – all these people (and many many more) are there waiting on the other end of their phones for our 140 characters. OK, waiting might be stretching the point, but available at least, to connect and chat. If you're putting off the online inevitable, you're missing out big time.

One of the major benefits to online networking is that we can do it in our pyjamas. Or in a park. Or while we're waiting in line at the supermarket. Having said that, despite the ease and accessibility, there are still strategies and potential pitfalls at play. And rather predictably, men and women seem to mirror their offline networking preferences when we flick, swipe and tap at others in the ether.

A study on the use of social networking sites by gender found that women prefer to spend their time on Facebook, Tumblr, Instagram and Twitter – the chatty, visual platforms. Whereas men lean heavier on LinkedIn, as it suits their straight-talking, business-focused minds.

While we're certainly more likely to hear about new jobs opening on LinkedIn, it would be short-sighted to say that this is the only channel to the top. If you work in travel, say, then images of far-flung beaches on Instagram might be just what your career needs. There are so many opportunities online, and while a photo upload or quick tweet can take just a matter of seconds, we can't possibly engage across all platforms all at the same time: sometimes, networking requires some skills of selection.

Social media is a new frontier and that's why we've called on the experts for the most up-to-date advice on how to be an effective social media networker.

INSTAGRAM

Amy Cole was Instagram's team member number six. She now leads its Brand Development for Europe, the Middle East and Africa. In her role, she works closely with marketeers across brands, agencies and other organisations to help inspire and advise on its strategies, to help Instagram deliver against its business and campaign objectives. For her, the power of Instagram is its worldwide, 400-million-person community and that it was built for mobile.

Here are Amy's tips:

'Instagram gives you the tools and the platform to communicate visually and build a personal brand. So start by asking yourself – what do I want to be known for? What makes me unique? Instagram suits all businesses that are all sizes: travel, retailers, car manufacturers; it's a place you can come to connect with your passion and for brands to tell their story. Its unique power is that it can transcend language and geography and become a meeting point for like-minded individuals.

'The way to build a strong account that facilitates the most number of followers is to make sure that each of your posts are consistent with your personal brand. They should give insight into your world. Use the filters, the types of photos or the perspective to craft the moments that you want to share. Two accounts that I love are @whatalexloves and @5ftinf. Both accounts are run by women who have been really clear and consistent with their own brand and the visual story they want to tell. Once you've drawn them in, the additional details you add – the location, people, caption – all help to tell a deeper story. For captions, don't use more words than you need to tell your story. There are great examples of accounts that use long-form captions – @natgeo, @time and even @instagram – but this is part of their overall Instagram brand identity. Make sure your captions are consistent in the tone and voice – your posts should be a reflection of you or your brand.

'People often focus purely on the number of followers they have, but it's more important to think about the quality and value of those followers. I would rather have five followers that I can build a relationship with – that know and love my brand, that will be advocates for me among their own network – than fifty followers who will never interact with my brand. When trying to grow your follower audience, I recommend first focusing on building awareness and interest.

'Be focused about the audience you want to reach, and then think about where they're spending their time and attention. Make sure you're talking about or linking to your Instagram account across the other communication channels you use – social and digital media, newsletters, websites. If you have a physical location or goods that are delivered, showcase your Instagram photos and include your Instagram username on displays or leave-behinds in the packaging.

'People on Instagram are careful about who they follow, so before building awareness you need to make sure the content you're posting is compelling and that you have a clear content strategy. If someone discovers your account but doesn't think the content is relevant or engaging, they will have no reason to follow you. You learn the most by just getting out there and testing what works, so get started. And more importantly, have fun with it! What's great about Instagram is that it makes it so easy to be creative, to get inspired and to connect with people from all over the world.'

TWITTER

Julia White Cohen has spent over a decade working in social media. The former Head of International Social Media for Yahoo UK now helps brands find their voice managing media partnerships for Twitter. She says the same principles she uses with brands like Innocent, the Royal family and even the Church to support, apply equally to individuals.

Here are Julia's tips:

'Success on Twitter is about voice and niche. The most important thing is to find your voice. Who are you? Then make it authentic. Be really honest with your followers. Now, let people in. Make yourself a full, rounded person on Twitter. So whatever you are doing, make sure that you are taking your followers along with you. Those exclusive moments. Or even if it's not exclusive, the nuts and bolts of your day. So, for example, if you're publishing a book and you see the first one come off the printer, share that with your network.

'The next thing is to identify your niche. Make yourself an expert on something. You might be very interested in politics, or your job might be about keeping fit or you're knowledgeable about fashion: be that point of contact so that in those conversations you're seen as that expert voice so you can join in to appropriate conversations and add value.

'Now you are ready to build your network. Remember Twitter is about LIVE conversation. So plot the conversation. Keep track of the conversations that are going on the platform and wade in when you have something appropriate and interesting to add.

'Follow people in your industry. Go after them. Following is one of the most direct forms of marketing you can do. They will get an email saying X has followed you and they will see your bio. So have your bio in shape. Make sure it sells you to the absolute max. Make sure it quickly conveys what your niche is and what your voice is. So that people can identify quickly whether you're of interest to them. Once you start following people you can build up your network within that community. Once you've followed them, don't be afraid to reach out to people on Twitter. We've seen some amazing examples where people have been bold. A recent example was another chef who tweeted Gordon Ramsay directly to say that he had been made redundant from his job on the same day he'd told them he had epilepsy. He tweeted Gordon and said, this has happened, what do you think I should do? And Gordon replied, DM me, I'll give you a job. So magical things can happen on Twitter. It can connect people who would never normally be connected. It makes the world a smaller place. It is absolutely accepted that you can use Twitter as a networking space and as a potential job-finding tool.'

LINKEDIN

Senior Manager of LinkedIn's Global Communications Programmes, **Danielle Restivo** drives global PR programmes for its communications team and oversees strategy, execution, campaigns and budgets. She's been at LinkedIn for five years and believes it can help professionals across the world achieve their career goals.

Here are Danielle's tips:

'Our data insights and scale help companies of all shapes and sizes to be more competitive and successful – whether you are a small or medium-sized enterprise employing one person or a multinational company with hundreds of employees. LinkedIn can help you find, attract and train the best talent, build and strengthen your brand and identify and connect with new customers. As an individual, social channels are obviously a great way to connect with your peers. Furthermore, they level the playing field so you can hear from some of the most senior leaders in your industry. As a result, places like LinkedIn can offer a great opportunity to keep in the loop with the latest trends and developments in your sector and keep pace with the changes happening in your industry.

'For businesses, social networks have changed the relationship between them and their next potential hire or customer. People are influenced by the views of their colleagues, connections and peers, which means selling and marketing look different here than they do elsewhere. The good news is that this offers an incredibly powerful platform for growth. LinkedIn is killing the cold call and changing the way brands engage with their target audiences. One example of this is the case of Jess Ratty from Cornwall, who used the power of her LinkedIn network to make a success of her business, Cornwall Camper Company, at the age of thirty. When the bank would not provide her with a loan she used the breadth of her connections to give her the knowledge she needed to set up and run a successful, sustainable business – from accounting to replacing engine parts. Networking is an incredibly important business tool.

'Your LinkedIn profile is a gateway for potential clients, employees and industry partners to contact you. The more complete your profile, the easier it will be for people to find you through search engines. Make sure your summary is complete, and include a photo of yourself to increase your credibility. Customise your public profile URL and claim your piece of digital real estate. Add skills to your profile to highlight your expertise and be found by others seeking those abilities. You can remind people who you are by keeping your profile active with regular status updates. Pair your LinkedIn and Twitter accounts and your LinkedIn status update can go out to both networks at the same time.'

WORKOUT Get Social

(1 minute) Having read the above, identify one network that tallies with you and your career goals. Not the one you like the best, the one that will actually help you with your work. One you don't use much or the way you should.

(4 minutes) Now spend four minutes honing your bio. Is it relevant? Up to date? Does it convey the tone, voice and message you need? And are you sharing the right links?

(5 minutes) Now list five things to share on that network this week. Five great photos for Instagram, five industry updates or five relevant tweets. The best social media strategy is planned in advance AND leaves room for spontaneity. Planning daily posts means the pressure is off and you are free to fill in the gaps and respond to daily events in a creative way.

THOUGHTS The Unspoken Line

As we've already mentioned, we're advocates of the blended approach to networking: both friends and acquaintances are valid contacts in the file. But what happens when the more intimate connections backfire? In networks, just as in life, some trusted, long-standing relationships can become troublesome. Perhaps a contact we felt obliged to do something with no longer suits our outlook or morals. Likewise, a contact in our network might offer a service that we aren't happy with, or (and this is especially true for startups) expect us to give them a cheap deal or some free corporate branding, just because we've known them since school.

Maintaining friendships and being liked are important for women, so how do we prevail when a dot on our network boomerangs? We do it with honesty.

A chef friend invites you for a meal at their new restaurant. You are thrilled until you receive your platter of food. The food is bad. Instead of just ignoring the chef's calls post meal you are honest because you like the chef, and want her in your network. It takes guts to tell it like it is sometimes, but when we can meaningfully engage across the dots on our web, our relationships strengthen. And that's called smart networking.

As a postscript to managing friendships within our networks, it is also worth remembering that we don't have to bring each member of our wider, male-dominated network into our circle of friends. It is OK to view these associations as just that. The best way to do this is to keep things professional. Because of our preferences for close friendships, women have a tendency to create intimacy by sharing. TMI is not always a good thing in networking circles. Yes, we want to sell ourselves, but that need not involve a detailed description of your latest waxing endeavours. All we're saying is be vigilant about which relationships are strictly professional.

THE TIPS

|1| Start small

How deeply we know that the best gifts come in small (preferably beautiful) packages. The same is true of networking. Forwarding a relevant article, highlighting an opportunity or making a quick introduction are all gifts that require little effort on your part but might make a big impact on your contact. Don't wait for the grand gesture. This week, reach out as you think of these and watch your network soar.

|2| Network up

If you need some bigger hitters in your network, don't think that you as the junior person have nothing to offer. Even heavy hitters value exposure, information and feedback. If you can identify what might be of interest to them you'll also be in a minority that have tried. So reach out to one today.

|3| Forget the scattergun approach

A combination of discomfort and enthusiasm means many new networkers aim their approaches far and wide. Yes, network size is important. But more important are depth, relevance and, crucially, synchronicity with your goals. Instead of turning up to an event with the biggest handbag you own and cramming it full of cards, rerun your goals before you enter. Then leave with the objective of securing three contacts that will really make a difference in getting you from A (now) to B (goals conquered).

|4| The deep connection

Networking isn't all about drinks and canapés. Sometimes it is appropriate to target a specific connection. This is best done through your network (see, it's working for you already) either in person or on social media. Once you get your intro, make sure you've done your homework. Being familiar with what that person has done and what you might be able to offer them before you meet sets you up for the most useful meeting possible.

|5| Ditch the elevator pitch

A common reaction to hating networking is practising an elevator pitch. Ditch it now. No one wants to be sold to straight away. Talking to contacts is not the same as pitching your latest project to your boss. Instead focus on common ground. Listening out for similarities between you will keep you relaxed as you focus away from yourself. Once you've found that connection – same alma mater, last holiday, love of a particular author – not only will they remember you better, but you have the perfect in for speaking next time.

CHAPTER 8

Look Good, Work Well

How we present ourselves really does impact on how we are viewed and treated in the workplace. For so many reasons (to pull a few from the book so far: confidence, authority and perceptions), your style decisions are important questions that need to be understood. In this chapter we will explore the complex rules of career dressing, before sharing the style secrets of our two fashion influencers.

THE BACKGROUND Work Style

Work style is a divisive subject. It is also a subjective subject. And for some, it is a minefield too. But what we wear to work matters. When we get it right, it sends positive messages to others: I'm confident, I can pick up social cues, let's do this.

In the same vein, sloppy clothes suggest sloppy work: when we don't take pride in what we wear, it puts our confidence on the back foot. Fashion is a tricky one because so many of us are wary of giving in to its capriciousness. The thing is that how we look really does inform others about who we are, what we do and whether we're worth backing.

In this chapter we will approach work style as we have done every other facet of career success: context, research and a practical How To guide. We will also sympathetically critique the work fashion choices of some of our favourite professional celebrities to help give tangible and visual support to our theories and advice.

And then because we couldn't leave you without some real expert tips, we've called in our most fashionable and knowledgeable friends in the shape of *Vogue* contributor and Fashion Director at the *Daily Telegraph*

Lisa Armstrong and personal stylist **Annabel Hodin**, who has dressed everyone from Daryl Hannah to Rachel Weiss, and also consults to London's top corporate firms on work style.

But first, some wise words from clinical psychologist **Dr Jennifer Baumgartner**, author of *You Are What You Wear: What Your Clothes Reveal About You*. 'What we wear to work impacts the way we respond to the self and the way others respond to us. Both alter our cognitions, emotions and behaviours, in and out of the workplace. We can use our work attire like an actor uses a costume. We are better able to inhabit the role, believe that we are the character we are playing, and convince the audience of the same. Our work clothes need to accomplish the following three things: allow us to physically and psychologically do our jobs, properly represent the brand, and convince others that we are the best person for the job. Overall, our attire should enhance and not distract.'

When we take care of our appearance, when we look our best, we feel more powerful – and more capable too. It's a lot to expect from a set of threads that may have been hanging in your wardrobe for some years, but clothes really do have the ability to up confidence and positively communicate with others when a conversation is out of reach. While this chapter certainly isn't a call to cull and then shop, we all need to accept that how we look at work impacts on our success – whether they spend their days in a photographic studio or a barrister's chambers, powerful, accomplished women just don't look dishevelled at work.

If you doubt this fact, mentally flick through the key women in your industry. Dissect what your role models wear, look on television and check out the Sunday supplements for images of influential working women. What you'll notice is that high-achieving types take care of their appearance; they wear clothes that are persuasive indicators of their industries – they look right, and they look comfortable too.

Christine Lagarde is the first woman to head up the International Monetary Fund. Her work is challenging and open to public criticism; she has a brilliant mind, carries an enormous degree of fiscal responsibility on her shoulders and exists in an industry almost completely devoid of style opportunities. Yet Lagarde always looks fabulous. She has to square up to some pretty intimidating (male) opposers during the course of each day, but Lagarde and her wardrobe aren't fazed. This is a French woman who is in control of her image, and her rocking set of suits provides a tailored backbone to a look that commands authority and never looks dull.

If you want the nitty gritty, Lagarde wears crisp shirts, neat trousers and adds a casual touch by throwing one of a series of psychedelic scarves artfully over her shoulder. Or, if she's in the mood, she'll tie it neatly at the neck. Her footwear is simple, modern and almost always flat; she carries big, fashion-y bags and in the evening, she can nail a tux with more panache than Bond.

Her style choices are so good – just the right side of daring – that they provoke healthy admiration in the rest of us. Simply by reading her style cues, we know that Lagarde is a woman with guts and a woman with brains. A woman with Miranda's aptitude, Charlotte's attention to detail, Carrie's joie de vivre and, somewhere in her knowing smile, there's a touch of Samantha's chutzpah too. Lagarde unashamedly utilises her personal style to enhance her career – and we couldn't respect her more.

We will explain later in the chapter how you can free your latent Lagarde. Before that, though, there's a lot more to explain on the subject. Like how what we wear can make us more confident. Because work style isn't just about opening a conversation with others; what we wear to the office also kicks off the dialogue we have with ourselves. How we look really does alter how we feel.

This is how Dr Jennifer Baumgartner puts it. 'When you decide to wear your favourite dress to work rather than your frumpy suit, you look in the mirror and you like what you see, which puts an extra spring in your step. On your way to work, you receive multiple approving glances and compliments, further improving your mood. At work you agree to lead a project that you may not have taken if you had not felt good about yourself that day. Your attire triggers a string of events that improves your confidence and improves on your ability to deliver your skill.'

Obviously, the opposite is true too. When we glance at ourselves in the lift mirror at work and the vision staring back at us makes us want to weep, it doesn't suggest a day of killer attitude and panache. Yes, morals tell us that what we wear to work shouldn't matter, that success is the culmination of efficiency, aptitude and pluck. The truth is, humans are a visual species and we make judgements on how everyone (ourselves included) looks.

This is no bad thing in fact, because while deep-rooted confidence issues and rookie networks can take months, years even, to get right, nailing work style can be a speedy game changer. Nothing lifts the mood and pushes away those niggling doubts like the right pair of trousers or a dress with attitude. Looking good is not a weakness. Just as looking good doesn't negate intelligence.

Amal Clooney, international human rights lawyer, activist, barrister and advisor to Special Envoy Kofi Annan on Syria, passes through each weighty day looking like a professional dream. Her sensitive work representing the likes of the former Libyan intelligence chief Abdullah Al Senussi, Yulia Tymoshenko and Julian Assange does nothing to diminish her weak spot for curvy dresses and bare legs.

Amal Clooney refuses to pick between her style and her substance. Many women working in tough corporate environments, in any work environment for that matter, restrict their fashion palette for fear of being deemed flaky. Not Amal. Her colourful, fashion-aware choices positively set herself apart.

And if Amal and Christine Lagarde can throw the odd bit of leopard or leather into the mix and remain venerated for their intellect, then you can too. Clothes are an extension of our minds; how we shop and the way we put together our outfits are indicators of how our minds tick.

STYLE DOES THE TALKING Coding

This is how **Leandra Medine**, one of fashion's most influential bloggers and founder of Man Repeller sees it: 'You make a choice about how you will present yourself, to wear a thing that will pick up slack where words might fail you, or conversely, surprise the onlookers who become your audience. It's an intellectual choice whether or not you're willing to see it and everyone participates in its power.'

And that power is transmitted across hierarchies and into every corner of the office. When we dress thoughtfully and aren't scared of standing out, our peripheral associates (bosses included) can quickly and correctly identify us. They notice what we wear because they have little else to go on. When we dress well, when we look right, we tell others that we're unique; that we aren't a grey, invisible person who only exists in relation to that job.

Work style, as with many of success's other building bricks, is part honesty and part make-believe. Dressing thoughtfully doesn't come naturally to everyone, so don't be hard on yourself if you need to copy, literally head-to-toe, what Michelle Obama wore last week. Dressing the part is much more important than pressurising ourselves to become the next Anna Wintour. What we need to be able to hone is an awareness of when and where our style requires an amp up or down.

Tweaking her look is something that medical oncologist **Debra Josephs**, who has a weak spot for pink mohair and backcombing, has absolutely perfected. When she's doing her ward rounds, Debra plays up the colour; patients love her bold choices and she feels comfortable and cheery. But when, for example, she has a verbal examination with a leading consultant, her more sober style comes into play.

'Whenever I do a verbal exam, I always wear my glasses and don't do my make-up.' She isn't deceiving anyone; Debra is just putting out the right codes for the right occasion. The great thing about clothes is that they are temporary; we say let them ebb and flow depending on what's going on.

As the dust fell after the American fiscal disaster of 2008, a new set of style rules rose out of the shaky ground. Almost immediately, anyone who worked in finance found that looking too flash felt vulgar. They pushed their expensive suits to the back of their wardrobes, and it became Dress Down Friday every day of the week. For women, inconspicuous wrap dresses took charge (thank you, Diane von Furstenberg) and everyone on Wall Street and beyond became a filtered-out version of their former selves.

The style indicators had shifted, and those who didn't keep up looked like they hadn't grasped the wider implications of the crash. Interestingly, the reverse is now true, and across America style consultants are being mobilised to re-educate city workers in the art of power dressing. The point illustrates the importance of reading and engaging in your industry and office style cues.

Architect **Deborah Saunt** knows only too well the impact of backing the wrong fashion horse at work. Generally when she's on a building site, Saunt is the only woman there. To start with, she dressed like one of the boys. She blended in. But blending in had the wrong effect.

'When I started out, I tended towards fashions that were less feminine: my style choices had decidedly butch overtones. But wearing jeans on a building site did not work for me. I was never going to be one of the lads, and dressing like them made nothing of my unique position as the only woman on the building site. I pretty quickly worked out that I needed to celebrate being a woman. I started carrying big, stylish handbags – everyone's behaviour towards me immediately changed. The guys suddenly respected me. Even today, my bags are an important weapon in my style armoury. I am accepted (celebrated even) as a woman and work is actually much easier. When I look feminine it prompts the best response in others.'

This is not about dressing for men. Nor is it about fashion kudos. As with everything else in this book, when we dress authentically, thoughtfully and with an eye to our success, others respond to the confident us that ensues. There are many languages at play in the workplace and when we can speak fluently with what we wear, it helps us control and manage how others respond to us.

STYLE DOES THE TALKING Enclothed Cognition
But what about how we respond to ourselves? What we wear changes how we feel.

Most of us can testify to the (unscientific) correlation between a pair of Jessica Rabbit heels and our degree of work oomph. And researchers have actually proved this link, and they did it with simple white lab coats. In their recent study, professors issued these standard white lab coats to all the participants. To some, they referred to them as doctor's coats and the rest were told they were painter's smocks. The participants were then asked to perform the same simple task.

What the researchers found was that during the execution of the task, the 'doctors' were more careful and attentive than their 'artist' peers. The reason for this, they believe, is simple: what they wore swayed how they felt, and that in turn fed in to how they completed the task.

'When we dress in a certain way, it helps shift our internal self,' explains Dr Baumgartner. 'We see that when we do makeovers, and even actors say that putting on a costume facilitates expression of character. The same is true for everyday life.' It is absolutely critical that we feel ourselves (preferably an emboldened version of our everyday) when we arrive at the office in the morning. And if that means you need to throw a slick of red lipstick into the mix, then so be it.

STYLE DOES THE TALKING The Fearful Dresser

It's no wonder so many of us hide under a shroud of black when we dress for work. Women have it harder because we have so many more style options to choose from. In most corporate offices, it's simple for men: ubiquitous jacket, crisp shirt, a neat trouser shape and they're done. Even in less formal settings, men find solidarity in understated staples.

For us, there are thousands of potential pressures and choices at play. And it's not just that we have more options to choose from. As with so many elements within career progression and satisfaction, when it comes to what we wear, we overthink things. We're also nervous risk takers (is the red pencil skirt too much?) and have a propensity to suffer from style overwhelm: too much choice + too little conviction = black shift dress every time.

We say (and the professionals agree) that the best way to fight the work style fire is with a go-to uniform. **Hillary Clinton** has had some fashion clangers in the past; she's tested our visual limits with giant silver polka dots and a plethora of tangerine suits, but these haven't stopped her. Clinton is a fearless beast and today she has arrived somewhere chic: sleek hair, sleek suit, sleek shirting and colours that don't make our eyes wobble.

If you get the heebie-jeebies when you think about what to wear to work, learn to be selective. Find your Hillary pieces, the ones that make you feel good, and then build a strong, organised career uniform around these.

STYLE DOES THE TALKING First Impressions

The cliché is true: first impressions are made in a snap: one research study says that we draw our conclusions on others in 0.1 of a second. We literally have the blink of an eye to tell people what we're all about – which is a lot of pressure on a silk chiffon blouse, if silk chiffon blouses are your thing. We don't want to sound dramatic here, but those of us who think that they can claw back some ground once they open their mouths and impart their wisdom are sadly, says the study, wrong. First impressions stick.

Apparently, these hasty first judgements, based just on our clothes, grooming and stature, are almost impossible to dent: no amount of talking or experience will budge that knee-jerk opinion based entirely on how we look. Being crumpled, not washing our hair, picking an inappropriately short skirt or wearing a heavy Friday morning hangover are all career dealbreakers served on a plate of sartorial clues.

STYLE DOES THE TALKING Hierarchy

Today, many of us work in less formal office settings. We sit in open-plan creative studios, write articles in busy newsrooms and trade stocks on rows of identikit computers: our days are spent in spaces that do not obviously delineate the bosses from the graduates. This playful interweaving of managers and interns is modern and sparky. It can also be highly confusing.

'Americans rely on clothing as an economic and social indicator because there aren't official marks of rank such as a caste system or aristocracy,' says Dr Baumgartner. It makes sense; we can't go around reminding everyone on the floor that we're the manager, just as the work experience shouldn't need to explain that she's just starting out. When we dress appropriately to our role – or better, the role we're eyeing up for the future – we help make sense of these undelineated, open-plan workspaces. We say aim for a look (don't forget grooming, accessories and make-up all feed into your appearance) that pushes you just above your parapet wall. Always notch up, not down.

Our clothes are visual career ambassadors, so make sure they're imparting the right message. Towards the end of the chapter, our experts will explain how to actually nail this. What's important at this point is to acknowledge the role of clothes in today's modern offices. And while you're thinking about your environment, be wise to your company's style tolerance levels. Is denim acceptable or abhorred? Are heels expected or can you jog in wearing trainers?

While we aren't expecting Amal Clooneys everywhere we look, it doesn't take too much to become a more sartorially alert version of your usual self.

STYLE DOES THE TALKING Sexy Beasts

On a Friday night, it is perfectly fine that sex and clothes (or a lack of them) are intrinsically interlinked. At work, though, sex and clothes are uneasy bedfellows. Research says that in high-status jobs, women who dress sexily in the office are deemed less competent and less moral than those who dress professionally. Like so much of this topic, there is no catchall guide for getting ready in the morning; each of our parameters has different degrees of tension. But we're pretty sure that there's a universal limit on cleavage and thigh exposure. What we're saying is tread gently.

HOW TO Get Dressed for Work

To arrive at a sleek, chic work look, we need to manage choice. As emancipated women with our names above the door we have the freedom to shake it all about on a career front, but what we've lost over the years is that go-to manual of how to dress for work.

Several decades back, working women had rubbish jobs and looked fabulous. Those 1940s fit and flare skirts and seamed stockings were the cultural norm; women knew they were expected to dress in a certain way because they existed (mainly to type and look good) in a male chauvinist society built on sexism and Bourbon.

Sixty years later, and some of us are confused. We're not sure what suits us, what's expected of us and how to nail smart-cas. Which is why it's worth engaging in a little objective self-appraisal. Here is a set of mildly interrogating questions to get your fashion ball rolling.

> Who looks good in your office and why?
> How would you rate your current work style: good, bad, ugly?
> Why do you make those choices in the morning?
> Are you comfortable at work?

For the record, we (that's us, the writers, Alice and Phanella) couldn't own two more opposing sets of work wardrobes. While Phanella is all glossy suits and heels, Alice generally spends her working days in harem trousers and a pair of Adidas kicks. Each of us feels good and slots smoothly into our unique office surroundings. When we work together, we seem to meet somewhere in the middle: Alice notches up the gloss, Phanella usually leaves her blazer at home, and while each of us still looks like ourselves, we become a *Step Up* unit that can take on the world, or so we like to think.

When we develop a strong, go-to look it helps us stand out and be noticed. A good way of doing it is by focusing on one key element. For Yahoo's Marissa Mayer it's a particular colour (green), while over at J Crew, Creative Director Jenna Lyons relies on a flexible combo of jacket, cigarette pants and geek glasses. Just as it's obvious who sits on the creative side and who is more corporate in our *Step Up* duo, when you start to reconstruct your work style, focus on a recognisable visual identity. When we get that right, it communicates to others that we are consistent, reliable and overflowing with self-knowledge.

WORK OUT The Strip Back

Instead of five separate workouts, in this chapter we offer you five workouts in one. Because dressing for work is a holistic process – you can't strip your wardrobe back (for example), without then going out to refill it.

STEP ONE Industry Analysis

One of the reasons our style tips are limited to the general is because, as we've said, each workplace and industry will have its own unwritten fashion rules. It is imperative you uncover yours. So spend ten minutes on day one of your style overhaul surveying the landscape.

First, check out your office. What do the successful women wear? How closely does your work wardrobe reflect theirs? We're not looking for identikit outfits but if your boss is in tailored Theory and you're rocking a denim Topshop mini, you may not be giving off the right vibes. How glossy do others look? How tailored do they dress? Don't neglect make-up, jewellery and shoes.

Then, take five minutes to surf the web. Check out well-known, successful faces in your industry. Carry out the same analysis. Understand how your industry dresses for success.

STEP TWO Style Analysis

Who wants to dissect their body shape? Not us. But, ultimately, our frames determine what we wear. With this in mind, we suggest ten minutes thinking about our best bits: legs, arms, height – or lack thereof – because when we dress to our own advantage we look better and feel more comfortable too. After all, there's no point wasting time on trousers if your body says dresses all the way.

STEP THREE Wardrobe Analysis

Now pull out all your work clothes and systematically try them on. The next few parts will (we admit) take more than your allotted ten minutes. But since they only need to be carried out once – and image is important – it's worth finding the time. Find a good pair of trousers

WORKOUT The Strip Back continued

(now might also be a good time to pull out a nice bottle of wine), and try them on with all your tops so that you can divide the keepers from the charity shop pile. Then reverse the process: keep on one good top and interchange your skirts and trousers. Look at how your clothes have worn too; no successful woman turned up to work in bobbles. As you work through your wardrobe, keep half your mind on what's missing. Perhaps go as far as making a few notes – there's nothing like shopping with a purpose to break through choice.

STEP FOUR Accessory Analysis
Don't neglect your accessories in this. And yes, it is worth trying them on too. Check for wear and tear – missing stones or scuffed shoes might work for weekends but don't say success at work. Accessories shouldn't be an afterthought. They are your secret weapons in your work style arsenal. Plain black trousers and fine knit = boring. But those same black staples with a great necklace, bag and heels = boardroom-ready. So be brutal about the accessories you own that don't say what you want about Work You. And remember to add the ones you need but don't yet have – killer work bag, great flats – to your list.

STEP FIVE Now Shop
Now that you've confidently analysed everything that you own, you can begin on the new strategic plan of action. Although we admitted at the top of this chapter that style can be a quick fix compared to, say, confidence, we aren't suggesting that you go out and buy an entirely new wardrobe tomorrow. Like so many of our career success principles, style can take time and effort to get right. Sure, an upgrade from jeans to a carefully chosen pair of slacks should give you an instant lift, but your bigger style picture will form properly over time. Don't rush or feel pressured into thinking otherwise.

A good tip if you do want to let rip in the shops is to sell on your old work gear. One woman's work wear nemesis is another woman's treasure, right? And with these extra funds, you can purchase and update guilt-free. Remember, when we buy better, we end up buying less.

When we theorise work style it becomes easier to digest and understand. If you're nervous in this area, win with maths and build your own work style formula: dress + cardigan + flats, say, or jeans + soft blazer + heels. A uniform, as we've already said, will put an end to that daily twenty-minute panic when we pull everything out of our wardrobes and then defer to the trusted black wrap dress, leaving our bedrooms cratered with clothes.

Role models are great when we're working out our style uniform. It doesn't matter whether she works in your office or not; is or isn't in the public eye; or whether she inhabits an altogether more fictional position (corporates might want to check out the restrained elegance of *House of Cards'* Claire Underwood) – when we find someone who inspires us it gives us hope and structure.

Try also looking over your old family photographs. In the Fifties, women found a new kind of smart fashion freedom. After years of war-enforced restrictions, they went wild for full skirts, dramatic grooming and colour. These style tips easily transcend time: a retro red lip on a casual entrepreneur makes jeans and trainers zing. Just as some artfully flicked black eyeliner can lift a simple corporate suit. It's all very well fitting the office mould, but don't forget to chuck a bit of personality into the mix. Natty, kooky and fun should be appropriate style adjectives wherever you sit on the career ladder.

Michelle Obama doesn't need to open her mouth for us to know that she has political nous and passion in equal measure. Those prom skirts, her agility with a studded belt, the way she mixes print and colour and her big sparkly necklaces tell the story of a powerful, independent woman who enjoys her work: her visual identity reinforces and reflects her position. Michelle Obama doesn't let a thing like the world's audience get in the way of how she asserts her individuality. And neither should you.

Neither, for that matter, does she only focus on her clothes. Michelle Obama has grooming down pat too. Her hair is always neat but bouncy, she indulges in the make-up department, but never too much and her nails are always perfect. With this in mind, we spoke to one of the world's favourite beauty gurus, **Bobbi Brown**, for advice on how to nail (sorry) work grooming. Because there's no point getting your fashion groove on if you turn up to work with dirty hair.

'Women are pretty with and without make-up, but they can be empowered to another level – both pretty and powerful – with the right products. Women want to look and feel like themselves, only a more confident version. The most compelling aspect of beauty is self-confidence. When you feel good about yourself there's no limit to what you can do. The secret to beauty is simple – it's about being who you are.'

When we take care of our appearance (in many cases this can cost almost nothing), it sends a message of attention to detail and all-round togetherness. We get it wrong when we look like we haven't taken the time or made an effort. Of course, fashion isn't everyone's thing, but we can all engage in simple, effective grooming.

HOW TO   Advice from the Top

There is nothing that personal stylist Annabel Hodin and fashion journalist Lisa Armstrong ('Whatever you wear to the office, make it good, make it subtle') don't know about style. Here are their tips on how to get it right at work.

GETTING READY
Annabel

> You can eliminate personal crises by being prepared and dressing appropriately and comfortably. You have to work twice as hard at being efficient if you're wearing an uncomfortable shirt or skirt.
> Before you get dressed, think about your commute: how will your travel plans (tube, bus, bicycle) impact on your comfort and style? Then consider if your day is going to involve any activities that might impact on your clothes. Be practical.
> On the bad days, when you're feeling insecure and weak, don't reach for the big sweater. Notch yourself up, not down. Put on a look that doesn't need touching even if it's too grand for the day ahead.

❭ Weddings, holidays and other fun social events tend to make us focus on what we wear and how we can look our best. Harness this focus and direct it towards your work wardrobe. It takes a lot of discipline, but being strategic makes things so much easier in the end.

❭ Appreciate where your job role sits in the company strata, and then dress as if you're aiming a few rungs higher, whilst sticking within the decorum of what's expected.

❭ Get things ready in advance and accept that you need a uniform. Why fight the inevitable? Men tend to have a suit as their core and then swap shirts and ties to keep things fresh and modern. You need to adapt this template so that the male suit becomes a dress, if that's your style, or a skirt and blouse, trouser and knit…

Lisa

❭ Don't draw attention to yourself through your clothes. If you look like you're someone who spends too much time caring about how you look, people won't take you seriously. American *Vogue*'s Grace Coddington wears all black because she is so consumed with focusing on her magazine pages. It's always best to spend your time on your work rather than your look – or at least, to make it appear that way.

❭ We all have different personalities and style; when you spend some time working out what your look is, you'll cut down on getting-ready time.

❭ In terms of your style, sometimes you have to compromise for work. But never feel like you should take on a false persona, as you'll end up looking awkward.

ARRIVING
Annabel

❭ When you walk in the door, what comes in is something that other people see. When you get it wrong, you have to undo that whole effect, which takes time and energy. Sometimes it's impossible to undo the damage. Realise the importance of first impressions.

❭ Smile at people. I don't love every job I do, but I always arrive as if I love it.

❭ Coats: you're not much good if you're wet or cold, so invest in a good coat. Understand what length and style works best with your core look. A straight boyfriend coat, say, will complement a trouser, just as a pea coat looks great over a dress.

Lisa

> You can't walk into a job looking a mess, because being able to co-ordinate an outfit is a sign of knowledge and organisation.

> You've got to tune into the influencers in the office, and slightly take your cue from them. Different offices have different unspoken codes. Some offices like to dress in a similar way, while in others you're expected to find your own look.

> You want to look polished, whatever that takes. And you want your clothes to reveal your personality too. Even those who wear identikit uniforms can set themselves apart by some artfully applied kohl above the eyes, or with a twist of their hair – an added something that feels authentic to you.

PERFECTING THE LOOK

Annabel

> Tailoring is still very important in the corporate world. Be aware of what is still formal but feels modern. Before, it would have been a stretch top under a jacket; today, it's all about breaking things up with a soft blouse.

> You can still look very smart when your jacket and skirt don't match. Play with soft complementing colours and you won't get it wrong.

> Looking unique is crucial, but actually it doesn't take a lot to look different. Your head and shoulders are already exclusively yours, so all you need to do is show that you're not completely lacking in character. The easiest way to do this is through your choice of accessories: go a bit bold here and the rest will follow.

> Learn to style yourself. Try rolling back your sleeves to reveal a nice lining, or pull them up towards the elbow for that modern three-quarter length. Or be a bit dramatic around the neck. A slim poloneck is a modern take on a shirt.

> It's the details that will give you the edge. A tiny bit of stitching here or a quietly embellished collar will visually set you apart from the white shirt gang.

> Dresses are important in corporate offices because they are feminine and can be extremely flattering. If you find a dress shape that works, look to invest in five or six of a similar shape. Then, you're home and dry.

> Understand fashion proportions: if oversize looks are in, don't do it head to toe. Make a nod to the trend with a wide coat, or a pair of blouson trousers, but in each case, counter the billow with something slim and sleek. Looking like you're ready for a catwalk show will not boost your credibility at work.

> You need to digest things, and that includes trends. If you suddenly see pink and fuchsia across your monthly fashion magazine, wait a while before you try it at work. Knee-jerk fashion is too impulsive – always appear considered and in control.

> If you love print, choose one you like and keep it contained. The best way to work print into a look is to pick a mid-tone colour within the design and keep everything else in that palette. Half shut your eyes when you look at the print and see which colour is coming through. When you manage print carefully you still look co-ordinated.

> Theme your style: try having a monochrome week, or a white shirt week. It gives you structure; it's less important to look different every day as it is to look sleek and pulled together.

Lisa

> Unless you're really good at it, don't choose too many wild colours. Even in the most creative office, the majority of well-dressed women keep their base clothes quite neutral. Of course, you can do black, but it's also quite nice to try those off colours that fall in between. Greys, nudes, creams and putty are good core colours.

> Big, bold patterns make clothes too memorable and it shortens their life span; details should be slyly eye-catching rather than conversation stoppers. Don't turn the dial up too much. Dark, raw-hemmed trousers = good; crimson raw hems = shouty, needy.

> Don't wear anything that restricts your movement or the way you sit at work.

> How do you tweak your look in an interesting way? By noticing the details. Choose your catwalk or street style cues carefully and then add them in with caution.

> Don't unbutton your blouse too far – it looks unsophisticated. The men in the office will be distracted and the women won't appreciate it.

SHOPPING

Annabel

> Shop in outfits, that way everything in your wardrobe should be effortlessly interchangeable. Once you've worked out your style core (this could be a shirt and trousers; a blouse and skirt; a shift dress; a suit) you should be able to pick and choose how to brighten or sober up your uniform depending on the day ahead.

> Know your trends. It's OK to discount skinny trousers if your thighs aren't up to the challenge, but if skinny trousers are back, put your flares on hold and opt for straighter cuts that still work with your body shape and core style. When you use fashion as a guide, colleagues will know you're aware of life beyond the office.

> You never want to look a mess at work. When I find things I like in a shop, I'll scrunch them up in my hand. If they crease, I put them straight back on the rails.

> Magazine fashion shoots might seem too showy to provide practical work inspiration but take away the accessories and crazy hair, and you're left with good, classic pieces. They might be classic pieces from Prada that are total bank-busters, but if you index them in your mind you'll shop better.

> It is very important to have a style icon. Make sure she's a bit like you, and then find pieces that are similar to what she wears. It's good to have a style role model because she'll keep you in line.

> Don't trust the opinions of shop assistants: flattery is the worst kind of advice.

Lisa

> Buy little but buy well. Even if you can't afford to buy lavishly, you can still make the effort to look polished and thoughtfully dressed.

> We all have different personalities and style. When you spend some time working out what your look is, you'll cut down on getting-ready time.

> Think navy and greys (obviously), but also teal, burgundy, khaki, bottle green, chocolate and cream. Save the orange and yellow for accent pieces.

> Don't bankrupt yourself for your work wardrobe. You can dress to look a million dollars if you know what you're looking for and you're not afraid of sales or outlets.

❯ Buy for the life you lead not the life you aspire to have. Buy for the person you are – learn what works, what basics you need, and slowly build your wardrobe to reflect and enhance yourself.

❯ If you're a trouser woman, then make sure the shapes you wear are really current. You can push it in ways that you couldn't before.

❯ Invest properly in coats, tailoring and accessories – a glossy leather belt with sleek gold hardware makes everything you wear it with look more glamorous and sleek. You'll still be wearing it in twenty years.

ACCESSORIES

Annabel

❯ A medium-height chunky heel is so much more professional than teetering around on stilettos. Flats are actually very good as long as they have a bit more weight than a ballet shoe; try loafers and simple leather shapes, steering away from anything too sloppy or moccasin-like.

❯ Never suffer and hobble in uncomfortable footwear.

Lisa

❯ A place to have some fun is through your accessories. There are two reasons for this; accessories rarely dominate, which means you can more easily play with colour and sparkle on a necklace or pair of shoes than you can on your go-to work blazer. Also, over time, accessories actually wear out, which means you're entitled to replace and start the fun all over again.

❯ Trainers: these days, you can get away with a really good trainer; just make sure they send out subtle messages.

❯ Flats are absolutely fine at work. Even better are flatforms – flat shoes with an extra-thick sole. These give you a bit of height, which is also a bonus, especially if you're working with men. Where possible, you do want to try to be looking at someone in the eye, rather than to their pecs.

❯ Keep your shoe shapes current. A square toe or a slingback could be the difference between being stylish and being stuck in a rut. The block heel is a perfect shoe for work: it's elevated, but practical and flattering, too.

❯ Save on the clothes and spend on the accessories. It's worth investing in accessories because you can always put them away for a few years when they feel out of date. The chances are, they'll be back on trend again and waiting for you at the back of your wardrobe just when you need a style pick-me-up.

GROOMING
Annabel
> If you struggle with make-up, get a lesson at a counter. Once you have some direction, use YouTube videos to perfect your technique. Done well, make-up can be a subtle but powerful grooming tool.
> Foundation on shirt collars, lipstick on teeth – carry a compact mirror in your bag to avoid make-up blunders.
> You have to invest in your hair if you want to look groomed and not messy. It can be casually cut (see Alexa Chung) but just make sure it improves your features. If you can tie your hair back, that looks good; layers need to be long and contemporary so that you have movement but it's controllable.
> Hair must always be clean.

Lisa
> Make-up should not be too distracting, and should always be well applied.
> If you have a manicure it should never be chipped. If you find manicures, or any other grooming device, too time-consuming or expensive, then don't do it.
> Invest in a flattering, low-maintenance haircut that doesn't yell 'HAIR-DO'.

CARE
Annabel
> De-fluff knitwear with brown tape; or the vacuum cleaner nozzle meant for carpets will also do the job.
> Look at your clothes in daylight. That way you'll notice stains, pulls and tears.
> Use a deodorant that doesn't go white.
> Hang clothes immediately when you get home and don't press on seams when you're ironing as it makes them go shiny.
> Soak white items overnight. Whites that don't look white any more must be degraded to weekend wear.

> Use hangers that won't damage clothes (slim wooden ones work well). And remember, a freshly pressed finish adds a refined touch, even to items reaching their expiration date.

Lisa
> Always polish your shoes.

So there you have it. Getting dressed for the office can be an assault course of trouser shapes, diamante and red nail varnish. From the outset, it can feel like a waste of time, effort and money to think so deeply about how we present ourselves each morning. The truth is, presentation is a vital element of success. Like it or not, we all have to act the part, and that means dressing right and dressing well. Without wishing – ever – to advocate that you become one of those women who appears to know what she's talking about because she looks so darn good but can't actually do her own work, it is equally foolish to ignore the influence of style altogether.

Have fun with what you wear. Don't assume because you're a woman in an austere profession that an encrusted belt must be passed over for regulation black leather. Often, the number of opportunities to be able to creatively express ourselves at work are slim. So Google Largarde, Clooney and Michelle Obama, and feed some of their fizz into your improved work uniform. You'll be amazed how others respond.

THE TIPS

|1| Preparation is key

If you struggle to hit the right style note in the morning, try your mum's old trick and lay tomorrow's ensemble out tonight. Planning clothes, jewellery and other accessories into a cohesive look before bed saves time, anxiety and that I-don't-feel-quite-right-in-this feeling that stays with you all day. If, on waking, you change your mind, that's fine, but being prepared is far preferable to throwing together a look for that big pitch in the three minutes between your shower and breakfast.

|2| Organise your closet

Another time-saving trip. Raise your hand if this sounds familiar: you have the perfect outfit in mind but no matter how hard you try, you just can't find that perfect black skirt. Sorting your closet will help you with your daily planning. Economy – no more finding you've gone out and bought the twin of something you already own. A sense of inner peace. The benefits are endless. So at the end of your workout, when you put everything back in your wardrobe, do it in a strategic and thoughtful way.

|3| Declutter your jewellery box

Arranging your accessories is even more crucial. Who hasn't perfected their look, headed to their jewellery box on their way out to retrieve a favourite necklace and discovered it's irretrievably tangled with myriad other necklaces? Ensure this never recurs by taking some time to organise your jewellery box. Individual pieces should be kept separate – ideally hanging or in pouches. Earrings ditto. And always keep your failsafe work pieces in the same place so you can find them when you need them.

|4| Trust your Instincts

Coco Chanel famously advised us to glance in the mirror and remove the most obvious accessory before leaving the house. We stand by that counsel. Similarly, when glancing, if you suddenly think your skirt might be a little short or your top a little see-through, heed your instincts. Others' impressions are made as quickly as our own so get in the habit of the glance and avoid any obvious work style bungles.

|5| Stay true to you

As with so many elements of this book, not least our definitions of success, our networking style and the way we approach work/life balance, career progression is a personal odyssey built on professional know-how. And the same is true with work style. All this advice is brilliant if it enhances your confidence and makes you feel like a stronger, more capable you. But if you're fretting or feeling uncomfortable about looking a certain way, then stop and take stock. Style is about authenticity; don't forget, in the mix of all this glossy advice, that to look your best you need to stay true to you.

CHAPTER 9

Making it Right to the Top

An advert for a sanitary pad is not an obvious place for female leadership reform. But that didn't stop Always. In 2014, the American female hygiene company launched its #LikeAGirl campaign with an emotive advert directed by Lauren Greenfield. In it, Greenfield asked pre-pubescent girls what it meant to run, jump and punch like a girl. Then she asked grown women.

The results showed the chasm between those old enough to be influenced by society and the blissfully uninformed. The untainted youngsters leapt and sprinted with gusto, with one five-year-old neatly summing things up from their perspective: 'It means to run as fast as you can.' The twenty-somethings, of course, had no such passion; to them, running like a girl meant being knock-kneed and shrieking. What the advert so brilliantly encompasses is the negative stereotyping we hold towards ourselves.

And it's this bias that stops us becoming leaders.

Today, we still associate leadership with men. Thanks to the #LikeAGirl campaign, and others like it, we are beginning to highlight this pessimism and challenge the skew by depicting girls as rough-and-tumble go-getters – as equal leaders of the future. In its launch week, the advert amassed 30 million online views.

Lauren Greenfield is an example of an exceptional female leader: she is brave and visionary; she rouses emotion in others and inspires devotion to her cause. She is also an exception in an industry led by men. Many women don't share Greenfield's resolve and many companies and industries don't have the courage to back women in our progression to the top. Which means, in terms of Leadership, we are still limited by society's hopes for the guys. Let-the-men-lead syndrome wins nearly every time.

According to one recent study of 3000 young women across the UK and America, 72 per cent said they felt that society put them into 'boxes' and that this had a negative impact on their lives. Below is the statistical impact of these boxes on female leadership.

> Percentage of women in the world's parliaments: 22%
> Women on UK FTSE 100 boards: 26%
> 90% of female FTSE board members are non-execs with no operational control
> Number of female CEOs of FTSE 100 companies: 5 (unchanged since 2011)
> Norway leads the way with 35% female directors in the OBX
> On boards in China's Hang Seng it's a feeble 11% for women
> In the US (where only 17% of directors in the NASDAQ are female), based on the slow rate of progress over the last three years, it will take twenty-five years to reach gender parity at the senior-VP level and more than 100 years in the boardroom
> Women start businesses with around one-third of the level of finance of their male counterparts, in every size and sector of business. And because these businesses are on a smaller scale they make less money (the entrepreneur gender pay gap is significantly bigger than the gender wage gap for employees)

When we bear in mind that women not only make up half the population and represent almost 50 per cent of the corporate pipeline – young people being recruited into companies at entry level – these statistics are especially uncomfortable. The manner in which we bring up young girls (nice ones don't rock the boat), how the workplace treats us, and not to mention society's unconscious bias towards men as leaders, equates to a great big hurdle in the leadership equality race.

For women who want to lead there are barriers at all levels and in all industries. And when we travel beyond Western countries or talk to women who want to spend extended time with their children, it gets more arduous and complicated.

What we're saying is that leadership has become more than the sum of its parts: yes, it's a crucial pillar of career success (much more of this to follow) but it is also a vehicle for change.

At Google, for example, pregnant employees would still be forced to park miles away from the entrance if Sheryl Sandberg (the first senior employee to be pregnant) hadn't stormed into Larry Page's office and demanded they install special parking near the entrance. And female Cabinet Ministers would still be without a maternity policy if **Yvette Cooper** – the first Cabinet Minister ever to take maternity leave in 2001 – hadn't used her position to approach then senior ministers Harriet Harman and Patricia Hewitt. Together the powerful triumvirate cleared the path for the next generation by pushing for and implementing a full policy for ministerial maternity leave. If we don't allow society to define our expectations of leaders by gender, then future generations (our unborn daughters, for example) will arrive at an untainted workplace where men and women rise because of skill and vision and not because of their sex.

The good news is that when women get to the top, we rock! Yes, research says that in companies where female leaders are well represented, profits rise and the workforce is happier. Which would be heart-warming if female leaders weren't so scant. But we don't have to accept the status quo.

THE FACTS Female Leaders

A problem is that the current leadership situation is subject to so many complicating pressures. One of these is precedent. The leader in every organisation massively impacts on that company's culture and values – the leader also affects who rises to the top. In companies where the leadership is male-dominated, where the precedent tells us that men are leaders here, then it's likely that that trend will continue unchallenged. We already know that we employ and network in our own image, and so in companies where men dominate at the top, the wall of male leadership ends up almost completely impenetrable.

The situation is daunting, but it's by no means a fait accompli. Yes, rebalancing the scales is going to take time, but that shouldn't be a reason to dissuade you if you've got leadership aspirations.

What we need to do is turn the problem on its head. Here's a *Step Up* promise: from this point on we aren't going to dwell on what's against us (OK, we might need to discuss it a little further); instead, let us be the ones who draw you towards leadership and all its opportunities and future promise for women.

We want to inspire you to make a difference in your own career so that you can fulfil the aspirations you hold for yourself. As well as that, we want your leadership flight to help reset precedents, so as to allow other women – our daughters, their daughters too – to lead in our wake.

Some of you may be about to flick to the final chapter, thinking, well, leadership isn't for me – I don't want to get to *that* top, I'm quite happy being led. The thing is, leadership has many guises. Leaders aren't just the ones who make up the C-suite in the boardroom. Leading is about motivating others; it's being visionary and strategic. Really wherever we sit on the career tree, in some capacity or other, we are all leaders – we just don't always label ourselves correctly.

When we present ourselves as capable, willing future leaders (even if we're very happy not directing Hollywood's next blockbuster movie) we single ourselves out as someone determined, capable, imaginative and confident. The crux of good leadership is not the number of people below us; it's how we're regarded and how we regard others back.

Having said that, many of us do aspire to the top, and so we should because in money terms, females fuel profits. In UK companies, senior-executive teams with greater gender equality repeatedly demonstrate better performance: for every 10 per cent increase in gender diversity, EBIT (basically profit) rises by 3.5 per cent. It's a proven fact that female leaders make a tangible difference, but here's the bitter irony: what makes us great at the job also holds us back.

We're nice.
We spend a lot of time talking to our colleagues.
We can over-analyse.
We're sensitive.
We want to inspire.

These are not leadership impediments; these are the qualities of
great leaders. Yet most of us assume our vulnerability is a fly in
our leadership ointment. We're conditioned to think that way – we
take it as truth as that's what we've been told – and it prevents us
from progressing. So here's step one to unleashing your leadership
campaign: readdress the typecast female leader in your head, because
the devil does not always wear Prada.

As a leader, **Deborah Saunt** fights adversity with kindness. 'Once
you're a leader, you can't turn it off, but that doesn't mean you
can't be nice and inspiring too. I need to be able to galvanise my
team to turn a piece of blank paper into a £100 million building
in just a couple of short years. I do this by being available, showing
my vulnerability and giving advice. Depending on the work at
hand, sometimes I'm a more approachable leader and sometimes
more hardcore, but I'm never lost in meetings or protocols –
my team still crave my time and let me know that I'm leading
successfully.'

Saunt revels in her role, but as we've said, many of us don't aspire to
top-level leadership. After all, those nearest the sky inevitably shoulder
extra stress and extra hours. Perhaps, for you, leadership just might
not be what you need at this moment in time. But (big BUT), it is
still important that we all learn to lead, because we never know what
we might want in the future and when we can motivate others, we
enjoy a new type of job fulfilment. Remember, leadership is as much a
behaviour as it is a job role.

What we're saying is that we are more likely to triumph in all
areas of our career when we can capably lead. The nub of a
successful business – yup, we've said this already – isn't money or
technological superiority, it's the effectiveness of the people within
it, and when we can positively influence the nub, we're winning.

For us, it's worth at least having leadership there in your mind; after
all, you can always turn it down if things become too stressful or it
doesn't suit your style of work. It's when there's absolutely no option
for leadership that women restrict their potential.

THE FACTS Disparities

Why aren't there more female leaders?

We think there are only three possible explanations to this simple question.

1. We are not capable of the work required
Not even dignifying this with any details.

2. We lose the will to get to the top
OK, there is some truth here. Many women just aren't interested in becoming leaders and that is absolutely fair enough. Experts call this the Ambition Gap. We're not so sure on the name (ambition and leadership don't necessarily equate) but it explains the underlying divide between wanting and declining the leadership option.

This term, though, doesn't account for the women who start off wanting to get there but don't reach the finishing line. When there is drive without accomplishment, other factors must be at play. Many women on their way to high-level leadership positions say that it's their different approach – compared to how the men do it – that's the obstacle.

We already know that men and women approach pretty much everything from a different angle when it comes to work. As we move up the ladder, research says that these variances become increasingly magnified. Further on in the chapter, we are going to throw gender completely out of the window, because being a great leader has nothing to do with our sex. At this point though, it's worth highlighting and appreciating these variances to help explain why society and precedent favour the boys.

As we touched on in our networking chapter, women are formidable collaborators: we work well together, we share expertise and we find strength in numbers. The problem is, leaders are single beings. With this in mind, when women work and shine collaboratively it can (wrongly) tell others that we are indecisive and submissive.

The way women express ambition – we question, we collaborate – can also have the superficial appearance of lacking ambition. We say that the Ambition Gap is in many ways just the ultimate misunderstanding.

3. External influences stop us

Centuries of male leaders mean that we're all more likely to imagine a leader as being male. No one is to blame for ancient leadership inequalities, but this imbalance is extraordinarily limiting for women – and many us can't face proving history wrong. We don't aspire to leadership because we are tired of trying to 'correctly' manage our approach to the role, especially when our efforts are judged against a culture that has been built by men, for men.

On top of that, we're scared. Yup, the old foe confidence – or lack of it. When we don't *believe* we can lead, we don't bother trying. For women working in male-structured and male-influenced environments it's wearing and depressing to be judged by different criteria, expected to perform in different ways and rewarded differently for the same accomplishments. Trying to be a female leader can sometimes feel like running a marathon in the wrong pair of shoes. We get there, but it hurts.

Amazingly, the expected and accepted face of leadership in the twenty-first century is still a white, middle-aged man. And that means that unconscious bias continues to keep women and ethnic minorities away from the top prize. And it's not just other people's unconscious biases that we need to fight through; we hold them against ourselves too.

Many women just don't see themselves as leaders. So we don't become leaders, even if we possess all the pertinent qualities. And as if unconscious bias hadn't aggravated the situation enough, another facet of its power is its emphasis on belonging: as humans, we feel safest with people who resemble ourselves. In terms of leadership, this means that a roomful of male private equity investors, say, are more likely to trust a male founder to reach his projections than a woman for the simple reason that in this entrepreneurial man, the investors see a little slither of themselves.

Whether we are barred from leadership because of these barriers, or we decide we don't want to get to the top because these barriers exist is a moot point. Which came first, the chicken or the egg? Whatever way it happened, today women contain their leadership aims because the road to glory is disproportionately stressful. We see a workplace skewed in favour of men and when we are brave enough to venture upward, organisational barriers hold us back.

Things *are* changing. Year on year, there are more influential female leaders and, as we've said, once we're ensconced at the top, impressive women are shaking it all up.

Women like **Susan Bright**, Managing Partner of global law firm Hogan Lovells in Africa and the UK. True to her gender, she manages her huge team in an authentically feminine way.

'I have developed my leadership style over time. I love talking with people one on one and that's great. But we have over 1600 people here in the UK, so it's not possible to do that with everyone. You have to find all sorts of different ways of communicating, both providing information and listening. I've also taken on leadership of our global innovation project which is looking at what we need to do differently to respond to the changing needs of our clients and to make ourselves fit for the future. We've identified a range of things we need to do – both in terms of new services and in delivering existing services differently and are now delivering those. We also decided that we needed to engage with everyone in the firm, ideally face to face. So we held a series of sessions around the world to which every member of the firm – over 5000 people – were invited. We had twenty-six sessions here in the UK. And we asked everyone for their ideas about what each of us can do differently, both individually and in teams. That for me has been crucial, because I am convinced that you can make huge strides in changing the way an organisation works if you harness ideas and engagement from everybody. So we went out to everyone, sharing our vision, and seeking input on what (and how) we should change.'

All leaders are equal, but some (female) leaders are more equal than others. Whilst companies and society as a whole (thank you #LikeAGirl) have a responsibility to remove the barriers that complicate women's aspirations for leadership, the only thing we can do is continue to look up. Arguably this whole book is about becoming a leader in your career.

Certainly, female leaders follow the same strategies that we endorse – getting a sponsor, promoting themselves, nurturing their networks, cultivating assertiveness – to get there. So if leadership drives you, then you're in for a treat, because when you successfully lead and that leadership results in the breaking down of male-skewed hurdles, you will enjoy success (and leave a legacy) on many, multi-coloured, sparkling levels. But we can't instigate seismic change unless we know how to lead. So keep reading.

THE FACTS Unconscious Bias

Unconscious bias is one of the stickiest hazards in our route to leadership progression. Think of a European border crossing: unconscious bias is the unhelpful policeman at the gate. We have our passport, our tickets are valid, there is no reason for any impediment to our holiday, and yet he does not let us pass. He is unconscious bias – he imagines someone else (a man in tiny Speedos perhaps?) on that summer adventure in Italy, and he holds us back.

The question isn't whether we do or do not have biases, but which biases they are.

Don't feel bad, by the way; these thought patterns, assumptions and interpretations – biases – help us to process information quickly and efficiently. They're our analytical autopilot and bias is useful and necessary for survival. But in a work situation, it's the pits; it causes us to make decisions that are not objective and leads to missed opportunities and unhelpful assumptions – and those biases against women as leaders. Here, let us prove this to you.

WORKOUT Find Your Bias

A father and his son are involved in a horrific car crash and the man died at the scene. But when the child arrived at the hospital and was rushed into the operating theatre, the surgeon pulled away and said: 'I can't operate on this boy, he's my son.'

How can this be?

Have you worked it out yet? How long did it take?

This story – called the surgeon's dilemma – is often used to demonstrate the way that unconscious bias works. Of course, the surgeon is the boy's mother.

If you didn't get the answer, don't worry – you are not alone. Less than half of those who try to solve the surgeon's dilemma struggle.

Women tend to struggle with gender bias just as much as men, which goes some way to explaining the most hidden barrier of all: the bias we hold against ourselves.

Having read this story, now fire up your computer. Search the web for Project Implicit. This is Harvard University's world-renowned Implicit Association Test – used by companies like Google – to measure bias. Spend ten minutes taking the test. Understand the biases you hold and that hold you back.

As we mentioned, reflexive bias means even women ourselves don't push towards leadership because we can't visualise a woman there in the first place. This is a major impediment and one that we hope this extended explanation of bias helps to cure. I am a woman. I am a leader. If you're ever in doubt, repeat the mantra.

Of course, as a woman, the further up the ladder we climb, the more slippery the rungs of leadership become. Our *Step Up* research tells us that women experience more obstructions and barriers in our path the more senior we become (border control on overdrive). Our *Step Up* study lawyers all said that while it was hard to get to be a partner, it was almost impossible to secure their spot on the management committee at the top of the partnership. And as if that wasn't bad enough, once they were there, our women continued to receive feedback that they didn't 'seem right' for the roles.

For the record, this bias also works against ethnic minorities and even short men. But it's not exactly comfort in numbers. In an everyday sense, unconscious bias results in managers that are less likely to endorse women, headhunters who put more men forward and executive committees that rarely elect women to their ranks.

But it's being held to a higher standard and having less leeway to express ourselves assertively – as a leader often has to do – that is the most bitter pill to swallow.

When female leaders are forceful and opinionated we are deemed emotional; when male leaders are forceful and opinionated they're high-five toughies. And even more galling than that is the perception of this emotion. For women, rather than passion, it's often read as 'temper' and no one wants a leader who loses that every time there's a disagreement in the office.

Even First Ladies aren't immune to these leadership constraints. When she was campaigning for her husband in 2008, Michelle Obama was painted with the same iniquitous anger brush used to depict many other aspiring female leaders. In regards to supposed (and still unproven) infighting between White House staff, Michelle Obama was cast as the baddie.

'I guess it's just more interesting to imagine this conflicted situation,' she said. 'That's been an image people have tried to paint of me since the day Barack announced, that I'm some kind of angry black woman.'

While anger is a sign of status in men, the opposite is true where women are concerned. Despite this obvious misrepresentation, many people noticed that Mrs Obama started softening her speeches to become more likeable, despite being a highly academic, Harvard-trained lawyer. Yup, society pushed the First Lady down.

Of course, we all (men and women) possess a complete range of emotions and behaviours. What makes it difficult for female leaders is what we have coined the Adjective Mix-Up. Front-running female emotions are nearly always of the weak, unhinged variety, despite the fact that we're equally ballsy and brave. Naturally, men forge ahead beneath the banners of Power, Strength, Boldness and Vision. Typecasting is an extension of unconscious bias, and for aspiring female leaders it's poison.

Sadly, we can't access the mental processes that create bias even when we know they exist. As Daniel Kahneman, a world expert on bias, says, 'It's difficult for us to fix errors we can't see.' In short, any strategy that requires us to catch ourselves being biased in the moment and correct it, won't work. What we need instead is to find strategies that break bias even when we don't think they're in operation.

WORKOUT Lose the Bias

Today you're going to focus on ridding yourself of these negative stereotypes that hold you back:

(3 minutes) Expose yourself to difference: Google at least five different images that counteract bias – for example female CEOs, construction worker breastfeeding her baby, female kickboxer. Looking at these images (and ideally saving them as your screensaver) subtly works against your personal bias against women in leadership roles.

(3 minutes) Find similarities: the Stereotype Inoculation Model suggests that if you are exposed to people who look like you (i.e. women) and who are also successful they act almost as a 'social vaccine' that inoculates you against some of your reflexive bias. Research has found that female students who were taught by a female maths professor felt more positively about both the 'female = leader' and 'female = maths' associations. This was also true in our *Step Up* research. Female partners were significantly more likely to be considered for management board roles in firms where there were already women in those roles. Their colleagues had been 'inoculated' against their bias against female leaders. To inoculate yourself, spend your three minutes

WORKOUT **Lose the Bias** continued

thinking of female leaders who have broken the barriers you see ahead. Then turn to our chapter on external influences to find out how to approach them.

(1 minute) Check your influences: Twitter (in its analytics section) will tell you the gender split of your followers. There are also tools that can analyse the gender of who you listen to by looking at your retweets. For example Twee-Q shows that in 125,000 Twitter accounts it has analysed, women are retweeted approximately half as much as men. Call yourself out if your 'Twee-Q' is low.

(3 minutes) Employ your imagination: research shows that just using your imagination can also counteract gender bias. In one study, students (of both genders) were asked to 'take a few minutes to imagine what a strong woman is like, why she is considered strong, what she is capable of doing, and what kinds of hobbies and activities she enjoys'. Now you do the same. No matter who they thought of, participants who engaged in this mental imagery exercise produced 'substantially weaker implicit stereotypes' compared with participants who engaged in neutral mental imagery or none at all.

When we become aware of the reflexive prejudices that hold us back, we free ourselves to achieve.

HOW TO See Ourselves as Leaders

Good leadership is portable. When we know how to lead, we can apply it to any and every type of job within all manner of careers and in our personal lives beyond. Leadership is a crucial skill for the simple fact that when we can positively influence others, we can make change.

So how do we lead as women? As with many other elements of career success, men and women often approach leadership from different sides of the court – and to get ahead, it's important that we understand the formations of both teams. Before that, though, we need to realise that leadership is an acquired skill, and while we can learn to lead as women, what's more important is to lead as ourselves.

In almost all cases, leaders share a suite of qualities that have helped springboard them to the mountain's summit. But there is not much point diligently perfecting the skills of leadership if we still can't place ourselves as Top Dog (Top Bitch).

Clearly, the art of vision isn't learnt in a day and internalising ourselves as a leader is an iterative process – we can't decide to do it, rather we learn it from experiences over time. When we start to act in certain ways (as a leader) or instigate specific actions that assert us as a leader, we slowly trick our mind into compliance. What we're saying is that becoming a leader (in every sense of the word) requires a series of small shifts and steps, which when repeated make us *feel* that we are a leader. When this happens, others begin to regard us in that light too.

German Chancellor **Angela Merkel** methodically worked her way up the ranks of the Christian Democratic Union party and, in doing so, became the protégée of the infamous Helmut Kohl. The big, vociferous Kohl referred to Merkel as 'mein Mädchen' ('my girl'), but that didn't stop Merkel asserting herself when the time was right. In late 1999, without warning, a letter written by Merkel appeared in the *Frankfurter Allgemeine Zeitung*. It told the German populace two things: that it was time for the party to move on without Helmut Kohl and that she was the compelling candidate for his replacement.

Merkel's letter did the job and in 2005, she progressed to become Germany's first female Chancellor (she is also its first leader from the former communist East Germany). Merkel made it to the top by taking steps that proved her leadership abilities to the German people – and it wasn't a subtle game.

Leadership capabilities grow and the opportunities to demonstrate these new skills breed too: when we decide to take leadership seriously, it becomes a positive cycle of affirmation. And like all of the cogs in this crazy watch called career progression, momentum keeps them turning: when we are treated as a leader we feel more confident, and when that happens, we find it easier to imagine ourselves taking charge. What we suggest is that you make those first few steps bird-sized, so that you aren't overwhelmed by the prospect ahead.

It is worth noting that the opposite is also true too. When we never put ourselves in a position of leadership (on whatever the scale) we never bask in its glory and, over time, whilst we're stuck in the shadows, our leadership identity flounders. It's the eternal self-fulfilling prophecy. So, if your heart tells you you'd make a great leader, put yourself in the driving seat.

Gemma Godfrey didn't let stereotypes or fear weaken her leadership aspirations. 'I believe you've just got to go out and do it. I haven't figured out how to be the ultimate leader, but what I can say is that me being a woman – a young woman – has been more of an issue for other people than it has for me. They find it difficult; it's the whole being assertive thing, men think I'm being defensive but I'm just being myself.'

So how do you do a Gemma and elegantly cut through the rubbish?

We say by acknowledging and playing to your own strengths. We all have them and really, any, when we apply them smoothly – and we're including empathy, kindness and other softer attributes to that standard list of vision, determination, self-awareness, and confidence – can form the basis of brilliant leadership. Because while humility, say, might not sound like a killer leadership attribute, when we look at the rise of, say, Aung San Suu Kyi and Mother Teresa, we can easily see that prominent and influential leaders come in many forms.

When we celebrate the traits we value in ourselves, we are well placed to start painting our leadership self-portrait. If you're great with clients, for example, let this be your leadership base layer – make it your first sphere of influence. Only the ability to lead and motivate others positively should matter.

HOW TO Be a Transactional Leader

Probably the most common form of leaders, transactional leaders rely on quid pro quos: you do something for me and I'll do something for you. If a newsroom graduate agrees to interview the neighbours of a grisly murder victim (known in the business as the Death Knock), then as a reward, the editor will give the Death Knocker a front-page by-line. This basic give-and-take style can be an effective form of leadership.

Traditionally, transactional leadership is seen as a masculine way of doing things, because men are more likely to act in their own self-interest and participate in a social interaction as if it were a negotiation – similar to their networking style.

We're stating the obvious here, but sex does not define the way we lead. Many women are competent and revered transactional leaders thanks to this method being both transparent and undeniably stimulating. And aside from gender or leadership style, being transactional is a necessity in certain situations.

Many women stumble on the transactional front, though, because of its directness – this mode of leadership is dependent on assertion because we need to feel confident as a leader to be able to broker the deal. Transactional leadership suits male personalities because it evolved through the dominance of men as leaders.

We don't agree with it, but the fact is that women who are overly aggressive (e.g. Margaret Thatcher) are not liked, and because we conflate aggression and assertiveness, being a transactional leader can feel uncomfortable.

But however tricky it feels, competent, rounded leaders need to be transactional (read: direct and persuasive) sometimes. It is OK if we don't make this candid give-and-take our go-to leadership method, but all leaders need it as a string in their bow.

One of the reasons that women find assertiveness uncomfortable is not because it's devoid from our personalities, but that it's been beaten out over time.

Bossy.

This little word has curbed a million dreams. If you're the type of woman who grew up with strong opinions and nascent leadership qualities then the chances are at least one of your school reports would have included the word bossy.

The humiliation and confusion of having your passion negatively relabelled as 'bossy' (as two grown women who have lived the deal we know the pain) has a simple knock-on effect in later life: it limits our brilliance. As adults, we don't aspire to leadership positions because we're scared of feeling small again; small when people on the outside label our ambition as bossy.

In a defiant stance against this fact, Beyoncé ('I'm not bossy, I'm the boss'), Sheryl Sandberg, Condoleezza Rice and Jennifer Garner launched #BanBossy. Their television, radio and magazine censorship advocacy campaign, which went live in 2014, has one single mission: to eliminate the use of the word bossy, due to its perceived harmful effect on young women.

#BanBossy wants to ringfence the negative and encourage girls to lead. To paraphrase the PR blurb, 'Words like bossy make girls less interested in leading than boys – a trend that continues into adulthood.'

WORKOUT Ban Your Own Bossy

The most successful leaders are not necessarily well-rounded individuals. They are clear on their strengths and play to those, bringing others in around them to support them where they are weaker. The women we coach often find it difficult to define those key strengths. Ask them to define their weaknesses, however, and the words flow.

WORKOUT **Ban Your Own Bossy** continued

But, interestingly, our perceived weaknesses often reveal strengths. Define yourself as over-analytical? So you're meticulous. Feeling too rigid or predictable? We'd define that as dependable and organised. So too with bossy. Our 'bossiness' is really just our natural assertiveness – and we already know how important that is – being viewed by society (and most importantly ourselves) as overdone.

So now we're going to embrace that power as a strength, not a weakness.

Some people swear by affirmations. But research shows that asking ourselves questions can be even more effective in creating deep-seated change.

Next time you hear yourself saying, 'I was being bossy,' spend ten minutes flipping that on its head.

'Am I bossy?' you ask. Then have the continuation of that conversation with yourself.

Ask yourself whether you really were bossy. How did others react? How do other people behave when they are being assertive? Do you feel bossed by them?

Using this interrogative self-talk, as researchers call it, each time you doubt your behaviour allows your subconscious to understand over time that you're not bossy.

Rather, you are capable and strong. Your team needs your support to succeed. People admire assertiveness. In fact, you're not bossy, you're the boss.

HOW TO Be a Transformational Leader

Where transactional leaders focus on their own power, and base their leadership style on give-and-take, transformational types lead by inspiring those around them to follow their cause.

A classic (non-work) transformational relationship is that of a mother and her child. The mother gives without expecting something in return, but of course, the child gives back without the need for transactions, because she is totally dedicated to her mother – her leader. This feeling of devotion that transformational leaders are able to inspire is what makes them powerful.

Transformational leaders inspire others and together they work towards a common goal. As people we like to feel part of something and to be motivated towards a cause, which is why research says that groups led by transformational leaders are happier and more productive than those coaxed by transactions.

The point of difference – and it's a surprising one as many of us assume we're driven by Number One – is employees with transactional leaders are inspired to transcend their own self-interest to achieve better results for the common good. Working for a transformational leader can be a wonderful and uplifting experience: these leaders are imbued with passion and energy and genuinely care about their team.

Transformational leaders are crucial in the workplace of tomorrow. They suit the intrinsic values and job satisfaction levels of younger workers and this is great news for aspiring female leaders. What modern employees want is to be motivated by the work they do and the people they work with on a daily basis. The concept of being paid a wage to progress and to gradually earn more as we rise without much thought to job satisfaction has become old-fashioned.

Transformational leaders reflect the changing landscape of today's careers because they suit the modern working mind and are adaptable to high levels of change. Speedy tech developments, a fervent movement towards entrepreneurship and the increasing number of complex portfolio careers all demand a type of leadership with more breadth than the simple give-and-take. Transformers are the leaders of today. This is fantastic news for women who are natural transformers.

Bow & Arrow's **Natasha Chetiyawardana** is as modern a leader as you can get. Not only has her growth agency Bow & Arrow carved out a new category in the market, with its unique fusion of design and consultancy (its clients include Google, Cadburys, O2, Barclays and

NewsCorp) but she leads it, with her partner Ben Slater, in cutting edge transformational style. Not least because she encourages this approach to leadership across all levels within the agency.

Natasha refuses to have a bottleneck at the top. To prevent this, she's instilled a culture of transformative collaboration. In the toilets, on the walls and slung on desks, there are expertly designed sets of company values that underpin how Natasha and Ben, along with all their team members, inspire each other to think, grow and be fearless. Here are just a couple:

'We look after each other as well as we look after ourselves'
'We never forget how lucky we are to be working together'

These aren't just throwaway thoughts; this is modern, transformational thinking. 'I want everyone at Bow & Arrow to be autonomous. I've seen so many small businesses where there's a bottleneck at the top, there's this one person that everyone else is accountable to and it makes everything so much less fluid. Plus they're not accountable to themselves, which means they aren't motivated properly and have less responsibility. I'll never use a directive leadership style because it just doesn't work. You end up doing things for your boss and not for yourself – you don't reach answers for yourself and the company doesn't grow and thrive. My team of nearly forty employees have all come through our internship programme. Which means they haven't been influenced by old-fashioned ways of doing things. Because of this, they're committed to the way we work and to the business as a whole. We all talk in "we" and not "I".'

As Natasha explains, this trend for female-friendly transformational leadership, with its emphasis on empowerment and alliance, suits today's young, creatively minded employees. What's most exciting is that because of transformational leadership's positive outcomes across all metrics of success, it means that at some point in the not-too-distant future, leadership should be seen as a domain most suited to women.

Transformational leadership thrives on shared success, empathy, collaboration and mutual encouragement. As we said earlier on, though, we can't just rely on transforming others; every great leader needs to be able to apply the rough and the smooth.

In the main, these types of empathetic, inspiring and agile leaders share four main characteristics. And to give the theory some context, we've matched each type with a well-known female leader below. Whilst we're not saying you need to be the next Malala Yousafzai to get ahead, borrowing some of her character traits should make others sit up and notice you.

MALALA YOUSAFZAI The Idealised Influencer

As the youngest ever Nobel Prize laureate, thanks to her tireless activism for female education, Yousafzai is an ideal leader to her many followers. She walks the talk and is admired for her ability to lead from within. Yousafzai is a collegial leader and embodies the values that she promotes to her (typically female) followers.

KATHRYN BIGELOW The Inspirational Motivator

With her film *The Hurt Locker* (2009), Bigelow became the first woman to win the Academy Award for Best Director. 'If there's specific resistance to women making movies, I just choose to ignore that as an obstacle for two reasons: I can't change my gender, and I refuse to stop making movies.' Inspirational Motivators create a vision that challenges followers to leave their comfort zones, communicate optimism about future goals, and provide meaning for the task at hand. This gives them charisma.

HARRIET GREEN The Individualised Considerator

Former CEO of Thomas Cook and current head of the IBM Watson Internet of Things business unit, Harriet Green's style of leadership speaks to the individual. 'People don't really remember what you say or what you do. But they always remember how you make them feel.' Green demonstrates genuine concern for the needs and feelings of her individual followers – she acts as their leader, supporter and mentor. This personal attention brings out the best efforts in others.

MARGARET THATCHER Intellectual Stimulator

Thatcher may have made mistakes and not been everyone's cup of tea politically, but she did one thing brilliantly: she challenged followers – and herself to be innovative and creative. Thatcher empowered and inspired Britons to seek their own creative solutions to their problems and she did this herself by becoming the first female British Prime Minister.

Hopefully, you can identify echoes of yourself in more than one of these great women. Leaders, all leaders, tend towards one or two character types. We all possess certain innate leadership qualities and whilst they aren't necessarily bestowed in the exact categories we describe above, these are useful guidelines. We say, find the leadership strengths you naturally possess within these types and hone them. Great leaders are often very strong in a few key areas – and then to fill in the gaps, they surround themselves with great teams.

HOW TO Envision

Visionary leaders are able to answer the question of where they are going. They do this for themselves but crucially they also articulate it for others too. By doing this, visionary leaders encourage creativity and innovation – they bring people along with them. Not only do they transform, but leaders with vision also trigger an elusive state in others: devotion.

If you've ever had the pleasure of eating **Ruth Rogers**'s Italian food you'll know that her heart is in everything that she does. At nearly seventy years old, Rogers is as committed (probably more so) to leading at the River Café, her restaurant on the Thames (she's soon to open her second outpost in central London), as she was in 1987, on day one.

'I'm here every day; I'm enthusiastic about being here because it's what I love to do. I have respect for the restaurant and for everyone who works here. I want them to come to work because they want to come to work, and I do that by having high standards that we're all proud of. They know that I am here to listen; leadership is about direction and listening to what your team has to say. As a woman I know my instinct is to want to please; I want to smooth things over and make everything better. It's taken me a while to build a sense of detachment so that sometimes I can make a decision that isn't popular but that benefits us all in the end. If you love what you do and you invest in your staff, it comes back so many times over.'

Ruth's style of passion and belief is paramount if you're going to be an authentic leader. Once you reach this happy place, next on leadership's checklist is vision. Vision is what separates leadership from management, something we'll discuss further on. Here though, this workout should help you see your vision more clearly.

WORKOUT Visioning Leader You

(10 minutes) If you are struggling to imagine yourself as a leader despite consciously acknowledging your strengths and making sure you are working on something you believe, use this exercise to bring your vision into focus.

First, grab a pen and paper. Close your eyes and imagine that you are a leader. Don't worry about the specifics yet, but imagine yourself leading a group. And, importantly, free yourself from realism. You are the leader of whatever or whomever you choose.

Start by imagining what you are doing. Use these questions to help get you started:

Are you leading your own business or are you in a bigger company?
What do you have for breakfast?
How do you get to work?
What are you wearing?
How do people respond to you when you get there?
What tasks do you do in the day?
How do you feel about being you?

Go through your entire day, from the moment you wake up until you go to sleep that night, and spend ten minutes writing down (in as much detail as possible) what you'd be doing.

Doing this exercise with its focus on the minutiae of a day in your life as a leader will help the image of you as a leader come to life.

When vision gets skewed we get North Korean-type situations that we certainly do not endorse. Played out with morality, though, vision is the key to the ultimate leadership gateway. According to research, women can struggle to be visionary. You don't need to ask why; yes, confidence and bias are its biggest suppressors. But we need it because having vision and being able to impart that vision is one of the most important qualities for a leader.

So what is vision? The distinction between management and leadership and being visionary is a matter of doing three things well:

> Sensing opportunities and threats in the environment: visionary leaders simplify complex situations and foresee events that will affect the organisation
> Setting strategic direction: visionary leaders encourage new business, define new strategies and make decisions with an eye towards the big picture
> Inspiring constituents: visionary leaders challenge the status quo by being open to new ways of doing things and by inspiring others to look beyond their limitations

Now a writer and coach, **Susie Pearl** was the founder and CEO of top PR agency Kazoo Communications, driving the Nineties entertainment scene with clients like Madonna, the Spice Girls, MTV and Sony. Susie grew the agency from a one (wo)man band to a top three agency through the power of her vision, which encompassed foresight, strategy and inspiration.

'I realised I was very good at visioning. I could have a strong vision and know I could keep going towards it, despite being surrounded by people who said I just wasn't being realistic. And particularly the numbers people would say that to me. But I wasn't looking at the situation today, I was looking at the situation as to how it was going to be once we had carried out the strategy I wanted to carry out. And I knew that if we changed the strategy, we would change the outcome. I did that through putting together a vision. I realised that putting together a team around you – who can be motivated by that vision, who can see it and join in with you in creating that vision, begin to feel it and be part of it – is crucial. That is a major part of the secret of success to me. It's about creating and motivating amazing teams around you. Because as an individual, no matter how creative, brave and resourceful you are, you can't produce an incredible business on your own. That's what I've learnt. The fast way to success is creating teams around you who can work with you and fill the gaps needed to create amazing things together.'

Susie's success demonstrates the power of vision both in reaching and making the most of her position as leader. This vision is vital; once we have it, we're ready to study leadership's next stage. Of course, all leaders impose their unique temperament, experience and wisdom on the job, but theory and tradition tell us that there are two key ways of approaching leadership: we either transact with others or we transform them. The ideal, of course, is a leader who combines these approaches in some kind of modern, leadership blender.

LEADERSHIP Hurdles: Envisioning

Being diligent: it's admirable, but for women, it's also the main impediment to being visionary. Instead of looking up and dreaming big, we're blinkered by getting the job done. For many women, hard work is a reliable crutch; we know where we are with it, there's a predictable beginning, middle and end, nothing says stable like the plodding through the To-Do list. This makes us great mid-level managers: our hard works grounds in others what is possible. Women are do-ers, not dreamers, and it blocks our route to leadership.

The reason that Beyoncé's gang are so set on their #BanBossy message is because wrapped up in its significance are the subtleties of restraint. Having had the 'be good and well-behaved' message drummed into our heads from childhood, we women have become conditioned to quieten our vision. In its place, we rely on competence and the art of being meticulous – not exactly visionary, right? Then we throw in our perfectionist tendencies and there is no space left for visioning.

According to a recent *New Yorker* article that overviewed the 2008 Democratic Presidential race, Barack Obama and Hillary Clinton were

equally capable. Obama had the edge, though, as he won the hearts
of the American people; he threw drama – vision – into the mix.
'Barack Obama was viewed as a visionary, a charismatic communicator
offering a more hopeful if undetailed future. Hillary Clinton was
viewed as a competent executor with an impressive if uninspiring
grasp of policy detail.'

Many aspiring female leaders – and Hillary Clinton is not exempt –
forsake rousing rhetoric for facts. This is the deal: most women
feel uncomfortable being viewed as visionary, as being too
Obama-esqe, because we assume (incorrectly) that it makes us
appear less competent and in control – facts and figures are our
comfort blanket.

But passionate leaders, the ones who successfully transform and
inspire others to their cause, need to have the confidence to stand up
and be bold – even if that means making statements of intent that are
unqualified and not tied to the latest sales figures. Thinking big gets
people going – it's what we want in our leaders.

Sure, when we go out on a limb, we're more likely to be challenged
by others and that's a scary place to inhabit – no one enjoys feeling
precarious and unmasked at work. Especially when negative
stereotyping, which tells us that when women act passionately many
perceive them as being flaky and unbridled, enforces that belief.
Men, of course, when they speak from the heart, are regarded as
someone with range; it's their added plus. Yup, another wretched
double bind, but one that should never prevent us from achieving
our goals. We say, the way to visionary freedom is to blend the big
facts with the big talk. And hey presto, you'll visioning like you've
never visioned before.

LEADERSHIP Bonuses: Collaboration

Collaboration, when combined with vision, is a leadership asset.
It inspires others to move outside their comfort zones and to start
to lead themselves. It is perfectly acceptable (ideal even) to rely on
a range of inputs to create our vision. Having said that, when we
vision in a collaborative sense, we need to beware that it doesn't

weaken our message. The trick is to harness collective vision whilst remaining the figurehead yourself.

Susan Bright used that collaborative bent to great ends when visioning Hogan Lovells as a law firm of the future. 'One of the challenges we face is collaborating globally. We couldn't have one person go to our forty-plus offices around the world, talking to everyone, so we've had to use distributed leadership. We put together a framework centrally, and then ask leaders locally to deliver these sessions, stressing that they had to own the material, to tell their own stories. Then I had to work out how to deliver this in my own region. And, again, I thought that the best way to go about it would be to involve a group of people to lead the sessions. This created some friendly competition in how they delivered them! We wanted them to be different from an ordinary meeting. Some people had music; some had afternoon tea, or drinks. It meant that each leader had to get out of their comfort zone, since this was nothing like a normal presentation to clients. The feedback has been fantastic. Well over 90 per cent of our people came along and there has been continuing momentum since then.

'Part of being a good leader is ensuring people understand and are engaged with the firm's vision and strategy, as well as gaining their input. But you also have to ensure that you feed back to demonstrate that you listen and adapt where appropriate. So we have created a loop back, saying, "This is what you have said to us; we've listened; this is what we're going to do." '

It is imperative that as leaders we are able to strike a balance between acknowledging the importance of collaboration and spotlighting ourselves. It takes confidence to be exposed as the protagonist. But if we do draw on the power of collaboration, we must remember to own the stage ourselves if we're to be viewed as solid leaders. When we make vision something that we are known for as a leader, it sets us apart from the rest, because vision, research says, is one of the most important uses of our time when we're in a leadership role.

Thankfully, vision can be learnt.

WORKOUT Embrace Your Visionary Self

First you need to get out of your comfort zone. So today change your routine. Take a new way to work or eat lunch in a different place with different people. You need to see something new.

(3 minutes) You need to practise visionary thinking. So brainstorm. Eventually, you'll apply this to your business but start with whatever is outside your window or something you see on your commute. Pick a question and start writing down ideas on something that bothers or interests you but you've not thought about deeply before: 'How would I improve the train system?' Or 'What else might people buy in the coffee shop?' In three minutes aim to find thirty ideas. Don't filter. No matter how wild or stupid, write it down. The first ten will be obvious, the second third will be challenging, the final ten are tough and often where the best ideas are.

(4 minutes) Now focus. Having practised thinking creatively, narrow the brainstorming to a focused question targeted at your job, team or business.

As you do it, notice assumptions. This is difficult because assumptions are hard to see. They are rules we don't even know we are following. To find assumptions ask yourself: Why can't I do this idea? How do I know that reason is still true? What would it look like if it wasn't true?

(3 minutes) Rank your ideas to find one worth pursuing. (Going outside the ten minutes, it can be useful to have those around you rank the ideas too.) The good ideas will become obvious.

N.B. Never let insufficient resources stop you. Fewer resources forces you to use what you have creatively in a VISIONARY way.

LEADERSHIP Thoughts

THE AUTHENTIC FEMALE LEADER

'It's really important to be yourself as a leader. If you show up and want to lead and it's not authentic then people won't respect you,' says **Natasha Chetiyawardana**. And **Yvette Cooper** concurs: 'In the end, if you do things you feel uncomfortable with in politics it shows, so you have to do it your own way.' Being true to who we are provides the best foundation for effective leadership, because however things progress we have a foundation of trust and honesty.

No one is the perfect leader. Beyoncé has bad days. Obama still wobbles. There will be times when Merkel can't find the right words. When we're authentic leaders, though, these stumbles don't matter because we've already got the team onside. In fact, vulnerability – getting things wrong, tripping up now and again – keeps us human; and employees dig that kind of thing.

Part of being an authentic female leader is not denying our femininity. We already know that society wrongly associates successful leadership with stereotypically masculine traits such as assertiveness and dominance. Often, female leaders are discounted because we violate these gender norms.

This is a dilemma, but at its core is a useful piece of advice: don't rise to the bait. We know that men are more likely to be seen as leaders, but that doesn't mean we need to fight fire with fire. Borrowing from the boys is a good idea. Taking inspiration from their way of doing things, their knack with flair and their skilful envisioning are all tricks that women need in their armoury.

As long as you don't confuse sharing with copying, then go forth and plough as much as takes your fancy. Copying is hazardous for female leaders because when we adopt too masculine a style in response to stereotype threat, research says we end up being rated less well by our subordinates. It's unfortunate but it is true.

Blending. We love it across so many career progression themes, and it's pertinent here too. Because while female leaders come across badly when they just duplicate the masculine style, when we mix together the best bits across the sexes, its makes us a more likeable and powerful force. Take as many cues from Barack Obama, Mandela and Martin Luther King as you do from Cooper, Merkel and Sheryl Sandberg.

Just make sure you are fiercely protective of your wonderful and unique womanliness – because it's what makes you sparkle.

THE TIPS

|1| Remember your gravitas

Confidence is a key leadership skill. And perhaps most important in that mix when it comes to leadership is gravitas. Powerful leaders tend to exude a sense of calm, control and total focus. So the next time you need to exert your leadership power, try being in the moment. Take five deep breaths beforehand, then enter the room able to focus completely on the matter at hand – not what you'll have for supper or whether you are good enough. Exude poise. Be taken for the leader you are.

|2| Ditch the micromanager

Our perfectionist tendencies can lead us – sometimes – to oversee others too closely. A great leader can let things go. Being focused and strategic when it comes to delegation allows you to get more done and inspires others to perform. In your next team meeting try being efficient and giving others full responsibility for what they need to bring to the table.

|3| Embrace empathy

We've touched on it, but our empathy is one of our greatest leadership strengths. Don't quash yours, embrace it. If you have been pushing yours to the sidelines, bring it back on board. Being perceptive helps us understand the needs of the team. Some teams value trust over creativity; others prefer a clear communicator to a great organiser. Building a strong team is easier when you know the values and goals of each individual, as well as what they need from you to lead.

|4| Get outside your comfort zone

The best leaders think outside the box. So, as uncomfortable as it feels, this week try taking on a new task: something unfamiliar to you. Being bold enough to get outside our job descriptions and come up with new solutions leads to both growth and recognition.

|5| Be an everyday leader

Leadership isn't just about being the boss. We know that now. But nor is it only about work. Many of the most effective leadership traits can be gained outside the office. So try showing leadership in the other parts of your life. Running a charity initiative, coaching your work softball team, even the dreaded head of the PTA – practising being a leader in different scenarios will give you an edge when it comes to leading at work.

CHAPTER 10

A Fine Balance

BALANCE The Facts

O f all the issues we discuss in this book, balance is the most emotive. It forces us to look at our own choices through the lens of choices different to our own. Balance brings us back full circle to the beginning of our book: *Step Up* is based on the belief that we must define our own success – and the same is true of balance. While we cannot possibly tell you exactly how you will find true and honest balance in your life, we will plainly set out the facts and then advise you on the best ways to achieve this mythical, often elusive state of being.

It is important that all of us assess and protect how we spend our time and energy in the spheres of work and life. Balance is important because when we are able to extend a more tangible control over our personal work schedules, we are happier, more productive beings. But happiness is a nebulous concept that doesn't always win out over hours in the office. A Mental Health Foundation survey found that more than 40 per cent of British employees are neglecting other aspects of their life because of work. This is not something to aspire to.

Work–life balance is an issue for everyone because technology ensures that most of us are never truly off duty. The internet, only ever a tap or swipe away thanks to the ubiquitous smartphone, is both the liberator and destroyer of our freedom. Monumental advances in online relations mean that whilst we sit in our offices (or lie in the bath, for that matter) we're able to be anywhere and everywhere on the planet. And that means that most of us are constantly available via calls, email and messaging. Hands up anyone who has had a swift peek at their phone during a romantic *tête-à-tête* dinner and realised that a pesky work problem is escalating elsewhere?

Not only is the world a smaller place these days, it now also spins within one homogenous time zone. When America wakes we can be there in a flash and that's a burden that not all of us enjoy. The patterns and demands of our work are more skewed than ever – the time when we could legitimately (and physically) clock off at 5.30pm has been buried beneath the throb of the World Wide Web.

On top of this, many of us choose to actively blend work and life. Tech entrepreneurs, lifestyle shopkeepers, organic bakers, lawyers with a passion for sport, graphic designers, fashion types, music industry women and hundreds of other types of creatives and professionals now realise the value – both in terms of success and self-promotion – of building a personal brand online.

Twitter, Instagram, YouTube, Periscope – there are many social media platforms to choose from, but they can all do the same thing to our lives: confuse matters. Social media is a wonderful invention that offers a never-ending stream of visual ideas and images, all seen, of course, through an artfully chosen filter. Yes, it's a unique and modern way to self-promote, market yourself and build networks. At the same time though, social media can become burdensome and stressful. Who can ever satisfy its infinite possibilities?

But at least social media doesn't have tantrums. Because the ultimate upenders of balance are children. They change everything again; they zap our time and our hearts and we become different beings who have extra responsibilities. Children can be wonderful instigators of renewed drive and determination, but they can just as easily require us to miss that tech summit because chicken pox hits.

Clearly, there's a lot to say on the subject of balance. First, though, let's address the term itself.

How we describe the equilibrium between work and life has become open to academic debate. While *Step Up* still values the use of the word balance to express life's never ending seesaw, according to other career folk, it is no longer the perfect metaphor. Others say that work and life have become so complicated that the scale would now constantly tip and dip in different directions, rendering the word balance unbalanced.

Other academics have criticised the term because it suggests that work is not integral to life. These ones have progressed to use the word integration, as the best expression of this already complicated subject. This, many feel, is a neater term for the pressured dance of careers and downtime – of the mix of our jobs and our loved ones.

But then, guess what, there's another school of thought too. These thinkers (please bear with us) criticise integration as the ultimate ideal, because it implies that the two spheres of work and life should be merged. This could, they say, lead to fears of a contamination of personal space by the demands of work. So, for the sake of simplicity, we're sticking with balance. Although we acknowledge that what we're not discussing is the equality of work and life nor, conversely, the complete segregation of these two areas of our lives.

Smartphones might have rocked balance's boat, but this is an age-old issue that many exceptional minds have struggled with: Sylvia Plath, Vincent Van Gogh, Agatha Christie and Michelangelo are just some well-known names whose mental health issues, many believe, were exacerbated by a visceral but often unmanaged commitment to their work.

Today, luckily, many of us work for companies that offer more flexibility so that we can enjoy a greater involvement at home and a more restful time away from our desks. Research says that those who take advantage of flexible working schemes improve their overall wellbeing.

And it's not just the employees who benefit; companies with flexible working policies (we'll discuss exactly what that means later) do better on all kinds of metrics, including employee turnover, stress, organisational commitment, absenteeism, job satisfaction and productivity. Of course, not all of us work in jobs or industries that have the capacity for modern flexi-working and different work patterns are suitable for different people at different times in their lives. What is undeniable though is that we cannot work constantly, or least not without major adverse consequences.

BALANCE A Woman's Issue?

One day in 2007, Arianna Huffington was at home working. She was taking calls and checking her phone at the same time, when she unexpectedly passed out. Huffington fell to the floor and later woke in a pool of blood, with a broken cheekbone. The media mogul, who had been working eighteen-hour days, decided that this must be a medical issue, and put herself through a series of doctor-led physical examinations. The results were simple: exhaustion.

Huffington's collapse was Huffington's wake-up call. Later on, it also inspired her to write the calming bestseller, *Thrive: The Third Metric to Redefining Success and Creating a Happier Life* in which she explains her thinking on the third tenet of success. We can't, she says, solely focus on money and power. To do that would be like trying to hold up a stool on just two of its legs.

In her opinion – and we wholeheartedly agree with her – none of us can progress, enhance ourselves, enjoy our lives and survive if we don't consider a third leg: balance. As women, we already possess and relish a nuanced definition of success. And the same principle is relevant here with balance. Because to be able to feel in control of all areas of life, women must stay true to our broad, diverse and unique female point of view. And for many of us, this will at some point include the subject of children.

Whatever the world says about equality, in the main, children complicate the notion of balance more acutely for women than they do for men. Because cultural norms and long-standing assumptions still underpin how we run our work and family lives (and – though not universally true – because many of us want to), women are still more likely to take responsibility for home and family alongside our paid work.

History tells us that the woman is the main caregiver and the man the main breadwinner – and this affects almost everyone whatever their position on childrearing and family ties. For one, we already know that the pressures of home life, with its constant and never-ending obligations, are part of the reason why women remain underrepresented at the top. And in a similar vein, children affect our pursuit of balance too.

The ability to cope with the triple whammy of life, work and seniority is the migraine of many working women. Should we 'lean in' and pay for childcare? Get senior enough to achieve more flexibility? Get our husbands to lean in and do the childcare? Or must we kick off our shoes and accept that we can't have it all? There aren't simple answers to any of these questions. And while society and the fathers of our children take their time in catching up, we still end up with a lap full of family responsibility.

There are myriad different ways to mix the complex fragrance that is life with work and children. The only thing that's simple is that there's no right way to do it. With this in mind, some of the suggestions that we introduce in this chapter will work for you, but there is no universally perfect solution.

BALANCE Time and Responsibilities

What makes balance especially complex is that it isn't a steady creature. The need for balance is constant, but its form, depth and potency vary widely during the course of our careers. With this in mind, we will use this chapter to help you to arrive at your breed of balance at this time in your life and secondly to provide a balance toolkit for its management henceforward, when work and life get out of kilter again.

For the sake of simplicity, we are going to divide balance into two subsets: balancing your time and balancing your responsibilities.

The first section will encompass everything relating to the universal need for time away from work, and the latter will discuss family responsibilities. Because while dependent parents and young children certainly rock the balance boat, there is no doubt that this subject runs deeper than just wanting to pick the kids up from school.

HOW TO Balance Your Time

This isn't so much a desirable as a necessity. No one can work constantly: scientists, vicars, even Presidents cannot engage their minds in work from the moment they wake until they go to sleep again.

As we've said, one good place to start in the pursuit of better balance, is by working more flexibly. Thanks to the internet and our perpetual accessibility, fewer and fewer of us need (or want) to be clocked in for an allotted number of hours each day. For many, especially those of us who don't work for big, old-school corporates, this is the dream: high-intensity gym class in the morning, high-intensity work time until mid-afternoon, quiet dog walk to collect our thoughts, then a final stint at the computer until dinner time.

When we work flexibly it doesn't mean we do fewer hours, it's just that we spread them more evenly – and enjoyably – across our days and lives. Amazingly, 90 per cent of UK companies now offer some form of flexible working and research says that when this is offered, the same number of men as women go from desktop to laptop.

For many of us, flexi-working is a win-win situation even if you only do a day or so of modern time-keeping per week. What's interesting though is that even if, on paper, this flexible working ticks all the balance boxes, it actually doesn't suit us all. Some people (this could be you, and we'll come to character preferences shortly) will grow tired of the blurred lines between work and home. With this in mind, it's worth keeping an open mind and even trying a few options before settling on your ideal balance-enhancing work style.

It isn't always possible to know whether an arrangement is manageable (not just in terms of time, but emotionally too), unless we give it a go. And while a complete dissection of every type of flexible working style is beyond the scope of this book, what is crucial here is to realise that a variable work option will impact on some of us differently to how it will on others.

HOW TO Be True to Ourselves

A central tenet of *Step Up* is difference – no one's balance fingerprint is the same. All of us harbour particular needs, hold tight certain desires and enjoy life circumstances that impact on our feelings of contentment, stress and overwhelm. What's universal, though, is that when our unique life keystones become out of kilter with how we want and need them to be, we lose our equilibrium.

WORKOUT How You Live

Spend some time (2 minutes) reflecting on how balanced you feel right now. Are you happy with the status quo or do you feel in your gut that things need to change?

For the next two minutes, look at the 'current' chart that follows and reflect on your life now. Balance is as much about how you feel as reality, so don't refer to your time study from Chapter 3. For each part of the circle put a line across the piece of pie. Zero, closest to the centre, means you have no focus on this in your life, ten is perfection in this area.

Put the chart to one side. This evening, take two minutes to look back at the chart. How does it tally with how you've felt today? The areas where you could get better balance should start to be clear.

Now spend four minutes mentally moving from present to future: go through each section of the chart again, trying to give a score on the 'ideal future' chart to where you would like to be in each area.

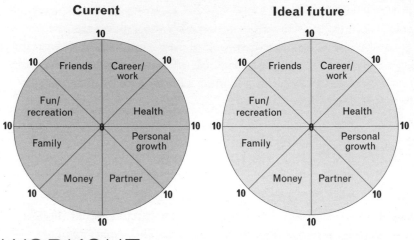

WORKOUT How You Want to Live

Now we're going to start moving towards your ideal wheel.

Spend two minutes identifying the areas where you're out of kilter comparing current to ideal future charts.

For each of the four most unbalanced areas spend two minutes (8 in total) writing down one sentence about what needs to change and two ideas for how to change it. So for example if you are low in the partner area, it might be because you are doing too much overtime. How could you change that? What about saying no to extra projects for a while (see confidence!)? Combine that with saying yes to invitations you would usually turn down in order to get out and meet new people and the scales will start to shift in the other direction.

[NOTE: Don't see these charts as yet another 'should' stick to beat yourself with. Not all elements of the pie are equal for everyone but we do need each of these pieces in our life in some way.]

When work starts overpowering every part of our lives we often struggle to see past it and that means we lose sight of why the other slices of pie still matter. Certainly, Huffington could not see the wood for the trees when she collapsed in front of her computer. Don't end up being one of those people, as research tells us, whose final regret in life was that they worked too hard.

While Step Up is committed to the importance of careers and how they positively impact on us as people, we'd never endorse them to the exclusion of absolutely everything else.

HOW TO Be the Way We Are

Do you find a constantly buzzing phone in your pocket a thrill or a stress? We all have our own ways of coping with the boundaries between work and the rest of our lives: the academics call these FlexStyles. These are not, to clarify, about flexible working, but rather they are character preferences that explain what sits comfortably for us as people when it comes to work space and personal space.

In this section, we are going to explore how the encroachment of our work on our lives makes us feel. And the easiest way to explain and unravel our feelings is by using these academic FlexStyles because balance is such a nebulous state that we can't always clarify or dissect it in our minds.

Now, within each FlexStyle, there are two subtypes (high and low contentment) that describe those of us who are comfortable resting in this category and those who are not. Generally, each of us stays within our character type across the course of our careers, but depending on time, pressures and a host of other disruptors, we will move up and down between higher and lower levels of contentment.

But of course, there are exceptions, and FlexStyles can shift over time and in response to changing life circumstances. So it is possible that the type you align yourself closest with today won't necessarily be the same one you affiliate yourself to next year.

Whilst writing this book, we have realised many things; one of them is the stark difference in how the two of us manage and approach our work. Phanella is an absolute, down-to-the-ground Separator. When spending time with her children she is energised by being fully there, undistracted. Similarly, when she's at work, she finds that giving it her full attention brings about her best results. In short, Phanella prefers to clearly delineate the times when she works, and the times when she is at home.

Alice, on the other hand, has a more blended approach; for her, anything goes and preferably all at the same time – she is a classic Integrator. Alice thrives when she is able to satisfy everyone's demands; this duality invigorates her and gives her the drive and energy to keep at it on all fronts.

So now it's your turn to discover your personal FlexStyle. As you read through our descriptions of the different types, hopefully you will start identifying yourself in one or another, but keep in mind that none are more or less desirable. This is not about trying to be something we're not, but accepting (again) who we are. Each type has benefits and drawbacks (we're all wonderfully imperfect beings); it helps to know our balance comfort zone because then we can justifiably operate within its expected parameters, and stop trying to be a woman that we're not.

Step Up's FlexStyles

	Integrators	Volleyers	Separators
CONTENTMENT	HIGH	HIGH	HIGH
	LOW	LOW	LOW

So, what type are you? Try our workout for extra clarification and then read on for our explanations and suggestions.

WORKOUT Find Your FlexStyle

Take ten minutes to think about how you organise your time. Then answer yes or no to these statements as honestly as possible.

A. I am happy to take private calls at work and work calls at home.
B. I feel uncomfortable sending work emails while with friends.

WORKOUT Find Your Flex Style continued

A. I prefer to work in the evenings so I can fit in some hobbies during the day.
B. My evenings are sacred and I prefer not to work after 6pm.

A. If possible I like to work from home.
B. I prefer to go into the office to do my work.

A. My family often complain that I take work calls in our free time.
B. I often wonder whether I am too focused on work or home.

A. Sometimes I feel exhausted by trying to do everything all at once.
B. Occasionally I miss out on work opportunities because I am unavailable.

Now add up your yeses. If they are mainly As, you're an Integrator. Mainly Bs, a Separator. Pretty evenly spread between the two (or sometimes one, sometimes the other) then you're most likely a Volleyer.

Now head to the appropriate section below to see the coping strategies that will work for you.

INTEGRATORS

Integrators happily blend their work and personal lives – there is no clear line between them. Integrators are the ones who gladly take work calls on holiday and can cope with nonstandard and erratic hours to be able to accommodate their personal needs and urgent work demands. Within this type, there are those who enjoy the blend and those who don't.

High Contentment Integrators see this merged world of work and life as a positive state – it makes them feel in control; they are willing and capable multitaskers who thrive on swapping between their professional and personal roles throughout the day – they see this as a way to stay on top of all things.

Low Contentment Integrators see this merged world of work and life as a negative state – they want more control over how and when they transition between work life and personal life; for them, multitasking is draining. They feel overwhelmed. This state often evolves because of a lack of support: they feel forced to address everything at the same time.

INTEGRATOR ISSUES

> **Long days.** The overlapping elements and constant switching are distracting and often slow us down.
> **Confusion**. Other people may not understand an Integrator schedule: are they are at work or at home? This can knock on into other, bigger issues including disappointment, frustration and upset.
> **Resentment from others.** Family may begrudge the Integrator's constant work intrusion, whilst colleagues may wonder about her priorities if the Integrator leaves early to attend a family event.
> **Exhaustion**. This constant switching between roles and tasks is difficult to sustain. Usually, the biggest loser is the Integrator herself who is running on overdrive.

INTEGRATOR SOLUTIONS

> **Be conscious.** When overwork, business and lack of sleep threaten your cool, be strict with yourself and borrow a leaf from the Separators. Even Integrators need to step back sometimes.
> **Communicate.** Maintain an open dialogue with those you love. Check in periodically to make sure they're on board with your schedule. If not, set boundaries you can all work within, together.

SEPARATORS

Separators, as the name suggests, keep their work and personal tasks and lives divided. They're at work when they're at work, and at home when they're at home.

Separators often use physical space and shrewd scheduling to keep things compartmentalised – they are hyper aware of any potential crossovers. Within this type, there are those who relish the separation and others who do not.

High Contentment Separators (they are either work-centred or home-centred) feel in control; they decide which part of their lives is of highest priority and then work around it, keeping everything else separate in order to focus and achieve: they are comfortable with the trade-offs that this type of prioritising requires.

Low Contentment Separators feel out of control; for them, the separation feels like a sacrifice – they don't want to favour one life element over the other. These captives often lack choice – the nature of their job might mean they are required in the workplace, or perhaps their company doesn't offer work-from-home options. Or, heavy personal commitments mean they struggle to dart away for a call or email.

SEPARATOR ISSUES
> **Blinkeredness.** Separators don't benefit from crossover opportunities that blend skill development and encourage widespread support.
> **Conflict.** Those who put work first may not have a strong social network outside of their jobs. They may also lack variety in the type of support available to them.
> **Regret.** Those who prioritise family often regret downshifting their career aspirations. Those who focus on work forgo precious personal time.

SEPARATOR SOLUTIONS
> **Challenge yourself.** Whether it's work drinks on a weekend or a project that's outside your remit, set yourself a target of integrating once a week. Occasionally stepping outside your comfort zone can reap big rewards.
> **Reassess.** Regularly check in with yourself to make sure your choices still fit with your preferences and goals. Is there a way to combine your options to minimise regret down the line? Your initial reactions might be right, but by opening yourself to the possibilities you might find a third way that's even better.

VOLLEYERS
Volleyers play the game; they switch back and forth between integrating and separating depending on priorities and circumstances at any given time. There are two types of Volleyers: those who enjoy the to-and-fro and those for whom it is more of a struggle.

High Contentment Volleyers thrive on the constantly shifting pattern of their lives: they will happily separate work and life to give their best to each role and then integrate at key times too. They understand the importance of quality time and feel in control. Their division might be broad (they might, say, work part of the year or rest the other) or more pedestrian (usual part-time work) but along these split seams they sew integration when necessary.

Low Contentment Volleyers lack control and have low satisfaction levels in regards to when and how they switch between integration and separation. Their jobs may require lots of travel away from home, or rotate around seasons in which the workload is particularly heavy. This is an imposition. They tend to resent what feels like forced integration or separation over daily or weekly periods.

VOLLEYER ISSUES
> **Brain power**. Switching between styles is hard on the mind – it requires more cognitive complexity and that is draining. Tasks and activities become more difficult to prioritise and fulfil because Volleyers are dealing with different demands at different times.
> **Confusion**. Both the Volleyer herself and those around her may feel like things are chaotic, because the Volleyer's behaviour is not predictable.
> **Fatigue**. Those who do not relish this flexibility in particular are susceptible to extreme tiredness and have to also manage the fact that because of the unruly nature of their lives, they're more vulnerable to support systems breaking down.

VOLLEYER SOLUTIONS
> **Embrace structure.** Even if it's just in her mind, the Volleyer will benefit from creating a format for how the day will pan out. Keep it loose, that's how you work best. But even a loose plan for what will happen when creates a feeling of control. And just like the Integrator, when exhaustion threatens to overwhelm, narrow the focus, turn off your devices and feel the benefits.
> **Clarify.** When those around you seem confused, tell them where you're at. To the Volleyer everything goes all at the same time, but friends and family might need more guidance as to what's going on in your head. Explain. Minimise conflict. Feel less stressed.

There are times when we all feel forced into a corner – when we end up on the lower end of the contentment scale. This usually happens because of pressures that are beyond our control. Sadly, much of our working lives involve managing control – we can't always have it, and that's when balance issues usually arise.

That said, even entrepreneurs who work for themselves (who might, in others' eyes, have the perfect, self-propelled set up) can't help but be at the will of others from time to time. We don't work alone in a void; other people's expectations and demands inevitably encroach on how and when we work, which can result in us losing control – and end up falling from the high end of the contentment table down to the bottom.

The point of all these FlexStyles isn't to confuse matters further – quite the opposite. When we have identified our type it releases us from attempting to work and exist within the other preferences – the ones that don't resonate with us. This is an exercise in pressure and expectation elimination – usually of our own self-imposed variety. Staying true to who we are (yes, we know, recurrent theme) means we don't waste our energies trying to live up to someone else's expectations.

SMARTPHONES

Balance isn't all about flexible working and childcare, far from it. Balance is about wellbeing, contentedness – and today, it also centres on connectedness. Many of us are constantly plugged into our phones – that flash of light, that ping – and while it seems fun and pleasantly distracting in the moment, phone addiction (even on a low level) impacts on our wellbeing and our sense of balance.

Research says that these days, many of us spend more time tending to the needs of our phones than we do our lovers. We aren't in a position to draw a conclusion on the state of modern romance, but we can at least highlight the fact that when we are in close, loving relationships with people, rather than technology, these bonds aid the pursuit of contentment.

Romance aside, the internet, social media and our phones – the biggest conduits of our online addictions – also interrupt how our brains best function. The upshot of having a mobile phone that constantly penetrates our peaceful (ish) lives, is that we become over-stimulated and overtired. They are a modern-day drug that leaves us needy and angsty when we don't get the next hit. In short, when we overuse technology it erodes our sense of balance, and our ability to perform or concentrate at a high level.

When it comes to technology in the home, some of us see it as an invader and some as a liberator. Many more of us have mixed feelings. It can, of course, be incredibly useful to be able to answer an email when it comes in, especially if this only requires a quick nip to the other room. But these constant interruptions can have a serious impact on our work and sanity. We must all, whatever our preference, type, job or lifestyle, learn to manage communication technology wisely. It is perfectly acceptable to make ourselves available where necessary, as long as we stay aware that the web doesn't become our dominant balance disrupter.

WORKOUT Digital Detox

WARNING: We've taken the liberty of including a workout that will take a little more than your allotted ten minutes. Bear with us. The space this workout will give you is worth more than the time it takes.

We believe in being connected to power ahead in your career, but don't burn out. One day this week (and as needed) try this digital detox. The compulsion to check phones is hard to resist.

Test this out by putting your phone by your hand whilst at work but not checking it for one hour even if you get messages.

Hard, right!?

So take the advice given to parents of teenage children and don't give yourself the option. When you're feeling particularly burnt out and stressed, just when it seems hardest, take all your devices and lock them in a drawer. Literally lock them. Then give yourself a time to unlock.

Whether it's a weekend, day or even your four-hour evening, taking that time to regularly disconnect will do more for your balance than Instagramming those same experiences ever will.

HOW TO Balance Your Responsibilities

Many of you may not have children yet nor will some of you have them at all. Statistically speaking, the majority of women do become mothers (in 2011 in the UK, 80 per cent of women aged forty-five years and over had at least one child and the figures are similar in the US) and so it's pretty likely that even if you aren't there yet, one day, children will become a dimension in your balance triangle. If you do have children, you will almost certainly have realised that while the need to integrate family and work isn't the preserve of the mother, we shoulder a disproportionate amount of child-rearing responsibility. And, whether we become mothers or not, these responsibilities extend past the small beings themselves into running the home and a duty towards extended family too.

DON'T HAVE IT ALL

One of the biggest antagonists to women balancing our responsibilities is the voice that tells us we need to have it all.

Originally the title of a life manual by the legendary *Cosmopolitan* editor **Helen Gurley Brown**, having it all refers to the idea that women can (should?) have a high-demand career, a gorgeous partner, well-rounded children, look great, reside in a *Grand Designs* home, host weekly dinner parties and retain, at all times, a cool, relaxed demeanour.

The thing is, the having it all woman is a caricature who lives in our imagination; we know she isn't real and yet her presence takes the wind out of our sails. A staunch feminist, who was passionate about the importance of careers for women's self-worth, Gurley Brown strongly disagreed with her book's title because of its sense of smugness and impossibility.

It was, after all, Gurley Brown who made *Cosmo* the radical, sex-loving magazine that it is today – not exactly a publication in line with these unrealistic female ideals. What Gurley Brown was telling her *Cosmo* readers, at a time when single women couldn't obtain a mortgage, was to celebrate their unmarried status and demand better lovers. We can

only assume that what she intended with her have it all concept was
not a yardstick against which we all continually fail, but a desire for
women to want more.

And that we agree with.

The problem is that having it all has become a shorthand criticism
used against women who work. It is a phrase today that embodies
our internalised guilt: we must live up to the hard choices and
expectations of women who have gone before us, whilst we must also
manage our own tendencies towards perfectionism.

Having it all also encompasses that malignant tendency we possess
to compare ourselves to other women, the ones who always, from
the outside looking in, *appear* to have all bases covered and shiny. Of
course, the chances are these women are no more sorted than you.
What we're saying is that when we accept the fact that appearances
can be deceptive, we move one step nearer to letting go of the
impossible expectations we put upon ourselves on a daily basis.

Anne-Marie Slaughter, the former US Director of Policy Planning, is
famously vocal on this subject. In her seminal article, 'Why Women
Still Can't Have It All', which, by the way, is the most popular article
ever published online by The Atlantic magazine (shows what a big issue
this is) and later in her book Unfinished Business: Women Work Men Family,
Slaughter is adamant that women just can't have it all.

Having landed her dream job in US foreign policy, she quickly
realised that holding a high-profile position in government brought
glory and complications in equal measure. It was impossible,
Slaughter said, to balance her responsibilities as a parent with
her responsibilities as a professional and meet her high expectations
of each role.

After two years in the top job, Slaughter handed in her notice. What
did she feel? Not resentment, but relief. With the structure of society
as it is today, Slaughter, and many other successful women like her,
strongly believe that women just can't have it all, all at once.

At the start of our careers we might think we're going to have a perfect family life with perfect work and the perfect everything to go alongside, but reality tells us otherwise. Overwhelmingly, other research supports this view too. So take heed and accept the truth, we promise it will have a positive effect on how balanced you feel. In a practical sense, this means learning to downgrade a little bit, because a mythical version of perfection just doesn't stack up in real life.

If we can't have it all, then what can we have? Well, 'all' is a subjective term. When we downgrade all from all-pervasive flawlessness to realistic satisfaction, from everything to enough, then all once again becomes a valid part of the balance equation. The trick is to know what our all is and to pursue only that.

We cannot tell you what your all is, just as we couldn't compose a universal formula for success in Chapter 1. What we can do is enlighten you about the impossible: you aren't going to be able to do an eighty-hour work week, pick the kids up from school, make dinner for the extended family, fit in a trio of gym sessions and get eight hours sleep a night. Something just has to give. For medical oncologist **Debra Josephs**, one facet of the universal work, family and social life trinity has had to go on the back burner for her to be able to fully engage in her job and children. 'Really, I don't see my friends – they are the people who suffer the most; it gets me down, but I just can't juggle all the plates all at the same time.'

That something doesn't need to be a complete element of life: Debra has a lot going on with her patients, research, seventy-hour weeks, toddler, new baby, husband, home, family and friends. If you aren't willing to forgo one life element completely, another tactic is to relinquish yourself from doing all to an A* standard. Because research says that when we lower the benchmarks just a fraction, we can still feel as though we're doing enough and we'll also be able to get more of a handle on our time management and balance too.

ACCEPT WHO YOU ARE

We can't go forth and feel centred when we are progressing in someone else's ideal. The reason that Mother Teresa and Ingrid

Bergman were drawn to such divergent paths in life, despite both being born in Europe around the same time, isn't due to place or time, it's because of their preferences.

The way we live, our aspirations and the values we put on work and life all come down to preference. We all possess different attitudes towards balance just as we all possess different tastes in style and food. In societies where basic barriers to career progression (education for girls, legislation against discrimination and availability of contraception) have been removed, we also differ in how much and how we choose to work.

'For me,' says Women's Equality Party Leader **Sophie Walker**, 'there are different balances on different days and at different times too. What I'm doing is very emotional and personal – politics is personal, right? – I just can't completely separate home from work. Plus, practically speaking, sometimes I know I'll need to work late and I'll bypass the childminder and take my children to a committee meeting because it's easier for everyone involved. When it comes to managing all the elements of life, you've got to be human. I wouldn't advocate my way of working for everyone – but it suits me.'

Our preferences usually slot into one of three broad character types that describe the importance we place on home life and work life. In the main, we are either home-centred, work-centred or adaptive, which describes those of us who straddle both camps – for whom work and life are equally important.

Below are descriptions of each type, alongside a well-known representative of the category. To be clear, these arch categories aren't there to box us in – after all, one of *Step Up*'s values is individuality; instead, we hope you find that they are a framework against which you are able to transcend the bind of comparison to others. When we know that we are different to our sisters, our friends and our mothers for that matter, it relieves some of the pressure to do it all, and should also help us inch towards a more finessed state of balance.

HOME-CENTRED (APPROX. 20 PER CENT OF WOMEN)
Jools Oliver
Describing herself as a 'Proud Mum of 4' (with a fifth child on the way at the time of going to press), Jools Oliver is a glowing example of a woman whose primary focus is their home and family.

WORK-CENTRED (APPROX. 20 PER CENT OF WOMEN)
Dame Helen Mirren
'I always did – and still do – value my freedom too highly [to become a parent].' An Oscar, a Golden Globe and a handful of BAFTAs to her name, work-centred Mirren is fully committed to her acting career. Dame Helen still needs balance, but she is unlikely to experience internal conflict in regards to how she balances work and home life.

ADAPTIVE WOMAN (APPROX. 60 PER CENT OF WOMEN)
Phoebe Philo
Celine fashion designer Phoebe Philo (ex-Chloé) only joined the LVMH-owned French brand on the condition that the Parisian studio was moved to London. Philo values her work and her family – and as such, cancelled an international fashion show because she was heavily pregnant. Philo may work full-time, part-time or flexibly but she still feels a visceral internal pull between her work and home lives. Philo and her peers want to fully succeed at work but they want to fully succeed at home too. Being this type of woman is tough.

The majority of women fall into Philo's adaptive category, which means it's likely that you're one of these types too. Although home- and work-centred women tend to court the most amount of public controversy, it's relatively easy for them in terms of internal conflict, because they're absolutely adamant about where their priorities lie. What's difficult is when we're a straddler, when our heart is in both camps but our time and energy restricts our efforts.

If you are adaptive, it's likely you'll always carry some degree of guilt, but there's comfort at least in knowing that many other women share your pain. Plus, when we accept our type, it helps quieten that comparison beast. There's just no point pitting ourselves against our work-centred best friend who flies all over the world on business, earns a packet and is happy to only see her children at the weekends, when we're adaptive and want to eat a meal with the family each night. It is a fact that if we acknowledge and accept our type, we begin to reduce tension within ourselves and become better placed to contain feelings of guilt too.

The trick with achieving balance is to strip away as many potential pressures and pitfalls as possible; all women struggle with balance so we might as well only struggle within our own category and not across the complete set. But it is true that those of us who hold a strong dual focus in our lives stand on wobblier, less balance-friendly ground.

HOW TO Stop Comparing

Yup, comparison is such a big issue, we've given it its own section. As an aside, preferences and work types aren't necessarily made in the womb. They are just as likely to be products of our inevitable psychosocial conditioning. However we arrived into our preference sphere, we still have them and we need to learn to live comfortably within their boundaries if we are going to achieve that mythical state of balance – if we want to ride our mythical unicorns.

Because when you aren't able to accept your inclinations and type, you devalue part of what makes you you – and that will inevitably lead to complications, stress, overwhelm and feelings of imbalance and guilt.

In comparison, a woman who understands her type will understand why she feels the way she does about the demands and strains of home and work. And when we're able to see this in ourselves we become more sympathetic towards other women and their preference types too.

Anne-Marie Slaughter learnt the hard – and public – way about what happens when we lack sympathy of others. 'I'd been the one telling young women at my lectures that you can have it all and do it all, regardless of what field you are in. Which means I'd been part, albeit unwittingly, of making millions of women feel that they are to blame if they cannot manage to rise up the ladder as fast as men and also have a family and an active home life (and be thin and beautiful to boot).'

One of the biggest complications to female career success is the way we put other women on a pedestal (usually a fictitious one) and then beat ourselves over the head with how she just does life better. This kind of thinking is poisonous on so many levels. In fact, comparison is not only detrimental but can often be just plain wrong. The external façade we see can often belie the reality going on backstage.

If you don't believe us, take it from food guru **Melissa Hemsley**, who with her sister **Jasmine** appeared to arrive at immediate success, despite many years of hard, private graft: 'Remember not to look at actors or celebrities and think they have had overnight success. It's never overnight. We've been doing this for seven years and we didn't do anything public for the first two years. For those two years we were cooking as private chefs for families, seven days a week. Then two years of blogging and building a platform for ourselves, then two years of really putting ourselves out there and being promoted by Ebury with our first book.'

Even that swanlike friend you think has effortlessly assumed all responsibilities – all while maintaining her figure and learning violin – might actually be more of a duck, who's able to appear all still and serene on the surface, but is still frantically paddling beneath.

Comparison is negative because, in our heads, it eats away at our confidence and when that goes, the dominos of networking, self-promotion and leadership topple in quick succession. And when we dig ourselves into a dark pit of harmful self-dissatisfaction and simple jealousy, our careers suffer, and so do our contentment levels, drive and everything else associated with a positive mental attitude.

We are absolutely wedded to the belief that if we want to get ahead in life and also, crucially, be able to leave a career legacy that is more favourable and open to our daughters, and their daughters after them, we must stand in solidarity as women.

So, rather than letting negative comparisons suck you into the pit, be proud of your female peers and allow yourself to work within your own type. When you are able to get those wheels spinning, you should enjoy a new strength of character that doesn't rely on negative comparisons, but rather accepts others as they are too.

If we all get ourselves to this happy place – a place without pedestals – then we will be able to stand together and instigate change. As **Catherine Hakim**, the creator of Preference Theory has said, 'It is our differences as women – and our criticism of those differences – that have allowed the patriarchy to flourish and if we can accommodate and understand each other, we will be in a better position to help each other and all of womankind rise.'

WORKOUT Comparison Free

Instead of comparing yourself to other people, create the habit of comparing yourself to yourself. If you feel yourself falling into a comparison freefall think back over the past year. How have you grown as a person? What have you achieved? What progress have you made towards your goals (see Chapter 2 for help setting them)?

For seven minutes you are now going to write in praise of yourself. Achievements this year, characteristics that make you proud, compliments you've received. For the whole seven minutes, your pen must flow and there's no stopping. Writing for seven minutes – even before you've read your ode to you – is proven to have a strong positive mental effect.

Then take three minutes to reread your ramblings. Soak up your success.

This habit has the benefit of creating gratitude, appreciation and kindness towards yourself as you observe how far you have come, the obstacles you have overcome and the great things you have done. You feel good about yourself without having to compare yourself with others.

HOW TO Take Our Time

'At the moment, women have fifteen years to go to university, get their career on track, try and buy a home and have a baby. That is a hell of a lot to ask someone. As a passionate feminist, I feel we have not been honest enough with women about this issue.' **Kirsty Allsop** is right. Time is another key ingredient in the pressure cooker of female careers. One that has the potential to ruin the dish entirely.

As Allsop says, many of us feel we need to progress as quickly as possible with few detours so that we can reach our success early on in life. There is absolutely nothing wrong with that – it's admirable in fact, to have such drive, commitment and vision – and it works as long as this time-pressured career path suits our vibe and our life plans.

Problems arise when things go awry. We are not here to tell you how to live your lives and we certainly don't want to bang on about babies, although statistically speaking most of you will end up having one. It's just that when we impetuously rush ahead without considering the whole picture, we are more likely to have negatively tipped the scales when it comes to balance.

These days, careers are wonderfully long and winding. Remember what we said at the start: as women we have so many opportunities ahead, not forgetting that re-energised second wind in our fifties and sixties. What we're saying is work hard and work tactically early on and you will build a strong foundation that can withstand any detours along the way.

Often, other people see the arrival of a baby as the ultimate career inhibitor. Actually, the opposite is so often true. Children can be wonderful career exalters; it's just that society doesn't take the broad view. It thinks (wrongly) that mothers = distracted employees. And while mothers can become distracted now and again, working mothers are also gritty, passionate employees who possess a renewed resolve for success.

For mother of two and *Desert Island Disks* host **Kirsty Young**, the arrival of her daughters fuelled her ambition fire. 'Before children, my life had been centred on work. Once I became a mother – and it's an entirely predictable change – I realised that if I was going to walk out of the door and leave this tiny person in the care of someone else, I had better be going to work on something that I enjoy; something that I really love and am good at. Strangely, having children has made me a lot more focused and ruthless in the choices I make in my career. I care more about my job now than I ever have.'

For many of us, like for Kirsty, additional responsibilities will fuel our drive, make us more strategic and renew our passion for our work. For others, they will prompt us to re-evaluate our choices and find success (and balance) a different way. The important thing to remember is that there is no right answer.

Nearly a decade ago, mother of four **Courtney Adamo** decided with a couple of her other mum friends to launch a quiet blog so that they could keep in touch across their geographical divides. The blog quickly morphed into a highly successful, market-leading shopping portal. The site's success is fuelled by Courtney's effortlessly good-looking Instagram account. But just as her fame and success went stratospheric, Adamo and her family sold their North London home and decided to take twelve months out of the rat race – a year as nomadic, blissful travellers. They did it to remove themselves from the pressures of work and modern living – and give their minds some space to wonder.

'I look back on the past twelve years in London, and not that I would change any of it (because it was wonderful!), but I just don't have any desire to return to that same busy lifestyle. And I think you really have to step out of it in order to come to this conclusion, because it can be so appealing while you're in the thick of it all. This year has been an enormous break for us and has certainly shifted our priorities, given us that big, deep breath and the ability to look at our lives with an entirely different perspective, not just with work but with life and family.

'I hate the term "rat race", but sometimes life can start to feel this way: working hard, trying to reach new goals, making more money, having a bigger, better house, keeping it perfectly tidy, staying on top of everything, accepting more and more onto your plate. I was definitely guilty of this "do everything and do it better" way of living, and I feel so much happier having stepped off that treadmill, slowing everything way down, focusing on what it is that makes me and my family happy and not worrying what impression I am giving, or how others view me and my "success". I have definitely been guilty of viewing my success based on what other people think, or even based on how my success compares to others. But this is really the worst thing you can do – it never makes you feel better about yourself, it only hinders your ability to be the best version of yourself and to be truly happy with the decisions you've made. Stepping away from it all has given me a clearer idea of what I want out of my career, irrespective of what others think or want.'

As Courtney implies, life isn't a hamster wheel that needs to spin in the same direction for eternity. We have the power to make our careers work for us and that includes having children (and myriad other responsibilities) and still feeling balanced. Hopefully, that thought alone has made you feel a tiny bit less frazzled already; after all, if we are going to be working for the next half a century, there is just no need to sprint the marathon. Your time is just that, yours – so remember to hold it tight and spend it your way.

HOW TO Get Support at Home

Sophie Walker, leader of the newly formed Women's Equality Party, mother of two daughters, autism campaigner and instigator of change, says she'd be unable to meaningfully engage in all the facets of her life without her husband. 'I couldn't do what I'm doing without a supportive partner: my husband and I are very similar, we're both hugely driven and ambitious. We both come from working-class, Northern families – we get each other. We have a very tight bond and that matters hugely.'

No person – man or woman – can spin all the plates of work, life and children all at the same time; when things become more complicated, we just can't progress or survive alone. Support is a vital component of attaining any type of balance: doing the dirty work needs to be equally passed around.

A good measure of how even things are in your house is the question of childcare payment: if it has been agreed that your salary will notionally cover this, then we propose that things aren't as equal as they could be. Do you have his and hers milk in the fridge? We guess not. Equality is as much about attitude as it is chores. Remember too that your return to work – even if it barely covers childcare – is an investment not only in yourself but in all of your futures.

When we build a level playing field at home, where responsibilities are even-handed (and you aren't the one who always takes the day off work because Baby Number One has croup again) then our glide towards personal balance should feel smoother.

And support, by the way, isn't just about partners. Friends, family, neighbours and, in particular, grandparents can all be gallant conduits of balance. In Japan, some companies have gone as far as to introduce special leave systems for employees so they can take care of their grandchildren. Whilst over in the US, nearly a third of grandparents watch their grandchildren for five days a week or more, according to Lori K. Bitter's new book, *The Grandparent Economy*.

Baby Boomers, she concludes, now spend their time and money making the lives of their children and grandchildren easier. There's no way the Duchess of Cambridge could support so many worthwhile causes and arrive at the job with no trace of baby puke on her shoulder without an army of helpers back at the palace – and her mum on speed dial. None of us should ever feel too proud to accept help.

Law firm partner **Tamara Box** could not have achieved her goals without the support of her husband and is a passionate advocate of planning how responsibilities might be shared before they happen. 'I cannot believe the number of women I talk to who don't have honest and open conversations with their partners about what they need, who don't even talk about how to divide up responsibilities. I think couples need to work out their parenting priorities. Each of you will have different roles – that's inevitable – but how do you support each other in those roles? What matters? How do you manage careers together? What kind of career do you both want? What is involved in that? Is there travel or relocation? What's really at the heart of your ambitions together? So many women are encouraged to think about men in a very one-dimensional way, and we are culturally conditioned to like powerful, strong, ambitious, perhaps even arrogant men, without thinking about the consequences of that on us.'

Box's questions are pertinent and meaningful. We must never just accept our lot; achieving a state of balance is a task in itself, and sometimes that needs to involve questioning the status quo at home. Box is also an advocate of embracing any help that our supporters offer us.

'You have to decide what you think is important. If you think it is important that one of you be there every night to put your children to bed but he either doesn't agree or doesn't want to do it, then you are the one who will have to take that responsibility. There is some fabulous research out there about the invisibility of privilege. Men have the invisibility of privilege at work in that they don't notice the extra advantages they are getting; they assume that they have gotten where they are by merit. With no experience in anything else, they assume that what happens to them happens to everyone. It doesn't occur to them that others don't experience things in the same way. Conversely, I think women have invisibility of privilege around child rearing. We seem to think that motherhood confers special knowledge and therefore we know best about everything involving our children. I'm afraid we won't see equality of parenting – and by extension, equality in the workforce – until women give up that privilege.'

So much of the female career progression formula – and we include balance in this – is based on not just equality, but in educating men to shift their opinions and cut us some slack and us doing the same for them too. Yes, we want parity, but parity doesn't equate to sameness. If you do have children, you might still end up the more dominant and involved caregiver. The crucial thing is that if you do, you do it by choice.

What we need to hold dear is that we are *allowed* to feel differently and we must never sacrifice our wellbeing for the sake of anything else. While having it all in the most literal sense might elude you, when we think clearly, plan well and don't surrender to pressures, we are all more than capable of enjoying everything we want out of work and life.

THE TIPS

|1| Manage your time

If after the workouts you still feel a victim of overwhelm, you need to trim. Missing out can be tough – particularly a great night out – but balance is all about choices. For help in making those choices, turn back to Chapter 3.

|2| Share the care

The support we can get from our partners, brilliantly, now goes beyond bath and bedtime. Shared parental leave in the UK means that maternity leave can now be split. Increasingly employers are acknowledging the importance of shared care with equal paternity pay too. If you have children – and ideally even before – have an open conversation with your partner about this option. Or if you live in a less dad-friendly place – USA, you have a lot to do on this front – then think about the other options. As we've said above, flexible and part-time working needn't be restricted to mothers. Traditionally, men felt taking extended leave or changing their hours reflected poorly on them. But times have changed. Help your partner – if he's not keen already – to embrace that change too.

|3| Just say no

The word NO doesn't always trip off the tongue. Not apologising for that no is even tougher. But in achieving balance, it is crucial. Next time you say no to a plan or catch-up, leave it at that. Don't explain, apologise or dither. You are otherwise engaged and that's OK. When we start to qualify our nos, we lose power and credibility. Plus we leave our choices open to negotiation. This week, let no mean no.

|4| Be well

Balance is all about wellbeing. Mental, physical and emotional. When one of these is out of whack, we aren't able to be – or work – at our most effective. So your task this week is to keep an eye out for yourself. Take the time to eat a proper meal, go for a walk, do something (not work) that you enjoy. Our careers are crucial, but not at the expense of ourselves.

|5| Inner peace

There are a few recurring themes in our book – difference, choice, enjoyment and authenticity being among the most crucial. We will never feel perfectly in harmony all the time. But if, even after following our tips in this chapter, you still feel imbalanced more often than not, the likelihood is you need to re-evaluate your choices, find things you enjoy more, celebrate your difference and embrace the authentic you. How? Full circle to the beginning of the book. What does success mean to you?

THAT'S A WRAP

Historian, author and The Ascent of Woman documentary-maker, **Amanda Foreman** has a clever knack of mining historical events to explain how women are viewed in today's society. We were lucky enough to hear her speak at a recent debate, The Future of Feminism, and at it, she told the 1000-strong audience (nearly all women, nearly all walks of life) this:

'Patriarchy is not a universal history. In 8000BC in Turkey, women did the same work, ate the same diet and were buried in the same way as men: so at the dawn of civilisation there was equality. The patriarchy came later – it was human made – and what has been made can be unmade.'

What Foreman said resonated. This female career odyssey, the one we have just spent ten chapters dissecting and celebrating, isn't solely a narrative for the singular woman – for you. It is also in some small way a vehicle for improvement for future generations too. To become truly equal in the workplace women need to rise and succeed for ourselves and for our gender as a whole – for our unborn daughters, and their daughters too.

What has been made can be unmade.

What's blatantly obvious is that we are just not meant to fit our smooth curves into all these man-shaped career holes that exist today. The ones with rigid hierarchical edges that only accommodate an insatiable desire for money and power: we need to cut out our own, freeform moulds. Ones that have breathing space for all of our individualities, our particular types of timings, our female-style authenticity, tenacity, vision and our aptitude for good old-fashioned multitasking.

With the small adjustments that we advocate and suggest within this book, we want to empower you to be your best – and then some. We want your careers to be fist-punchingly fantastic (and rainbow-coloured to boot). Only once we begin to feel unencumbered will we be able to unmake male dominance at work.

Today is a crazy exciting time to be a career woman. We don't have to be a CEO or a startup whizz to make a difference for ourselves, and for women as a whole. Change doesn't come from above, it exists at the grassroots: it exists with you.

OK, so that's the big, stirring picture. In an everyday sense though, this book was very much written to give you the knowledge, tools and inspiration to take your career, put it under a microscope and then javelin-throw it skywards. We don't care where you are heading, as long as you get to the place you want to be – the place that you dream about, the one that you think it is impossible to reach.

It's not. That place is there waiting for us to stand tall and mean business.

Women often feel invisible in the seas of change. But Foreman says this is absolutely not so. Even the tyrant that was Lenin, she recounted, told others that all uprisings need women. 'Throughout history, every revolution has needed women to support it, but in the end women have always been oppressed and betrayed by men – until the twentieth century, when there was a female-led revolution [the Suffragette movement]. Why? Because male revolutions were about shifting power from one structure to another, but women's are about subverting the order of power altogether and making it accessible to all. That engendered real change. And that was not only good for women, but for men too.'

Female career empowerment and success isn't about haranguing the men for how over time they have unwittingly (we hope) built obstacles in our paths. Equality at work – capturing your success unicorn – relies on drawing men in, educating them to this necessary change, and then working together to the same end.

To an end where we can truly pick and choose what we do and how we do it: when that day comes, by the way, we're absolutely certain that women's struggles with confidence will start to ease, because we'll be able to shine in just the way we want. So many of our barriers to success reside inside our heads; we are insecure because we've been made to feel that we're losing before we've even started the race.

Now all you need to do is work hard, network ferociously, nab a mentor and remember that it is OK to tell the world that you've just done something good – or even that you're just there. You are not a number on a timesheet; you are a brilliant example of what it means to be a woman today and it's OK to disrupt the order of things as long as you maintain integrity and poise.

We hope that by bringing together so many interwoven strands of this female progression story that things will change in your career – and in your life too. Because we want women to have a better journey to success; to a success that is built in our own image and is valued for what it is and not how it conforms.

Now go out and get 'em. Go on. It's only you that's stopping you.

If you like what is in our book, find us on all the major
social media platforms @thestepupclub for more advice,
encouragement and sparkling tales from the top.
(Yes, we've just shamelessly self-promoted.)
(Gotta practise what we preach, and all that.)

Endnotes

CHAPTER 1 – THE TRUTH ABOUT WOMEN (AND MEN)

'diversity also equals prosperity': Gender-balanced investment teams have been shown to provide better results and a more balanced approach ('What Makes Teams Smarter', *Harvard Business Review*, July 2011). Organisations with gender diverse senior leadership teams also show more successful growth across a range of measures including operating results, public image, employee satisfaction and stock price (several studies, for example, 'The Bottom Line: Corporate Performance and Women's Representation on Boards (2004–2008)', *Catalyst*, March 2011).

'for men and women there are brain wiring variations': Ingalhalikar, M., Smith, A., Parker, D., Satterthwaite, T., Elliott, M., Ruparel, K., Hakonarson, H., Gur, R. E., Gur, R.C. and Verma, R., 'Sex differences in the structural connectome of the human brain' (2014), *PNAS*; see also 111(2), 823–828. Ruigroka, A., Salimi-Khorshidib, G., Laia, M-C., Baron-Cohen, S., Lombardoa, M.V., Tait, R. J. and Suckling, J., 'A meta-analysis of sex differences in human brain structure' (2014), *Neuroscience & Biobehavioural Reviews*, 39, 34–50.

'some recent studies suggest no significant difference in crucial parts of the brain at all': Tan, A., Ma, W., Vira, A., Marwha, D., Eliot, L., 'The human hippocampus is not sexually-dimorphic: Meta-analysis of structural MRI volumes' (2016), *Neuroimage*, 124(A), 350–366. This study, for example, suggests that the hippocampus (the centre of emotions and long-term memory) and the corpus callosum (a group of fibres that links the two parts of the brain which affects languages processing) are not significantly different between men and women.

'the most recent research leads to the centre of the brain': Daphna Joel, Zohar Berman, Ido Tavor, Nadav Wexler, Olga Gaber, Yaniv Stein, Nisan Shefi, Jared Pool, Sebastian Urchs, Daniel S. Margulies, Franziskus Liem, Jürgen Hänggi, Lutz Jäncke and Yaniv Assaf, 'Sex beyond the genitalia: The human brain mosaic' (2015), *PNAS*; published ahead of print 30 November 2015.

'The most successful person in the workplace, research says, is the woman who retains her female brain but who isn't afraid to borrow some stereotypically male traits when the opportunity requires it': O'Neill, O. and O'Reilly, C. A., 'Reducing the backlash effect: Self-monitoring and women's promotions' (2011), *Journal of Occupational and Organizational Psychology*, 84(4), 825–832.

'the map of association in our childhood brains is sculpted so that the function of the hardware is constantly altered by experience': This refers to neuroplasticity, whereby our brains create new neural pathways to adapt to our experiences.

'Hormones also play a part in this lifelong divide': See, for example, Baron-Cohen, Simon, *The Essential Difference: Men, Women and the Extreme Male Brain*, Penguin, 2012.

'as does parental nurture': Eliot, Lise, *Pink Brain, Blue Brain: How Small Differences Grow Into Troublesome Gaps And What We Can Do About It*, OneWorld Publications, 2012.

'a recent study using Asian-American women': Shih, M., Pittinsky, T. L. and Ambady, N., 'Stereotype susceptibility: Identity salience and shifts in quantitative performance' (1999), *Psychological Science*, 10(1), 80–83.

'in reality women aren't actually worse at maths': Lindberg, S. M., Hyde, J. S., Petersen, J. L. and Linn, M. C., 'New Trends in Gender and Mathematics Performance: A Meta-Analysis' (2010), *Psychological Bulletin*, 136(6), 1123–1135.

'gender pay gap': See for example http://ec.europa.eu/justice/gender-equality/gender-pay-gap/index_en.htm (as at 20 May 2016) for gender pay gaps across the EU, which range from 3 to 29 per cent (unadjusted). The gender pay gap in the US was 21 per cent in 2014: See Ariane Hegewisch, Emily Ellis, Heidi Hartmann, Ph.D, 'The Gender Wage Gap: 2014: Earnings Differences by Race and Ethnicity' (March 2015) http://www.iwpr.org/publications/pubs/the-gender-wage-gap-2014-earnings-differences-by-race-and-ethnicity#sthash.rMEFSw09.dpuf.

'**disparity between the number of women at entry-level jobs versus the number higher up the tree**': The statistics on this point have been widely quoted and vary according to industry but see Sandberg, Sheryl, *Lean In*, WH Allen, 2013, pp.5–6 for a good global summary.

'**One huge recent study of student assessments**': Guiso, L., Monte, F., Sapienza, P., Zingales, L., 'Culture, gender, and math' (2008), *Science*, 320,1164–1165.

'**blind auditions were introduced; when the judges weren't able to see the gender of the musicians playing before them, something remarkable happened: women suddenly accounted for 40 per cent of the orchestras**': Goldin, Claudia and Rouse, Cecilia, 'Orchestrating Impartiality: The Impact of "Blind" Auditions on Female Musicians' (2000), *American Economic Review*, 90(4), 715–741.

'**At entry-level jobs, women are nine times more likely than men to say that they do more childcare**': For background to the statistics in this paragraph see McKinsey, 'Women in the Workplace Report 2015' (http://womenintheworkplace.com as at 20 May 2016).

'**In France**':

'**In Japan**': *Womenomics 3.0*, Goldman Sachs, 2010 (http://www.goldmansachs.com/our-thinking/investing-in-women/bios-pdfs/womenomics3_the_time_is_now_pdf.pdf as at 20 May 2016).

'**Just last year in the UK, the government-backed Davies Review**': *Women on Boards*, Davies Review, Five Year Summary, October 2015, https://www.gov.uk/government/publications/women-on-boards-5-year-summary-davies-review

'**Lenny Letter newsletter**': http://www.lennyletter.com/work/a147/jennifer-lawrence-why-do-i-make-less-than-my-male-costars/ as at 20 May 2016.

'**research shows that positive career behaviours (we have hundreds waiting henceforward…) are far more significant than hard graft alone**': There are many studies that demonstrate this principle in relation to the many career behaviours we advocate in this book, for example obtaining a mentor or sponsor (e.g.

Allen, T., 'Career Benefits Associated with Mentoring for Protégés:
A Meta-analysis' (2004), Journal of Applied Psychology, 89(1), 127–136)
or networking (e.g. De Vos, A., De Clippeleer, I. and Dewilde, T.,
'Proactive Career Behaviours and Career Success During the Early
Career' (2010), Journal of Occupational and Organizational Psychology, 82(4),
761–777). There is also evidence that more general positive career
initiative-taking is good for career progression. For example, Seibert,
S., Kraimer, M. and Liden, R., 'What do Proactive People Do? A
Longitudinal Model Linking Proactive Personality and Career Success'
(2001), Personnel Psychology, 54(4), 845–874 found that proactivity in
terms of career initiatives led to better salary growth and number of
promotions.

CHAPTER 2 – DEFINING SUCCESS

'UPBRINGING': The development of gender is a complex subject but
there is no question that parental, societal and cultural expectations
and behaviours play a huge part in determining gender roles. For
a full examination of gender development see, for example, Owen
Blakemore, J., Berenbaum, S. and Liben, L., Gender Development, Taylor &
Francis, 2009 (reprinted 2015).

**'the typical woman gives birth to her first child at thirty years old,
compared to twenty-six years old forty years ago in both the UK
and Australia (twenty-six now and twenty-one then in the US)':**
UK data: http://www.ons.gov.uk/peoplepopulationandcommunity/
birthsdeathsandmarriages/livebirths/bulletins/
livebirthsinenglandandwalesbycharacteristicsofmother1/2014-10-16
Australian data: http://www.abs.gov.au/ausstats%5Cabs@.
nsf/0/8668A9A0D4B0156CCA25792F0016186A?Opendocument US
data: http://www.cdc.gov/nchs/data/databriefs/db232.pdf

**'Men, on the other hand, are usually driven by Summit Fever
from the off':** The 2014 Harvard Business Review study, 'Manage Your
Work, Manage Your Life' (by Groysberg, B. and Abrahams, R.)
consisted of 4000 interviews and 80 surveys with senior executives.
The study confirmed that men continue to place more emphasis on
organisational achievement, whereas women are more likely to define
success as individual achievement and fulfilment. Men were also

more likely to list financial achievement as an aspect of personal or professional success.

'Current research has revealed a shift though, as men who make up Gen Y and to some extent Gen X, begin to take their cues from our zigzagged career graphs': See for example Clarke, M., 'Dual careers: the new norm for Gen Y professionals?' (2015), *Career Development International*, 20(6), 562–582.

'Kaleidoscope career model': Mainiero, L. A. and Sullivan, S. E., 'Kaleidoscope Careers: An alternate explanation for the "opt-out revolution"' (2005), *Academy of Management Executive*, Vol. 19, Issue 1, 101–123.

'The most recent large-scale studies': See above under 'Summit Fever has traditionally driven men' and the 2015 *Today's Professional Woman Report* by Citi and LinkedIn (http://www.citigroup.com/citi/news/2015/150325b.htm as at 20 May 2016), which similarly shows women are more likely to define success as pursuing a passion and making a difference, whereas relatively few (17 per cent) equate reaching the top of their profession with success. Balancing career and family is also a major concern, as is appropriate financial reward.

'Women who have reached this kind of role have typically been driven and worked continuously and full-time': Research tells us that despite the kaleidoscopic nature of our lives, for women to reach senior management positions they still need to operate within a traditional, typically male career framework. See for example O'Neill, D. A., Hopkins, M. M. and Bilimoria, D., 'Women's careers at the start of the 21st century: Patterns and paradoxes' (2008), *Journal of Business Ethics*, 80(4), 727–743.

'Arianna Huffington': Arianna Huffington writing in *The Huffington Post*, 'Beyond Money and Power (and Stress and Burnout): In Search of a New Definition of Success', 2013: http://www.huffingtonpost.com/arianna-huffington/third-metric-redefining-success_b_3354525.html. The Third Metric conference which this blog post promotes subsequently gave rise to her acclaimed book, *Thrive: The Third Metric to Redefining Success and Creating a Happier Life*, WH Allen, 2015.

'When we know our work type': Our terminology is based on that used in Bank, A. and Vinnicombe, S., *Women With Attitude: Lessons for Career Management*, Routledge, 2002.

'short-term career goals': There is extensive evidence that goals positively affect action. See Locke, E. A. and Latham, G. P., *New Developments in Goal Setting and Task Performance*, Routledge, 2013 for a summary of recent theories and developments in this area.

'Research tells us that those who actually write their strategy or goals down score more winners': Dr Gail Matthews' 2015 research into goal-setting, writing and accountability found that those who write down their goals are significantly more likely to achieve them. Those who shared written progress reports on their goals' achievement were even more likely to achieve those goals than those who simply wrote them down for themselves (http://www.dominican.edu/academics/ahss/undergraduate-programs/psych/faculty/assets-gail-matthews/researchsummary2.pdf as at 20 May 2016).

CHAPTER 3 – INTERNAL INFLUENCES

'Strategy: how you think about work': There is very little academic research into personality traits of successful women. These facets are collated from Phanella's own extensive practice and research. However, they are also informed by Caliper's 2014 *Women Leaders* research paper: http://uk.businessinsider.com/personality-traits-of-high-performing-women-2015-1?r=US.

'Men, by the way, have an almost identical set of traits for success': Whilst there is a lack of female-specific research in this area, there are however lots of studies into what makes a successful person. Most of these study senior leaders who are predominantly men. Unsurprisingly, these studies (for example, Pfeffer, J., *Power: Why Some People Have It and Others Don't*, Harper Business, 2010) show similar traits in successful men that we find in successful women, except for the absence of confidence as a specified trait for men.

'The confidence gap': see Kay, K. and Shipman, C., 'The Confidence Gap', *The Atlantic*, 2014.

'Being conscientious … is one of the most important personality factors when referring to success': Behling, O., 'Employee selection: Will intelligence and conscientiousness do the job?' (1998), *Academy of Management Executive*, 12, 77–86; Mount, M. K. and Barrick, M. R., 'Five reasons why the "Big Five" article has been frequently cited' (1998), *Personnel Psychology*, 51, 849–857; Dudley, N., Orvis, K., Lebiecki, J. and Cortina, J., 'A Meta-Analytic Investigation of Conscientiousness in the Prediction of Job Performance: Examining the Intercorrelations and the Incremental Validity of Narrow Traits' (2006), *Journal of Applied Psychology*, 91(1), 40–57.

'Women are expert stress heads' and **'Women and men experience different types of stressors in the workplace':** Richardsen, A., Traavik, L. and Burke, R., 'Women and Work Stress: More and Different?' in *Handbook on Well-being of Working Women*, ed. Connerly, M. and Wu, J., Springer, 2015.

'a body of research in the field of law': Phanella's postgraduate research into the career development of female partners in City law firms.

'Holy Grail of success: work focus': In our study, career planning and ambition (or work focus) were the final two crucial internal factors for career success. In terms of career planning, it was very clear that more junior women were much less likely to plan their careers than junior men and this had a negative impact on their careers. Other research confirms this, for example a study by Penna found that 45 per cent of women don't plan ahead in terms of career goals compared with a third of men: http://www.penna.com/ news-and-opinion/news-details/2015/01/29/women. In another study (Schulz, D. and Enslin, C., 'The Female Executive's Perspective on Career Planning and Advancement in Organizations; Experiences With Cascading Gender Bias, the Double-Bind, and Unwritten Rules to Advancement' (2014), *SAGE* Open 4 (4)), the authors found that women must plan their career and take responsibility for implementing that plan in order to find career success.

'they are all self-aware': see for example, Tjan, A., 'How Leaders Become Self Aware' (2012), *Harvard Business Review*.

'take a personality test': Type theories split individuals into personality types as opposed to determining individual traits. See Bernstein, D., Penner, L., Clarke-Stewart, A. and Roy, E., *Psychology*, 8th edition, Houghton Mifflin Company, 2008, for a full discussion. An example of a test using this model would be the MBTI published by OPP: https://www.opp.com/en/tools/MBTI

'Feedback Analysis': This workout is based on Drucker, P., 'Managing Oneself' (2005), *Harvard Business Review*.

'a woman of relative intellect could, research tells us, be good at pretty much any job': Hunter, J., 'Cognitive ability, cognitive aptitudes, job knowledge, and job performance' (1986), *Journal of Vocational Behavior*, 29(3), 340–362.

'Job crafting': Job crafting is the process through which individuals alter their own job roles to better suit their skills and interests, thereby increasing their job satisfaction. For a fuller discussion, see Tims, M. and Bakker, A., 'Job Crafting: Towards a New Model of Individual Job Redesign' (2010), *SA Journal of Industrial Psychology*, 36(2), 1–9.

'Academics define stress': Lazarus, R. S., *Psychological Stress and the Coping Process*, McGraw-Hill, 1966.

'when we are able to raise our stress tolerance': Stress tolerance shows a strong correlation with job performance. See, for example, Evers, A., Anderson, N. and Smit-Voskujil, O. (eds), *The Blackwell Handbook of Personnel Selection*, Wiley-Blackwell, 2005.

'Women who conduct stress more effectively': Burke, R. and McKeen, C., 'Training and Development Activities and Career Success of Managerial and Professional Women' (1994), *Journal of Management Development*, 13(5), 53–63.

'Cognitive Behavioural Therapy': CBT is an evidence-based talking therapy that has been proven to treat a wide range of conditions by looking at how we think about a situation and how this affects the way we act. There are many excellent resources about CBT both online and in print which can be easily found using your internet browser, library or book shop. If, however, you experience severe anxiety or worry that affect your mood or ability to function you should always see your doctor who may consider referring you to a mental health specialist.

'Stress really does': Baum, A. and Polsusnzy, D., 'Health Psychology: Mapping Biobehavioral Contributions to Health and Illness' (1999), *Annual Review of Psychology*, Vol. 50, 137–163.

'Research tells us that people who walk outside in a natural setting': Bratman, G., Hamilton, P., Hahn, K., Daily, G. and Gross, J., 'Nature experience reduces rumination and subgenual prefrontal cortex activation' (2015), *Proceedings of the National Academy of Sciences of the United States of America*, 112(28), 8567–8572.

'scripts that we carry through life': Script theory was developed by Silvan Tomkins (Tomkins, Silvan, 'Script Theory' in *The Emergence of Personality*, Joel Aronoff, A. I. Rabin and Robert A. Zucker (eds), Springer Publishing Company, 1987, 147–216) and then Roger Schank (Schank, R. and Abelson, R., *Scripts, Plans, Goals and Understanding: An Inquiry into Human Knowledge Structures*, Erlbaum, 1977). The theory suggests that human behaviour falls into a number of patterns or 'scripts' which determine how we think and react. Jeffrey Young's Schema Therapy translates the idea of scripts into an effective therapeutic intervention. For a self-help guide to using schema to effect positive change see Young, J. and Klosko, J., *Reinventing Your Life: The Breakthrough Program to End Negative Behavior and Feel Great Again*, Penguin, 1998.

'Brigid Schulte': Schulte, B., *Overwhelmed: How to Work, Love and Play When No One Has the Time*, Bloomsbury, 2015.

'Laura Vanderkam': Vanderkam, L., *I Know How She Does It: How Successful Women Make the Most of their Time*, Portfolio Penguin, 2015.

'Stephen Covey': Covey, S., *The Seven Habits of Highly Effective People: 25th Anniversary Edition*, Rosetta, 2013.

'Research into positive psychology': See for example Seligman, M., *Flourish: A New Understanding of Happiness and Wellbeing and How to Achieve Them*, Nicholas Brealey Publishing, 2011.

'Flow': Research shows that being in flow when we work increases work enjoyment or happiness (Salanova, M., Bakker, A. B. and Llorens, S., 'Flow at work: evidence for an upward spiral of personal and organizational resources' (2006), *Journal of Happiness Studies*, 7(1), 1–22).

CHAPTER 4 – CONFIDENCE

'we suffer more greatly from deficiencies in the confidence department': Alongside Phanella's experience coaching hundreds of successful women who suffer from low confidence, empirical evidence supports the idea that women tend to be less confident than men. See for example, Kling, K., Shibley, J., Showers, C. and Buswell, B., 'Gender differences in self-esteem: A meta-analysis' (1999), *Psychological Bulletin*, 125(4), 470–500. For a fuller discussion of this topic see also *The Confidence Code* (Kay, K. and Shipman, C., Harper Business, 2014). See also *Ambition and Gender at Work*, Institute of Leadership and Management, 2011 (https://www.i-l-m.com/~/media/ILM%20Website/Downloads/Insight/Reports_from_ILM_website/ILM_Ambition_and_Gender_report_0211%20pdf.ashx as at 20 May 2016).

'undersell our abilities': Bench, S., Lench, H., Liew, J., Miner, K. and Flores, S., 'Gender Gaps in Overestimation of Maths Performance' (2015), *Sex Roles*, 72(11), 536–546.

'hold us back from applying for the perfect job': The statistic that women need to fulfil 100 per cent of job criteria before applying (as opposed to 60 per cent for men) comes from an internal HP report and has been extensively requoted. Our experience confirms that women do tend to be more reluctant to apply for jobs where they don't fulfil the majority of criteria. Tamara Mohr in a recent *Harvard Business Review* article suggests this is due to social conditioning and misunderstandings around the hiring process amongst women rather than confidence (Mohr, T., 'Why Women Don't Apply for Jobs Unless They Are 100% Qualified' (2014), *Harvard Business Review*). However, we would suggest the impact of that social conditioning is a lack of confidence in a woman's individual ability to surmount barriers such as lack of certain hiring criteria.

'we frequently misattribute our success': See for example, Clance, P. R. and Imes, S., 'The Imposter Phenomenon in High Achieving

Women: Dynamics and Therapeutic Intervention' (1978), *Psychotherapy Theory, Research and Practice*, 15(3).

'less predisposed to overconfidence': Sutter, M. and Rützler, D., 'Gender Differences in Competition Emerge Early in Life' (2010), IZA Discussion Paper No. 5015. Available at SSRN: http://ssrn.com/abstract=1631480.

'success correlates with confidence': Self-esteem has a significant and positive impact on leadership role occupancy for both genders vs. no significant impact for general mental ability (Li, W-D., Arvey, R. and Song, Z., 'The influence of general mental ability, self-esteem and family socioeconomic status on leadership role occupancy and leader advancement: The moderating role of gender' (2011), *The Leadership Quarterly*, 22(3), 520–534). Self-esteem has also been found to have a significant prospective impact on real-world life experiences (with a small to medium effect on job performance) and high and low self-esteem are not mere epiphenomena of success and failure in important life domains (Orth, U., Robins, R. and Widaman, K., 'Life-span development of self-esteem and its effects on important life outcomes' (2012), *Journal of Personality and Social Psychology*, Vol. 102(6), 1271–1288).

'imposter syndrome': As first described by Clance and Imes (1978), see above.

'men experience imposter syndrome less often': See Clance and Imes (1978) above.

'Transactional analysis': For an accessible guide to the theories of TA and how they can be applied in real life see Berne, E., *Games People Play: The Psychology of Human Relationships*, Penguin, 1964, reprinted 2016.

'Gravitas: Communicate with Confidence, Influence and Authority': Published by Ebury (Random House) 2014.

'Amy Cuddy': Cuddy, A., *Presence: Bring Your Boldest Self to Your Biggest Challenges*, Orion, 2015.

'as another clever research study proves, we draw our conclusions on others before they speak a syllable': Ambady, N. and Rosenthal, R., 'Half a minute: Predicting teacher evaluations from thin slices of nonverbal behavior and physical attractiveness' (1993), *Journal of Personality and Social Psychology*, 64(3), 431–441. For a fuller discussion of first impressions see Ambady, N. and Skowronski, J. (eds), *First Impressions*, Guilford Press, 2008.

CHAPTER 5 – THE INFLUENCE OF OTHERS

'Over the course of our year': http://www.newyorker.com/culture/culture-desk/seeing-nora-everywhere as at 20 May 2016.

'a whole gang of career supporters': Higgins, M. and Kram, K., 'Reconceptualizing Mentoring at Work: A Developmental Network Perspective' (2001), *Academy of Management Review*, 26(2), 264–288.

'Mentors also increase our work resilience': Kao, K-Y., Rogers, A., Spitzmueller, C. and Lind, M-T., 'Who should serve as my mentor? The effects of mentor's gender and status on resilience in mentoring relationships' (2014), *Journal of Vocational Behavior*, 85(2), 191–203.

'they imbue us with inner strength': An effective mentor increases career satisfaction (DeCastro, R., Griffith, K., Ubel, P., Stewart, A. and Jagsi, R., 'Mentoring and the Career Satisfaction of Male and Female Academic Medical Faculty' (2014), *Academic Medicine*, 89(2), 301–311). A mentor also increases self-esteem, helps us become more self-efficient and reduces worry about work–family conflict (Dutta, R., Hawkes, S., Kuipers, E., Guest, D., Fear, N. and Iversen, A., 'One year outcomes of a mentoring scheme for female academics: a pilot study at the Institute of Psychiatry, King's College London' (2011), BMC *Medical Education*, 11, 13).

'helps with office politics too': Internal networks are crucial to career progression and mentoring relationships with powerful senior people are one way of helping women gain access to these networks (Ramaswami, A., Dreher, G., Bretz, R. and Wiethoff, C., 'Gender, Mentoring and Career Success: The Importance of Organizational Context' (2010), *Personnel Psychology*, 63, 385–405. See also Hewlett, S. A., Peraino, K., Sherbin, L. and Sumberg, K., 'The sponsor effect: Breaking through the last glass ceiling' (2010), *Harvard Business Review*.

'at least ten jobs by the age of forty': The average person born in the latter years of the baby boom (1957–1964) held 11.7 jobs from age eighteen to age forty-eight, according to the US Bureau of Labor Statistics (http://www.bls.gov/news.release/pdf/nlsoy.pdf 20 May 2016).

'Careers have evolved … into something wavier and more mercurial': This is referred to by academics as the post-corporate (Peiperl, M. and Baruch, Y., 'Back to square zero: The post-corporate career' (1997), *Organizational Dynamics*, 25(4), 7–22) or boundaryless career (Arthur, M. B. and Rousseau, D. M., *The Boundaryless Career*, Oxford University Press, 1996).

'we must remember not to discount men': Research shows that men tend to offer more career support to protégés whereas women tend to offer more relational, psychosocial support: O'Brien, K. E., Biga, A., Kessler, S. R. and Allen, T. D., 'A meta-analytic investigation of gender differences in mentoring' (2008), *Journal of Management*, 36(2), 537–554.

'diagram': based on Shea, G., *Mentoring*, Crisp Publications, 2002.

'earn more money': 'The Promise of Future Leadership: A Research Program on Highly Talented Employees in the Pipeline', *Catalyst*, 2012. It benefits not only protégés but leads to career advancement and compensation growth for those providing the assistance – $25,075 in additional compensation between 2008 and 2010, according to the report.

'WORKOUT Feedback Time': With thanks to Nancy Darling Ph.D writing in *Psychology Today* (https://www.psychologytoday.com/blog/thinking-about-kids/201002/are-you-good-giving-feedback exercise-in-clapping as at 20 May 2016).

'we earn more and progress more quickly': Center for Talent Innovation (CTI)) research shows sponsors positively impact three crucial things: pay raises, high-profile assignments, and promotions. For example the percentage of women who will ask for a pay rise increases by nearly 10 per cent if they have a sponsor. The same 10 per cent effect is true for getting a great project or assignment. Sponsored women are also approximately 10 per cent more likely to be satisfied with their career progression. So you can see sponsorship is key.

'sponsors help to cut through this stalemate': Dougherty, T., Dreher, G., Arunachalam, V., Wilbanks, J., 'Mentor status, occupational context, and protégé career outcomes: Differential returns for males and females' (2013), *Journal of Vocational Behavior*, Volume 83, Issue 3, 514–527.

'Deutsche Bank is a sparkly example': see *Sponsoring Women to Success*, Catalyst, 2011, http://www.catalyst.org/system/files/sponsoring_women_to_success.pdf

'male/female sponsor combination is the deadliest on the block': Research shows that juniors with senior male champions earn more than those without but also that this effect is stronger for women than it is for men. In one study, women with senior male sponsors received more compensation not only than women without sponsors but than men with senior male sponsors (Dougherty, T., Dreher, G., Arunachalam, V., Wilbanks, J. (2013), as above).

'look to other women': Lockwood, P., 'Someone Like Me Can Be Successful: Do College Students Need Same-Gender Role Models?' (2016), *Psychology of Women Quarterly*, 30(1), 36–46. In this study, female students were more influenced by the gender of role models than male students. Female students reported greater motivation after reading about an outstanding woman than they did when they read about an outstanding man. Male students were also inspired by reading about successful people, but their level of inspiration is not affected by the gender of the person in the story.

CHAPTER 6 – SELF-PROMOTION AND NEGOTIATION

'women who publicly talk up their achievements and ask for what they want experience less discrimination and obtain more promotions': See Moss-Racusin, C. A. and Rudman, L. A., 'Disruptions in women's self-promotion: the backlash avoidance model' (2010), *Psychology of Women Quarterly*, 34(2), 186–202. Self-promotion has been found to predict perceptions of competence (Jones, E. and Pittman, T., 'Towards a general theory of strategic self-presentation' in Suls, J. (ed.), *Psychological Perspectives on the Self*, Vol. 1, pp. 231–262, Erlbaum, 1983) and thereby contribute to hiring and promotion decisions (e.g., Janoff-Bulman, R. and Wade, M. B., 'The dilemma of self-advocacy for women: Another case of blaming the victim?' (1996), *Journal of Social and Clinical Psychology*, 15, 445–446).

'one recent study has gone as far as to say that making our achievements visible is the only behaviour directly correlated

with pay growth for women's Carter, M. and Silva, C., The Myth
of the Ideal Worker: Does Doing All the Right Things Really Get Women Ahead?,
Catalyst, 2011.

'most men are natural self-promoters': Men are more likely to self-
promote and are more successful at self-promotion: Moss-Racusin,
C. A. and Rudman, L. A., 'Disruptions in women's self-promotion:
the backlash avoidance model' (2010), Psychology of Women Quarterly,
34(2), 186–202. Men's advantages have also emerged for related
behaviours including self-citation (King, Molly M., Correll, Shelley J.,
Jacquet, Jennifer, Bergstrom, Carl T., West, Jevin D., 'Men set their
own cites high: Gender and self-citation across fields and over time',
working paper – draft; West, Jevin D., Jacquet, J., King, M., Correll, S.,
Bergstrom, C., 'The role of gender in scholarly authorship' (2013),
PLOS ONE, 8(7)).

**'when they were little boys during those precious first few years
at school':** See Chapter 1 for a discussion of the impact of gender
difference and nurture.

'we're riddled with self-doubt': See Chapter 4 for a discussion of
gender differences in confidence.

'The academics call this the Backlash Avoidance Model': Rudman,
L. A., 'Self-promotion as a risk factor for women: The costs and
benefits of counter stereotypical impression management' (1998),
Journal of Personality and Social Psychology, 74, 629–645; Moss-Racusin, C.
and Rudman, L., 'Disruptions in women's self-promotion: the
backlash avoidance model' (2010), Psychology of Women Quarterly,
34(2), 186–202.

**'the study on university students who were asked to predict
their future grades should convince you':** Heatherington, L., Burns,
A. B. and Gustafson, T. B., 'When another stumbles: Gender and
self-presentation to vulnerable others' (1998), Sex Roles, 38(11–12),
889–913; Heatherington, L., Daubman, K. A., Bates, C., Ahn, A.,
Brown, H. and Preston, C., 'Two investigations of "female modesty"
in achievement situations' (1993), Sex Roles, 29(11–12), 739–754.

**'women were more prone to underestimation when they knew
that their guesses would be publicly discussed':** Daubman, K. A.,

summariz1e

Heatherington, L. and Ahn, A., 'Gender and the self-presentation of academic achievement' (1992), Sex Roles, 27(3–4), 187–204; Heatherington, L., Daubman, K. A., Bates, C., Ahn, A., Brown, H. and Preston, C. (1993), as above.

'Stereotype Threat Theory': Inzlicht, M. and Schmader, T. (eds), Stereotype Threat: Theory, Process and Application, Oxford University Press, 2011.

'we are less likely to overrate our abilities': Betsworth, D. G., 'Accuracy of self-estimated abilities and the relationship between self-estimated abilities and realism for women' (1999), Journal of Career Assessment, 7(1), 35–43; Furnham, A. and Rawles, R., 'Sex differences in the estimation of intelligence' (1995), Journal of Social Behavior and Personality, 10(3), 741.

'less likely to credit ourselves for our successes, more willing (expecting, even) to receive blame': Berg, J. H., Stephan, W. G. and Dodson, M., 'Attributional modesty in women' (1981), Psychology of Women Quarterly; Levine, R., Gillman, M. J. and Reis, H., 'Individual differences for sex differences in achievement attributions?' (1982), Sex Roles, 8(4), 455–466.

'negative estimations of our general intelligence too': e.g. Furnham, A., Hosoe, T. and Tang, T. L. P., 'Male hubris and female humility? A cross-cultural study of ratings of self, parental, and sibling multiple intelligence in America, Britain, and Japan' (2002), Intelligence, 30(1), 101–115.

'we leave university with better degrees': Despite underperformance in the CAT in the US, women outperform once at college: Mau, W. C. and Lynn, R., 'Gender differences on the Scholastic Aptitude Test, the American College Test and college grades' (2001), Educational Psychology, 21(2), 133–136. Women are also more likely obtain a degree than men: US Census 2015 (http://blogs.census.gov/2015/10/07/women-now-at-the-head-of-the-class-lead-men-in-college-attainment/?cid=RS23). In the UK, women outnumber men at every type of university, are more likely to obtain a good pass and less likely to drop out: Male and Female Participation and Progression in Higher Education, HEPI, 2009 (http://www.hepi.ac.uk/2009/06/05/male-and-female-participation-and-progression-in-higher-education/).

'and this applies to self-promotion too': O'Neill, O. and O'Reilly, C. A., 'Reducing the backlash effect: Self-monitoring and women's promotions' (2011), Journal of Occupational and Organizational Psychology, 84(4), 825–832.

'less than 1 per cent of the UK's consultant cardiologists are women': Census of Consultant Physicians and Higher Specialty Trainees in the UK 2013/14 (https://www.rcplondon.ac.uk/projects/outputs/2013-14-census-uk-consultants-and-higher-specialty-trainees as at 23 May 2016).

'office politics': Heath, K., Office Politics: A Skill Women Should Lean Into (2014) (https://hbr.org/2014/02/office-politics-a-skill-women-should-lean-into).

'carried out a test': Smith, J. L. and Huntoon, M., 'Women's bragging rights overcoming modesty norms to facilitate women's self-promotion' (2013), Psychology of Women Quarterly, 0361684313515840.

'Although the majority of us feel we are underpaid at work, less than half of us have ever dusted ourselves down and gone in to ask for a rise': see Babcock, L. and Laschever, S., Women Don't Ask: Negotiation and the Gender Divide, Princeton University Press, 2009.

'In the United Kingdom, the gender pay gap remains at 20 per cent': See Chapter 1 for discussion of the global gender pay gap.

'in a study into people buying new cars': Neale, M. and Lys, T., 'More Reasons Women Need to Negotiate Their Salaries' (2015) (https://hbr.org/2015/06/more-reasons-women-need-to-negotiate-their-salaries).

'In another study, over 150 managers were asked to allocate a fixed pool of money': Belliveau, M. A., 'Engendering inequity? How social accounts create vs. merely explain unfavourable pay outcomes for women' (2012), Organization Science, 23(4), 1154–1174.

'When women believe that we are worth the same as men, we are just as likely to negotiate': Riley, H. C. and Babcock, L., 'Gender as a situational phenomenon in negotiation' (2002), in IACM 15th Annual

Conference; Babcock, L. and Laschever, S., *Women Don't Ask: Negotiation and the Gender Divide*, Princeton University Press, 2009.

CHAPTER 7: NETWORKS

'our network … opens doors': A large body of empirical research provides evidence of the central role networks play in the career development process: Ibarra, H. and Deshpande, P., 'Networks and Identities: Reciprocal Influences on Career Processes and Outcomes', in *Handbook of Career Studies*, H. Gunz and M. Pieperl (eds), Sage (2007), 268–282. Both current salary and growth of your salary over time are positively impacted by successful networking (Wolff, H-G. and Moser, K., 'Effects of networking on career success: A longitudinal study' (2009), *Journal of Applied Psychology*; Lalanne, M. and Seabright, P., 'The Old Boy Network: The Impact of Professional Networks on Remuneration in Top Executive Jobs'). Not only is there extensive empirical evidence as to the many career benefits of networks including job satisfaction (Seibert, S., Kraimer, M. and Liden, R., 'A Social Capital Theory of Career Success' (2001), 44(2), 219–237) but valuable relationships are also important in their own right as a measure of success (Gersick, C. J., Dutton, J. E. and Bartunek, J. M., 'Learning from academia: The importance of relationships in professional life' (2000), *Academy of Management Journal*, 43(6), 1026–1044).

'Around 75 per cent of new jobs are found through networks': US Bureau of Labor Statistics using figures taken from the Job Openings and Labor Turnover Survey (JOLTS) http://www.bls.gov/jlt/.

'For small businesses, networks produce around 83 per cent of new profitable fruit': Verizon and Small Business Trends' Survey, 2014.

'when we have access to influential people, it actually makes us more powerful ourselves': See Chapter 5.

'we'll be moving and shaking our way to the top': See Chapter 5.

'by 2028, experts expect women to be controlling close to 75 per cent of discretionary worldwide spending': *Women, The Next Emerging Market*, Ernst and Young, 2015.

'women are already up against it on the accessibility front': Fisher, V. and Kinsey, S., 'Behind closed doors! Homosocial desire and the academic boys club' (2014), *Gender in Management: An International Journal*, 29(1), 44–64; Gamba, M. and Kleiner, B. H., 'The old boys' network today' (2001), *International Journal of Sociology and Social Policy*, 21(8/9/10), 101–107.

'Queen Bee is most secure ensconced within her Bee friends': Ibarra, H., 'Personal networks of women and minorities in management: A conceptual framework' (1993), *The Academy of Management Review*, 18, 56–87; Ibarra, H., 'Paving an Alternative Route: Gender differences in managerial networks' (1997), *Social Psychology Quarterly*, Vol. 60, No. 1, 91–102.

'a small body of research that wholly disagrees': Fang, L. H. and Huang, S., 'Gender and connections among Wall Street analysts' (2011), available at SSRN 1962478.

'Here is a visual explanation of how things stand at the moment': adapted from Ibarra, H., 'Homophily and differential returns: Sex differences in network structure and access in an advertising firm' (1992), *Administrative Science Quarterly*, 37, 422–447.

'Quiet: The Power of Introverts in a World That Can't Stop Talking': Cain, S., Crown, 2012.

'appreciate their preference for the internal': See Petrilli, L., 'An Introvert's Guide to Networking' (2012), *Harvard Business Review*.

'Collaborations are enormously beneficial': Vongalis-Macrow, A., 'Two Ways Women Can Network More Effectively' (2012), *Harvard Business Review*.

'A study on the use of social networking sites by gender': See https://www.brandwatch.com/2014/03/social-media-and-women/ (as at 23 May 2016).

CHAPTER 8: LOOK GOOD, WORK WELL

'*You Are What You Wear: What Your Clothes Reveal About You*': Baumgartner, J. J., Da Capo Press, 2012.

'**one research study says that we draw our conclusions on others in 0.1 of a second**': Ambady, N. and Rosenthal, R., 'Half a minute: Predicting teacher evaluations from thin slices of nonverbal behavior and physical attractiveness' (1993), *Journal of Personality and Social Psychology*, 64(3), 431–441.

CHAPTER 9: MAKING IT RIGHT TO THE TOP

'**one recent survey of 3000 young women across the UK and America**': Always Survey 2015, http://always.com/en-us/about-us/our-epic-battle-like-a-girl (as at 17 March 2016).

'**it will take twenty-five years to reach gender parity at the senior-VP level and more than 100 years in the boardroom**': *Women in the Workplace* (2015), LeanIn.org and McKinsey.

'**Women start businesses with around one-third of the level of finance of their male counterparts, in every size and sector of business**': Carter, S. L. and Shaw, E., 'Women's business ownership: Recent research and policy developments' (2006).

'**the entrepreneur gender pay gap is significantly bigger than the gender wage gap for employees**': Economic Policy Institute, 2015 http://www.epi.org/publication/women-still-earn-less-than-men-across-the-board/?utm_source=Economic±Policy±Institute&utm_campaign=7ad17298f4-EPI_News_04_10_154_10_2015&utm_medium=email&utm_term=0_e7c5826c50-7ad17298f4-58003869 (as at 17 March 2016).

'**research says that in companies where female leaders are well represented, profits rise and the workforce is happier**': S&P 500 companies led by women perform better across a range of factors including job satisfaction (Dezső, C. L. and Ross, D. G., 'Does female representation in top management improve firm performance? A panel data investigation' (2012), *Strategic Management Journal*, 33(9), 1072–1089). Stock performance of companies with gender diverse leadership is also better than that of companies with homogenous leadership teams (Credit Suisse, *Does Gender Diversity Improve Performance?*, 2012).

'for every 10 per cent increase in gender diversity, EBIT (basically profit) rises by 3.5 per cent': *Diversity Matters*, McKinsey, 2015.

'Experts call this the Ambition Gap': see Sandberg, S., *Lean In*, WH Allen, 2013.

'External influences stop us': Ibarra, H., Ely, R. and Kolb, D., 'Women rising: The unseen barriers' (2013), *Harvard Business Review*, 91(9), 60–66. See also *Women in the Workplace* (2015), LeanIn.org and McKinsey.

'because of these barriers': For more on barriers see for example Whelan, J., 'The barriers to equality of opportunity in the workforce: The role of unconscious bias' (2013), *Understanding the Gender Gap*, 55.

'Project Implicit': https://implicit.harvard.edu/implicit/takeatest.html (as at 17 March 2016).

'this bias also works against ethnic minorities': Rosette, A. S., Leonardelli, G. J. and Phillips, K. W., 'The White standard: racial bias in leader categorization' (2008), *Journal of Applied Psychology*, 93(4), 758.

'even short men': Blaker, N. M., Rompa, I., Dessing, I. H., Vriend, A. F., Herschberg, C. and Van Vugt, M., 'The height leadership advantage in men and women: Testing evolutionary psychology predictions about the perceptions of tall leaders' (2013), *Group Processes and Intergroup Relations*, 16(1), 17–27.

'having less leeway to express ourselves assertively': Brescoll, V. L. and Uhlmann, E. L., 'Can an angry woman get ahead? Status conferral, gender, and expression of emotion in the workplace' (2008), *Psychological Science*, 19(3), 268–275.

'As Daniel Kahneman, a world expert on bias': Bottom, W. P., Gilovich, T., Griffin, D. and Kahneman, D., 'Heuristics and biases: The psychology of intuitive judgment' (2004).

'Expose yourself to difference': Workout devised with reference to Banaji, M. and Greenwald, A., *Blindspot: Hidden Biases of Good People*, Delacorte Press, 2013.

'Find similarities': Dasgupta, N., 'Ingroup experts and peers as social vaccines who inoculate the self-concept: The stereotype inoculation model' (2011), *Psychological Inquiry*, 22(4), 231–246.

'Employ your imagination': Blair, I. V., Ma, J. E. and Lenton, A. P., 'Imagining stereotypes away: the moderation of implicit stereotypes through mental imagery' (2001), *Journal of Personality and Social Psychology*, 81(5), 828.

'internalising ourselves as a leader is an iterative process': Ibarra, H., Ely, R. and Kolb, M., 'Women Rising: The Unseen Barriers' (2013), *Harvard Business Review*.

'transactional leaders rely on quid pro quos': Bass, Bernard, *Bass & Stogdill's Handbook of Leadership: Theory, Research and Managerial Applications* (4th ed.), The Free Press, 2008.

'transactional Leadership is seen as a masculine way of doing things': Eagly, A. H. and Johannesen-Schmidt, M. C., 'The leadership styles of women and men' (2001), *Journal of Social Issues*, 57(4), 781–797.

'women who are overly aggressive (e.g. Margaret Thatcher) are not liked': Rudman, L. A. and Glick, P., 'Prescriptive gender stereotypes and backlash toward agentic women' (2001), *Journal of Social Issues*, 57(4), 743–762.

'launched #BanBossy': banbossy.com (as at 20 March 2016).

'transformational types lead by inspiring those around them to follow their cause': Burns, J. M., *Leadership*, Harper & Row, 1978; Bass, B. M., *Leadership and Performance Beyond Expectation*, Free Press, 1978.

'research says that groups led by transformational leaders are happier and more productive': Alimo-Metcalfe, B., 'An investigation of female and male constructs of leadership and empowerment' (1995), *Women in Management Review*, 10(2), 3–8; Barker & Young, 1994; Eagly, A. H., Johannesen-Schmidt, M. C. and Van Engen, M. L., 'Transformational, transactional, and laissez-faire leadership styles: a meta-analysis comparing women and men' (2003), *Psychological Bulletin*, 129(4), 569; Kark, R., Shamir, B. and Chen, G., 'The two faces of transformational leadership: empowerment and dependency' (2003), *Journal of Applied Psychology*, 88(2), 246; Trinidad, C. and Normore, A. H., 'Leadership and gender: a dangerous liaison?' (2005), *Leadership & Organization Development Journal*, 26(7), 574–590.

'Transformational leaders are crucial in the workplace of tomorrow': *Women Matter 2*, McKinsey 2008 (as at 21 March

2016: https://www.google.co.uk/url?sa=t&rct=j&q=&esrc=s&source=web&cd=1&ved=0ahUKEwiOhrjAn9LLAhUKWxoKHcl3A98QFggdMAA&url=http%3A%2F%2Fwww.mckinsey.com%2F~%2Fmedia%2FMcKinsey%2FBusiness%2520Functions%2FOrganization%2FOur%2520Insights%2FWomen%2520matter%2FWomen_matter_oct2008_english.ashx&usg=AFQjCNESbgukCk4p4FLmijSRnQ7LuQ6-KQ&sig2=8XZrmCQKvFHej9bsV3y0pg)

'While many of these transformational characteristics are often already part of our feminine DNA': In fact, women are more likely to display a transformational leadership style (Eagly, Alice H., Johannesen-Schmidt, Mary C. and Van Engen, Marloes L., 'Transformational, transactional, and laissez-faire leadership styles: a meta-analysis comparing women and men' (2003), *Psychological Bulletin*, 129(4), 569–591). See also Gerzema, J. and D'Antonio, M., *The Athena Doctrine*, Jossey-Bass, 2013.

'women can struggle to be visionary': see Ibarra, H. and Obudaro, O., 'Women and the Vision Thing' (2009), *Harvard Business Review*.

'when we vision in a collaborative sense, we need to beware that it doesn't weaken our message': Flynn, J., Heath, K. and Davis Holt, M., 'Collaboration's Hidden Tax on Women's Careers' (2011), *Harvard Business Review*.

'because vision, research says, is one of the most important uses of our time when we're in a leadership role': See for example Tuomo, T., 'How to be an effective charismatic leader: lessons for leadership development' (2006), *Development and Learning in Organizations: An International Journal*, 20(4), 19–21.

'that doesn't mean we need to fight fire with fire': Research suggests women often react to masculine leadership stereotype threat by adopting more masculine behaviours and communication styles (von Hippel, C., Wiryakusuma, C., Bowden, J. and Shochet, M., 'Stereotype threat and female communication styles' (2011), *Personality and Social Psychology Bulletin*, 0146167211410439; Kray, L. J., Thompson, L. and Galinsky, A., 'Battle of the sexes: gender stereotype confirmation and reactance in negotiations' (2001), *Journal of Personality and Social Psychology*, 80(6), 942).

'**research says we end up being rated less well by our subordinates**': see von Hippel, C., Wiryakusuma, C., Bowden, J. and Shochet, M. (2011), as above.

CHAPTER 10: A FINE BALANCE

'**when we are able to extend a more tangible control over our personal work schedules, we are happier, more productive beings**': Work–life balance is important. A greater sense of control over our own work schedules has been shown in research to lead to improved mental health (MacDonald, M., Phipps, S. and Lethbridge, L., 'Taking its toll: The influence of paid and unpaid work on women's well being' (2005), *Feminist Economics*, 11(1), 63–94).

'**A Mental Health Foundation survey**': see https://www.mentalhealth.org.uk/a-to-z/w/work-life-balance (as at 22 May 2016).

'**Work–life balance is an issue for everyone**': Jones, F., Burke, R. J. and Westman, M., *Worklife Balance: A Psychological Perspective*, Psychology Press, 2013; Allard, K., Haas, L. and Hwang, C. P., 'Family-supportive organizational culture and fathers' experiences of work–family conflict in Sweden' (2011), *Gender, Work & Organization*, 18(2), 141–157; Kvande, E., 'Work–life balance for fathers in globalized knowledge work: Some insights from the Norwegian context' (2009), *Gender, Work & Organization*, 16(1), 58–72.

'**we're able to be anywhere and everywhere on the planet**': Globalisation of competition, changes in the patterns and demands of work, and the fast pace of technological innovation have put a lot of additional demands on employees (Coughlan, A., 'Family-friendly/work-life balance policies' (2000), Irish Business and Employers Confederation, Dublin; Fisher, H., 'Investing in People: Family-friendly Work Arrangements in Small and Medium Sized Enterprises: Work Life Balance in the New Millennium' (2000), Equality Authority). In particular, with advances in communications technology we are constantly available by phone, email and messaging and through social media in particular, our work and home personas are inextricably bound (Felstead, A., Jewson, N., Phizacklea, A. and Walters, S., 'Opportunities to work at home in the context of work-life balance' (2002), *Human Resource Management Journal*, 12(1), 54–76).

'other academics have criticised the term': e.g. Rapoport, R., Bailyn, L., Fletcher, J. and Pruitt, B., 'Beyond work-family balance: Advancing gender equity and workplace performance' (2002).

'criticise integration as the ultimate ideal': Lewis, S. and Cooper, C. L., *Work-life Integration: Case Studies of Organisational Change*, John Wiley & Sons, 2005.

'those who take advantage of flexible working schemes improve their overall wellbeing': Greenhaus, J. H., Collins, K. M. and Shaw, J. D., 'The relation between work–family balance and quality of life' (2003), *Journal of Vocational Behavior*, 63(3), 510–531; Burke, R. J., 'Workaholism in organizations: Concepts, results and future research directions' (2000), *International Journal of Management Reviews*, 2(1), 1–16.

'companies with flexible working policies (we'll discuss exactly what that means later) do better on all kinds of metrics, including employee turnover, stress, organisational commitment, absenteeism, job satisfaction and productivity': Bloom, N. and Van Reenen, J., 'Measuring and explaining management practices across firms and countries' (2006), National Bureau of Economic Research; Frone, M. R., Russell, M. and Cooper, M. L., 'Antecedents and outcomes of work-family conflict: testing a model of the work-family interface' (1992), *Journal of Applied Psychology*, 77(1), 65; Parasuraman, S., Purohit, Y. S., Godshalk, V. M. and Beutell, N. J., 'Work and family variables, entrepreneurial career success, and psychological well being' (1996), *Journal of Vocational Behavior*, 48(3), 275–300; Parris, M. A., Vickers, M. H. and Wilkes, L., 'Caught in the middle: Organizational impediments to middle managers' work-life balance' (2008), *Employee Responsibilities and Rights Journal*, 20(2), 101–117; Veiga, J. F., Baldridge, D. C. and Eddleston, K. A., 'Toward understanding employee reluctance to participate in family-friendly programs' (2004), *Human Resource Management Review*, 14(3), 337–351.

'Thrive: The Third Metric to Redefining Success and Creating a Happier Life': Huffington, A., Random House, 2014.

'women are still more likely to take responsibility for home and family alongside our paid work': Hochschild, A. and Machung, A., *The Second Shift: Working Families and the Revolution at Home*, Penguin, 2012.

'we still end up with a lap full of family responsibility': Even women without children tend to take on more family responsibilities. For example, the average caregiver in the UK in 2015 is a woman in her forties, caring for her mother in her sixties who does not live with her. She is married and employed. Although men also provide assistance, female caregivers may spend as much as 50 per cent more time providing care than male caregivers (https://www.caregiver.org/women-and-caregiving-facts-and-figures - as at 22 March 2016).

'90 per cent of UK companies now offer some form of flexible working': Institute of Leadership and Management (2013), *Attitudes to Flexible Working* (https://www.i-l-m.com/Insight/Inspire/2013/May/flexible-working-infographic - as at 22 March 2016).

'the same number of men as women go from desktop to laptop': Institute of Leadership and Management (2013), *Flexible Working: Goodbye Nine to Five* (https://www.i-l-m.com/~/media/ILM%20Website/Downloads/Insight/Reports_from_ILM_website/Research_flexibleworking_march2013%20pdf.ashx - as at 22 March 2016).

'the academics call these FlexStyles': Kossek, E. E. and Lautsch, B. A., *CEO of Me: Creating a Life that Works in the Flexible Job Age*, Pearson Prentice Hall, 2007.

'Statistically speaking, the majority of women do become mothers (in 2011 in the UK, 80 per cent of women aged forty-five years and over had at least one child and the figures are similar in the US)': See http://www.ons.gov.uk/peoplepopulationandcommunity/birthsdeathsandmarriages/livebirths/bulletins/birthsummarytablesenglandandwales/2015-07-15 (as at 22 March 2016) and http://www.census.gov/hhes/fertility/ (as at 22 March 2016).

'Originally the title of a life manual by the legendary Cosmopolitan editor Helen Gurley Brown': Gurley Brown, H., *Having It All: Love, Success, Sex, Money Even If You're Starting With Nothing*, Simon & Schuster, 2012.

'In her seminal article, "Why Women Still Can't Have It All" . . . and later in her book *Unfinished Business:Women Work Men Family*': Slaughter, A. M., *Unfinished Business*, Oneworld Publications, 2015.

'The way we live, our aspirations and the values we put on work and life all come down to preference': Hakim, C., 'Women, careers, and work-life preferences' (2006), *British Journal of Guidance & Counselling*, 34(3), 279–294. It is important to note that Hakim's Preference Theory, although influential, has also been widely criticised (see Lewis, P. and Simpson, R., 'Understanding and researching "choice" in women's career trajectories' (2015), *Handbook of Gendered Careers in Management: Getting In, Getting On, Getting Out*, 44). However, despite clear organisational and societal biases against women at work, we believe from our research and practice that there is a strong element of choice in women's work–life decisions.

'Lori K. Bitter's new book': Bitter, L. K., *The Grandparent Economy: How Baby Boomers Are Bridging The Generation Gap*, Paramount Market Publishing, 2015.

Index

Acknowledgements

To all the people who believed in this book and have made *Step Up* happen.

For one, our wonderful families, particularly Toby, Rich, Noah, Otto, Pearl, Lulu and Tallulah; our agent Mildred Yuan for her brilliant advice; our editors Morwenna Loughman and Sam Jackson for their enthusiasm, support and belief in the Step Up message; Rosy Tsai and Charlie Hay at Campbell Hay for their beautiful cover design and general sharp eyes; Malika Favre for her gorgeous illustration; and, of course, a huge thank you to our incredible interviewees for their openness and wisdom.

PHANELLA: I would like to thank the psychologists, coaches and clients who have educated and inspired me. And my parents, for teaching me early on that gender equality is worth fighting for.

ALICE: Mum and Dad, thank you for always encouraging my love of writing, Grandma, here's to powerful (and glamorous women), and laptop, cheers for not losing any *Step Up* chapters.